AF505942

National Conversations

National Conversations:
Public Service Media and Cultural Diversity in Europe

Edited by Karina Horsti, Gunilla Hultén and Gavan Titley

intellect Bristol, UK / Chicago, USA

First published in the UK in 2014 by
Intellect, The Mill, Parnall Road, Fishponds, Bristol, BS16 3JG, UK

First published in the USA in 2014 by
Intellect, The University of Chicago Press, 1427 E. 60th Street,
Chicago, IL 60637, USA

A catalogue record for this book is available from the
British Library.

Cover designer: Stephanie Sarlos
Copy-editor: Emma Rhys
Production manager: Tim Elameer
Typesetting: John Teehan

ISBN 978-1-78320-175-4
ePDF ISBN 978-1-78320-285-0
ePub ISBN 978-1-78320-286-7

Printed and bound by Short Run Press Ltd, Exeter

Contents

Acknowledgements

The editors would like to thank the Publications Committee of the National University of Ireland for their generous grant in support of this publication.

Introduction

National Conversations: Public Service Media and Cultural Diversity in Europe

Karina Horsti, Gunilla Hultén, Gavan Titley

Introduction

This book is shaped by an awareness of the somewhat paradoxical position of public service broadcasting (PSB) and public service media (PSM) in Europe. As has been the case in most western European contexts since at least the 1980s, PSBs face a significant and intensifying range of challenges: digitalization and convergence, audience fragmentation and transnationalism, fragile funding models and ideological relegation. However, the consistent and often intensive contest over their relevance and mission, even in a world of communicative abundance, suggests that for many they still represent a normative vision of what mainstream media ought to strive to achieve in terms of pluralism and societal representation. In-depth examination of PSB and PSM institutions, strategies and programmes remains critical to media analysis, both because of their continuing centrality in national polities, but also because discussions of public service, by their nature, open up a range of further interesting questions about society, media ecology, technology and politics.

One such critical question is that of recognition and representation in societies characterized over time by migration and settlement, and by public debates about difference, belonging and legitimacy. This book aims to explore the shifting landscape of PSB and PSM in relation to migration, sociocultural change and the politics of 'diversity'. Focusing on how public service media have re-interpreted their general mission to foster both 'national conversations' and a pluralist spectrum of perspectives in migration societies, it positions media developments as a lens on sociopolitical change, and as implicated in some of the most fractious political debates in contemporary Europe. In turn, by examining how institutional shifts towards 'diversity' and 'integration' policy and programming are inseparable from wider pressures relating to digitalization, neo-liberalism and audience fragmentation, this book positions the politics of diversity as a lens for understanding the ongoing transformation of public service broadcasting and media.

The thematic chapters in the first section place contemporary issues and debates in an historical context in Europe, and develop the political, theoretical and policy issues engaged in the empirical studies gathered in section two. These nationally-focused empirical case studies analyse the responses of public service media to the politics of representation shaped by migration and cultural diversity, in a context where economic and technological changes have further complicated the ethos of public service broadcasting, and where the dominant European political emphasis on 'integration' (see Guild, Groenendijk and Carrera 2009) manifests specific demands for national broadcasters.

All that is solid?

Central to the development of national radio, and subsequently television services in the early to mid-twentieth century, public service institutions have proved remarkably resilient. It has been a commonplace in both academic literature and public debate for decades that their marginalization, if not demise, may be inevitable. In part this is because the dominant organization of public service broadcasting through significant national institutions has resulted in structures that are symbolically associated with the western nation-state itself, and with the public culture of representative democracies. A combination of monopoly conditions and ideological conviction allowed for several post-war decades of national pre-eminence in most sites, where, as Hallin and Mancini note, 'broadcasting has been treated as part of the res publica, as an institution whose influence on society is too great to be left under the control of private interests' (2004: 164). Even allowing for distinctive national differences, the centrality of a public interest mission has been based, according to Jay Blumler's early 1990s summary, on the shared foundations of comprehensive remit, generalized mandates, emphasis on diversity, pluralism and range, and a self-consciously cultural and political role (1992).

The cluster of reasons for the relative weakening of public service broadcasters, and the unsettling of the paradigm of public service, are also well known. As relative monopoly conditions rapidly dissolved in the 1970s and 1980s through broadcast deregulation, intensified and ideologically buoyant commercial competition, and the fraying and extension of national media spaces through cable, satellite and media globalization, the broadcasting landscape shifted irrevocably. According to Papathanassopoulos and Negrine:

> While in the past they [PSB] might have been regarded as part of the infrastructure of informed democratic polities, untouchable and permanent, they have long ceased to be the only organizations of broadcasting that matter [...] as these others [commercial competitors] provided news, sport and entertainment, the position of public service broadcasters began to erode, as they often lost their share of the audience, and their sole access to sources of public funding could be questioned.
>
> (2011: 25)

This line of questioning has, of course, intensified in a digital media era where the rapid convergence of information and communication technologies (ICTs), telecommunications and broadcast media raises profound questions as to how public service remits could be re-shaped and meaningfully delivered in a multi-platform era. The ethical and pragmatic futures of public service in a digital era have, unsurprisingly, dominated both recent academic research and public discourse. In many sites, and particularly in the Nordic countries, commercial competitors have argued that the 'mission creep' of public service broadcasters into digital platforms and online services extends the historical unfairness of the compulsory licence fee into a convergent media environment where advertising is increasingly shifting online, and all revenue generation models are contingent and fragile. As against this, proponents contend that PSBs utilize long established methods of audience feedback and outreach, and that new modes of participation deepen an existing commitment to 'connecting' with the audience. The – uneven – digital strategies shaped in a context of competing for audiences in a multi-platform media environment, while seeking legitimacy for this expansive renewal, have resulted in the emergence of the label 'Public Service Media' (PSM) (see Donders 2012; Iosifidis 2012 [2007]).

The concept of public service media is not a precise analytical term or institutional description, and for this reason the studies in this book employ the concepts of public service broadcasting and public service media dependent on the context, content and medium. It is used to loosely describe an emphasis on modes of content delivery in a digital environment, as well as suggesting a more definitive, future policy project based on these shifts (Donders 2012: 2). The Council of Europe expert group on 'Public service media in the information society' frame this project as the deepening of democratic participation through enhanced digital capabilities for multi-layered audience reach and interaction, and where 'PSM must increasingly strive to move away from one-way communication to reinforced dialogue and afford the public access to varied information as well as a possibility to engage and participate in the democratic debate' (2009: 7). These extensive digital media possibilities, however, must be evaluated in a context where digitalization is seen, inter alia, to further erode the principled necessity for public service media. As Gregory Ferrell Lowe and Jeanette Steemers outline in their most recent *Regaining the Initiative for Public Service Media* (RIPE) study:

> Although dark clouds are nothing new, the magnitude of this storm is stronger and more threatening. The public media sector is being challenged on nearly every front at the same time. Publics and politicians alike have come to see the commercial approach as the 'normal' way of organizing broadcasting. There are strong pressures for downsizing PSM organizations, limiting investment options, restricting online and digital opportunities, narrowing remits to genres and audiences that are not commercially attractive, and for implementing increasingly intrusive assessment procedures. The principles of public service in media no longer seem to resonate very widely, and there is growing criticism about a decline in PSM distinctiveness as these organizations compete aggressively with commercial rivals.
>
> (Lowe and Steemers 2012: 3)

One dimension of this criticism suggests that the representative, and for many critics, paternalistic mission of public service broadcasting is fundamentally unsettled in a media era defined by dramatically increased participation in media production and content dissemination. For all their stated ideals in relation to the (interactive) audience, PSBs structurally inhabit one side of the divide between what Leah Lievrouw (2011) terms the 'pipeline' view, and the 'frontier' opened up by the precise affordances of the 'new' in 'new media' (widely available devices for generating and sharing meaning and content, widespread expectation of and engagement in new communication practices and activities, and the 'larger social arrangements' built in and through these possibilities):

> The pipeline view tends to see media technologies and content in terms of property and gatekeeping, production and consumption; the frontier view is more likely to value reputation, credibility, creativity, reciprocity, voice, and trust as well as ownership, and to see media and information technologies as opportunities to create and communicate as well as consume.
>
> (Lievrouw 2011: 3)

If the 'increasing unknowability of the media audience in the digital age' (Couldry 2012: 21) is added to expectations derived from cultures of interactivity and participation, it is clear that public service media face a dilemma in ensuring accountability and legitimacy, and retaining the public service core values underpinning their existence, when the nature of the public addressed is fundamentally altered. Yet as Nick Couldry notes, 'in the multiple-outlet digital media era, "centrality" becomes an even more important claim for media institutions to make, as they seek to justify the wider "value" they provide' (2012: 23). What Couldry discusses as an inevitable tactical response to communicative abundance also provides a suggestive basis for theoretical and programmatic re-imaginings of de-centred institutions. Graham Murdock, for example, has argued for more emphasis on communicative rights in conceptualizations of citizenship (1999: 28), and subsequently linked this explicitly to the central position of public broadcasting in providing the shared cultural spaces required for fuller participation (Murdock 2005). He attempts to redefine the role of public service broadcasting within what he calls a 'digital commons'. In his view public broadcasting is 'the principal node in an emerging network of public and civil initiatives that taken together, provide the basis for new shared cultural space' through a commitment to 'values of diversity and deliberation' (Murdock 2005).

As Donders and Pauwels point out, public broadcasting does not itself guarantee the production of public service programmes (Donders and Pauwels 2012: 80). Thus a new 'centrality' must involve realizing core values such as respectful conversation with the audience, citizen empowerment and societal credibility (see also Bakker 2012). They conclude that the imperatives of market competition rather than public service values provide more of an incentive to public service broadcasters to develop digital services, but ultimately the provision of these services must be seen to extend an established mission rather than simply provide more digital services (Donders and Pauwels 2011: 92). Thus 'regaining the initiative' (Lowe and Steemers 2012) at a time of a 'crisis in legitimacy' involves developing new and diversified forms of funding, negotiating a balance between existing services and new, probably commercialized services, and reinventing public service media to include services tailored to digital media technologies and interactive platforms (Debrett 2009). Yet it will also by necessity involve engaging in sustained argument as to why a common communicative sphere is a necessity in a fragmented and individualized media environment, and why public service media can be trusted to organize it, given how problematic the realities of 'pluralism' have been in past iterations.

Legitimacy, representation and cultural diversity

It is widely acknowledged that the national media of daily newspapers and public service broadcasting have historically played a constitutive role in integrating citizens into everyday practices of national belonging, not through forced homogeneity, but through the ritual and repetitive definition of sociability, common interests, and what Michael Billig has termed the 'banal nationalism' of routine practices of shared belonging and communal heritage (1995). In a discussion of national media and 'boundary work', Roger Silverstone (2006) distinguishes between what he terms *centripetal* and *centrifugal* phases of broadcasting. In the decades when single or relatively unchallenged public service broadcasters dominated the national media space of western European countries, a centripetal power worked to reflect and shape boundaries of national and local belonging. In the centrifugal phase ushered in by, among other factors, deregulation, globalization and accelerated technological change, the integrative role of broadcasting and the national press is diluted, with the result that 'this boundary work is becoming even more significant, if not more complex and challenging' (2006: 19).

This book is concerned in large part with this question of 'boundary work' in a centrifugal mediascape. Public service broadcasting evolved from the 1920s onwards to provide programming 'for all', and to produce programming that speaks to an assumed national, cultural commonality, if not necessarily homogeneity. Particularly in smaller nation-states in north-west Europe, the centripetal drive underpins the goal of language maintenance. It remains a central driver of PSB legitimacy, and audiences appear willing to pay for the services from public funds on the basis that few other actors will provide adequate programming in national languages. In, for example, Finland and Norway, YLE (*Yleisradio*, The Finnish Broadcasting Corporation) and NRK (*Norsk rikskringkasting AS*, Norwegian Broadcasting Corporation) are the main providers and contractors for national and minority language production (Lowe and Steemers 2012). For public service media, boundary work in postcolonial societies such as the United Kingdom and the Netherlands has long implied complex questions around ethnic minority recognition, representation and participation. In the other national contexts discussed here, in recent decades immigration and the attendant and fractious political questions of legitimacy and belonging have added a significant dimension to the re-anchoring of PSM in a 'centrifugal' phase.

John Ellis's periodization (2000) of media systems may be specific to the United Kingdom, but it has a wider heuristic value in insisting on placing the problematically simplistic narrative of a shift from 'cultural homogeneity to heterogeneity' in wider sociopolitical relief. For Ellis, the high era of public service broadcasting is that of an 'era of scarcity', that of the post-war industrial state, mass consumer society and political projects of national consolidation. What he terms as the 'era of availability' is marked by increased commercial competition and increasing technical possibilities for media content delivery, but also by an increased awareness of emerging 'post-industrial social formations' and consumer society. Writing in 2000, his 'era of plenty', characterized by 'time famine and choice fatigue', describes an abundance that scarcely features the online and the convergent. However, what is important about such a schema is that it frames the general unsettling of the representative role of PSB by emphasizing the tension between institutional form and sociocultural formation. Holding on to such a framework lessens the temptation to regard migration and its implications as uniquely challenging to the 'imagined community', a reduction that is both sociologically inadequate and politically toxic.

That said, precisely because, as Arjun Appadurai puts it, no nation-state is 'free of the idea that its national sovereignty is built on some sort of ethnic genius' (2006: 3), the process of recognition has always been fraught with political tensions. The studies collected here proceed from the fundamental recognition of what Ben Pitcher terms the 'facticity of difference', that is, 'an already-existing sociopolitical reality of which cultural difference has become a defining feature' (2009: 2). He continues:

> the existence of cultural difference – whether understood in terms of race, ethnicity or religion – has become fully acknowledged as a constituent part of the societies within which we live today. In this most basic of senses, and irrespective of the extent to which it is tolerated, celebrated or condemned, multiculturalism describes the widespread recognition that we can no longer be in any doubt as to whether or not cultural difference is here to stay.
>
> (Pitcher 2009: 2)

Yet this facticity is a subject of political discourse, and, more fundamentally, of *mediation*: it is shaped, framed and represented by media sources and channels; flows of information and opinion; images; stories and voices; headlines and sidelines; inclusions and exclusions; and so forth. As a consequence, it makes little sense in migration societies to argue as to whether media should 'respond' to migration and multiculture, as it is constrained to do so, explicitly or implicitly. The question, rather, is one of representation, or as Sarita Malik puts it in this volume, of 'recognition in a media democracy tasked with equality of representation'. The idea of recognition has enjoyed a philosophical resurgence in recent decades, both in normative theorizations of multiculturalism (Taylor 1994) and broader explorations of social justice (Fraser and Honneth 2003). The close relationship between ideas of recognition and what is at stake in the 'politics of representation' is reflected in a significant literature within media studies. Nick Stevenson (2003), for example, summarizes issues central to the literature on recognition for communication theory:

Our integrity as human beings does not flow from our access to material resources, but is dependent upon processes of *cultural domination* (being represented as inferior), *non-recognition* (being excluded from the dominant imagery of one's culture) and *disrespect* (being continually portrayed in a negative or stereotypical way).

(2003: 47)

The studies in this book examine media institutions grappling with the task of recognition, and they narrate experiences that are often strikingly similar, if unfolding at different speeds and intensities, and over varying time spans. In most cases, the initial paradigm of what was broadly termed 'multicultural programming' focused on 'niche programming' for specific groups, while also seeking to 'explain' minorities to the national audience. Almost uniformly, this generation of public service programming came up against a key question for recognition-based approaches: what happens if ethnic minority audiences do not find themselves adequately represented in the media work aimed at them and about them? Annabelle Srebreny's (1999) study, *Include Me In*, conducted for the British Broadcasting Standards Commission, found that audiences are 'multiculturally aware' and experience their society as cross-culturally connected, and individuals' lives as involving multiple attachments and identities. However they believe 'that even the standard descriptions of minority ethnic audiences do not do justice to the cultural mixes in which people live their lives' (Srebreny 1999: 3)

A similar study, *Multicultural Broadcasting: Concepts and Reality* (Millwood Hargrave 2002) – commissioned by the British Broadcasting Corporation (BBC) and several other media institutions – stressed a 'general need to be seen' and linked it to feelings of belonging in British society and increased understanding between communities. Inadequate representation was held to encompass questions of tokenism, negative stereotyping, and unrealistic and simplistic portrayals of communities. At the same time, policy-making and programme strategies are subject to political evaluation, and are porous to and sometimes influenced by wider political discourse, atmosphere and policy prerogatives. Several of the studies here reflect the point made by Simon Cottle, that 'political ideas of assimilation, integration, pluralism, multiculturalism and/or anti-racism can all variously inform the regulatory frameworks and cultural climates in which mainstream and minority productions can either flourish or founder' (2000: 17).

As approaches associated with 'multiculturalism' have been critiqued by audiences as too flat and limited, and within wider political discourse as exacerbating differences and undermining 'integration' (for a general critique see Lentin and Titley 2011), most of the studies are located within a paradigm of 'diversity'. According to Yudhishthir Raj Isar (2006), diversity has become a 'normative meta-narrative' widely deployed

with a view to supporting the 'right to be different' of many different categories of individuals/groups placed in some way outside dominant social and cultural norms, hence including disabled people, gays and lesbians, women, as well as the poor and the elderly.

(Raj Isar 2006: 373)

What must be noted however, is that merely supporting the right to be different tells us little about either difference or rights. In other words, institutional practices of diversity vary enormously, and diversity is a fluid idea.

Ben O'Loughlin's (2006) study of the 'operationalization of the concept "cultural diversity" in British television policy and governance' provides a useful comparative analysis to the approaches contained here. In the 1970s and 1980s, policy debates centred upon issues of 'including diverse and marginalised voices' in the 'national conversation' by focusing on including a diversity of contributors and dedicated programmes, and on the politics of representation. Organized under the rubric of 'multiculturalism', programming energies were directed towards 'recognising, and managing different – essentialised – identities and voices' (2006: 3). By the 1990s, O'Loughlin argues, the idea of cultural diversity had begun to replace multiculturalism. Politically, there was an increased emphasis in the United Kingdom on discourses of 'social cohesion' in the aftermath of the Cantle report into the urban uprisings in northern England in 2001.

At the same time, 'diversity' was seen as congruent with governmental requirements to develop individual capacities in complex societies and competitive 'knowledge economies'. Thus by the 2000s, the 'concept of cultural diversity as a mode of thinking about identity' was informed by the need to have 'plural overlapping conversations within and across the differing political, social, cultural and economic spaces within which people living in Britain are located and locate themselves' (2006:3). Concomitantly, it involved a shift to a 'flowing concept of cultural diversity' where the 'policy goal has been to increase the social capital of individuals in Britain as a means to ends such as democratic renewal, social cohesion, and economic productivity'.

As the studies here detail, within European public service broadcasters, diversity is understood as a series of commitments to 'diversify' across three key areas: in *programming* (questions of representation and plurality of voice), in *employment* and in *organizational development* (training people to appreciate/learn from diversity). Diversity frameworks have provided what Håkon Larsen (2010) terms a 'legitimation strategy' for public service broadcasters, promising to reconcile this dimension of their public mission with the exigencies of commercial competition and audience share. In general, multicultural formats have been replaced by strategies designed to develop 'cross-cultural forms', as dedicated formats are seen not only as having a limited relevance to more diversified minority audiences, but also to represent a politically unacceptable parallelism. Similarly, the focus on ethnic minority recruitment is to a significant extent being replaced by the idea of diversity as a reflexive 'competence' – a way of perceiving and working that any journalist or broadcaster can cultivate.

Andra Leurdijk (2006) has conducted qualitative research with producers in Austria, Belgium, Germany, the Netherlands and the United Kingdom; and to a lesser extent, with producers in Finland, Ireland, Italy and Sweden. 'Multicultural programming' emerges as a fluid category underpinned by an educational message: 'In general programmes are based on the assumption that cultural diversity and multicultural society are not (yet) sufficiently or adequately represented in the programme schedules and require separate attention, special staff and dedicated time slots' (Leurdijk 2006: 27). At the time of her study, in all but the United Kingdom and the Netherlands, multicultural programming was based around the allocation of dedicated programme slots, a situation that has shifted, in large part because of the criticisms her research investigates: dedicated slots are seen as box-ticking, limited television, and in some instances, as a compromising of quality standards. When the contemporary politics of 'integration' are added to this picture, it illustrates why the smaller public service broadcasters featured here are moving away from conventional slot-based magazine programmes to various forms of 'integrated' approaches.

'Cross-cultural appeal' is a notion that combines the aspirations of a unifying public service with a sharp awareness of the competitive environment, and drives programme makers to 'search for subjects of common interest or to find clever ways of presenting a subject in such a way that it appeals to viewers with different ethnic and cultural backgrounds' (Leurdijk 2006: 30). In this context the 'strong individual story' has emerged from the putative suffocation of group-based representation, where a focus on personalities, experiences, emotions and human stories is regarded as the necessary basis for 'cross-cultural' programming. As many studies here explore, the hybrid generic possibilities of 'reality television' formats has centred a focus on daily life, modalities of social existence and stories of 'exceptional people', to an extent that viewers are familiar with the idea that 'the particular stands for general social or human problems and displays something about present-day multicultural societies' (Leurdijk 2006: 34).

While these new approaches are widely contrasted with the overly 'paternalistic and educational' approach of magazine and slot-based programmes, it may not amount to more than substituting a commodified, cosmopolitan, lifestyle 'diversity' for the equally flat, if less sexy, world of 'multicultural programming'. Similarly, while the individual particular story may say something about wider social experiences and relations, just as easily it may not – this is a function of treatment, not merely form. As Leurdijk concludes:

Multicultural programmes do not necessarily imply a specific political stance, philosophy or ideology on multicultural societies or on the issues concerning immigration and integration. However at a more abstract level, the underlying concepts do express a certain way of thinking about multiculturalism [...] [the early programmes] functioned as a sort of compensation for the under-representation or misrepresentation of minority perspectives in mainstream programming. In trying to gain larger audiences, stressing the universality of human emotions and experiences became the next important strand [...] 'multicultural' came to stand for showing incidences and locations of contact and communication between minority and majority groups, despite differences in cultural backgrounds [...] in its latest inflections, the term 'multicultural' refers to a mixture of cosmopolitan styles most visible in urban youth culture, or to subject matter that deals with cultural identity as an important field of both pleasure and anxiety in modern western societies. Of course the development and present reality of multicultural programming are not as clear-cut as this categorization suggests. Different approaches coexist over time and rarely are programmes informed by well-considered and philosophically-grounded concepts of multiculturalism.

(2006: 42)

These different approaches, and their commonalities across institutions and contexts, are explored in this book. The concerted focus on policy-making and programme development is outlined below, but it also draws attention to an astonishing gap in 'cultural diversity' policies. In his work on 'reinventing public service communication', Petros Iosifidis (2010) emphasizes the possibilities of interactive digital media for enabling 'public service media to reflect the multi-cultural and multi-ethnic composition of contemporary European societies'. At this moment in time, however, these studies reflect the near absence of attempts to use PSM possibilities to engage diverse audiences and to overcome the burden of representation.

An overview of the book

The political, economic, institutional and discursive transitions sketched above raise a number of critical questions that are explored through a focus on north and west European contexts – Flemish, Dutch, Irish, Swedish, Finnish and Norwegian PSM – in which broad state intervention and strong public service broadcasting systems are typical (Moe and Syvertsen 2009). While this rationale underpins the choice of case studies, it is worth noting that the choice has also been shaped by pragmatic considerations as to where significant histories of such policy development exist, and whether research was or had been conducted in context. Estonian public service media has developed in a post-Soviet media landscape, and while it provides an interesting case study in its own right, it also illustrates the pressures generated by an accelerated process of working through these issues, particularly in an EU framework. More prosaically, the choice of contexts was shaped by contingent pragmatism; the absence of considerations of other western, central and eastern, and southern European countries is dictated by the absence of available research during the course of this project.

Sarita Malik's chapter sets out an important conceptual landscape by examining three overlapping areas that pertain to the question of representation: *audience representation* (what is provided, and how do audiences evaluate it, particularly in the context of the rise of 'post-national' diasporic TV); *textual representation* (the encoding and construction of meanings associated with cultural diversity through communication); and the encompassing *politics of cultural recognition in public communication.* Attention to these dimensions, Malik writes, 'can help us to understand public service broadcasting as a principal signifying system in contemporary society, which actively and continuously depends on the representational process'. Through a discussion of the BBC – regarded by many other PSBs as a key influence in this area of media work – Malik's analysis details the development of a 'post-multiculturalist' era emphasizing integration and shared citizenship.

The institutional shaping of this 'post-multiculturalist' era is explored in Karina Horsti's examination of collaboration between public service broadcasters on cultural diversity policies at a European level. As Tarlach McGonagle's subsequent chapter demonstrates, there is no direct legal regulation, at the European level, in this particular policy area of cultural diversity. Nevertheless, European broadcasters have collaborated, shared experiences and made policy recommendations among themselves, and in collaboration with or under pressure from NGOs (non-governmental organizations) and journalist associations. Echoing Malik's diagnosis, this chapter details a shift from overt discussions of anti-racist intent to a discourse of cultural diversity that de-politicizes difference, and that identifies 'non-integration' of 'migrants' as the main problem. Horsti's chapter also notes that European diversity initiatives focus on diversity in media content, and to a limited extent in recruitment, with little attention paid to access to education, distribution of public funding, alternative ways of organizing journalism and relations between mainstream and minority media in the digital media environment. Her conclusion that European broadcasting collaboration is withdrawing from cultural diversity policy-making, is borne out in several national case studies.

Tarlach McGonagle's contribution focuses on regulatory frameworks for cultural diversity and cultural provision, and examines the regulatory instruments applicable at the European level. As he documents, there is an extensive European regulatory framework for public service broadcasting/media, encompassing legal and policy instruments from the European Union and the Council of Europe, but also involving the standard-setting measures developed by UNESCO (United Nations Educational, Scientific and Cultural Organization) and others. In arguing that PSBs and PSM can and should develop measures that ensure that programming and other related services correspond to the needs of culturally diverse audiences, the chapter surveys the regulatory instruments available in the European context and evaluates their contributions to possibilities for representation, access and participation.

The second part of the book presents national case studies. A recurring theme in these studies is the pressures on cultural diversity policy and public service media in the context of increasing right-wing populism and political hostility. Isabel Awad and Jiska Engelbert examine these pressures in relation to Dutch broadcasters, which, as with the BBC and the United Kingdom, have been influential in the shaping of cultural diversity policy in the European mediascape, and have an impact on the thinking of policy-makers elsewhere. Nevertheless, as Awad and Engelbert show, their guiding concepts of *pluriformity* and *diversity* are mapped onto specifically Dutch categorizations, of autochthonous ('natively' Dutch) and *allochtonen* (migrant-descended) differences, where autochthonous differences can be conceived of as social resources, while non-autochthonous differences are discouraged.

The flow of transnational exchange in policy-making and institutional ideology is taken up by Alexander Dhoest's study of the Flemish VRT (Vlaamse Radio en Televisie). He notes the influence of Dutch and British PSB approaches to cultural diversity, but documents how, in comparison to their neighbours, Flemish initiatives have been highly limited in scale and sporadically implemented. And in a theme that is rendered familiar as the book progresses, he examines how the wider political context, and in particular the appeal of far-right actors, has inhibited and intensively politicized the development of diversity policy and programming. However, the chapter teases out a situation where 'good intentions' are at least constant, if constantly in tension with their translation and impact.

Gavan Titley's chapter examines RTÉ (Raidió Teilifís Éireann) in Ireland and its policy and programme development during a period of intensive public focus on migration and sociocultural change. Like Dhoest, his study details institutional good intentions and also reflexivity, as RTÉ developed and published 'intercultural indicators' for their diversity commitments, and accelerated through exploring the generic possibilities accumulated in other PSBs over much longer periods of time. However, his study illustrates perhaps the most dramatic instance of the European turn away from cultural diversity policy. Titley places this in the context of the 'semiotic commitments' that characterized the governance of difference during the so-called Celtic Tiger period in Ireland, commitments rapidly disassembled and forgotten with the onset of economic recession and political crisis.

This rapid inflation and deflation contrasts with Gunilla Hultén's study of Sweden's largest public service actors' – Swedish Television (Sveriges Television –SVT) and Swedish Radio (Sveriges Radio – SR) – long-standing engagement with cultural diversity in their programming and staffing. Through an examination of policy documents and interviews with managers in the institutions, she examines how the policies are interpreted and put into practice, and the interviews reveal discrepancies between the principles and practices of cultural diversity policies. Hultén shows how 'benevolent' attempts to bring diversity into the newsrooms are in conflict with the prerogative of securing market share, a conflict that renders diversity a 'vulnerable value'.

Karina Horsti's study of Finland's YLE and its 'politics of a multicultural mission' examines the ways in which the public service broadcaster articulates its position and responsibility to cultural diversity in the shadow of a long-running, politicized and polarized 'immigration debate'. YLE followed Swedish SVT in its cultural diversity policy, and shifted from 'niche programming' and an affirmative action form of multicultural policy to the idea of 'mainstreaming' diversity in all of its programming. In so doing, the company attempts to balance between vulnerability to increasing anti-immigration sentiments and populist politics, on the one hand, and a commitment to the democratic responsibility to serve minorities and recognize them as equal members of the society. The chapter offers an assessment of this balancing act.

Whereas, as the previous two chapters examine, the broadcasters in Sweden and Finland have abandoned distinct 'ethnic minority' programmes and editorial offices, Gunn Bjørnsen's study illustrates how Norway presents a somewhat different experience of Nordic public service broadcasting. The Norwegian NRK has expanded its 'niche' editorial office, Migrapolis, and for Bjørnsen, this commitment is bound up in a dual articulation of the cultural function of Norwegian public service broadcasting; attempting to define the 'classic Norwegian' experience while attempting to include new perspectives on 'ways to be Norwegian'.

The final national case study differs from the others in many ways. Andreas Jõesaar and Saame Rannu analyse how Estonian public broadcasting caters for 'linguistic minorities' in a context of post-Soviet adoption and adaptation of public service media approaches. Of particular consequence here is how the Russian-speaking minority in this small nation is represented and recognized in the national Estonian media, and where Russian speakers have access to the enormous and highly proximate Russian media landscape. The chapter analyses four major tensions in the development of Estonian PSB's cultural diversity policies: between Estonia and Russia as nation-states; between Estonian and Russian media outlets; between Estonian and Russian speakers within Estonia; and between the European Union and Estonia concerning the role and function of PSB.

The afterword, by Andrew Jakubowicz, synthesizes questions emerging from the national cases studies, and in reprising what is at stake in contested understandings of the public, identifies key trajectories of change – tensions in the 'European project', concomitant and resurgent nationalisms, migration and diaspora as dimensions of the transnationalization of the nation – which confront media institutions locked into national frameworks, and are committed to complex projects of national address. In framing this synthesis, Jakubowicz's survey draws attention to the particularities of debates emerging from northern Europe, and underlines how studies focused on the same issues in southern Europe – in a conjuncture where both public resources and democratic institutions are threatened by neo-liberal crisis – would look radically different. His thoughtful response contrasts the constraints and debates surveyed in northern Europe with Australia, and concludes with a statement of the common challenge facing representative media systems seeking to engage with globalizing, societal change in a hostile political economy:

As the tensions in European public media demonstrate, the transformations in global populations, the huge displacement of refugees and economic immigrants, and the pending pressures from environmental, political, economic and social crises, suggest that the public media have an increasingly important part to play. They will need to explain, interpret, engage with, and inform many different people, and do so in ways that remain respectful, authoritative and effective. The evidence suggest that, unless they seriously rethink their roles in maintaining social cohesion and ensuring communication rights, they will have their work cut out for them.

References

Ahmed, S. (2000), *Strange Encounters: Embodied Others in Post-Coloniality*, London: Routledge.

Ahmed, S., Hunter, S., Kilic, S., Swan, E., & Turner, L., et al. (2006), *Integrating Diversity: Race, Gender and Leadership in the Learning and Skills Sector*, Lancaster: Centre for Excellence in Leadership.

Appadurai, A. (2006), *Fear of Small Numbers*, Durham: Duke University Press.

Bakker, P. (2012), 'Expectations, experiences & exceptions: Promises and realities of participation on websites', in G. F. Lowe and J. Steemers (eds), *Regaining the Initiative for Public Service Media: [RIPE@2011]*, Gothenburg: Nordicom.

Billig, M. (1995), *Banal Nationalism*, London: Sage.

Blumler, J. G., (1992) 'Introduction', in J. G. Blumler (ed.), *Television and the Public Interest*, London: Sage.

Cottle, S. (2000) (ed.), *Ethnic Minorities and the Media*, Buckingham: Open University Press.

Couldry, N. (2012), *Media, Society, World: Social Theory and Media Practice*, Cambridge, UK: Polity.

Debrett, M. (2009), *Reinventing Public Service Television for the Digital Future*, Bristol: Intellect.

Directorate General of Human Rights and Legal Affairs (2009), *Report Prepared by the Group of Specialists on Public Service Media in the Information Society*, Strasbourg: Council of Europe Publishing.

Donders, K. (2012), *Public Service Media and Policy in Europe*, Basingstoke: Palgrave Macmillan.

Donders, K. and Pauwels, C. (2012), 'Ex ante tests: A means to an end or the end for public service media?', in G. F. Lowe and J. Steemers (eds), *Regaining the Initiative for Public Service Media: [RIPE@2011]*, Gothenburg: Nordicom.

Ellis, J. (2000), *Seeing Things: Television in an Age of Uncertainty*, London: I.B. Tauris.

Faist, T. (2009), 'Diversity – a new mode of incorporation?', *Ethnic and Racial Studies*, 32: 1, pp. 171–90.

Fraser, N. and Honneth, A. (2003), *Redistribution or Recognition? A Political-Philosophical Exchange*, London: Verso.

Guild, E., Groenendijk, K. and Carrera, S. (eds) (2009), *Illiberal Liberal States: Immigration, Citizenship and Integration in the EU*, Farnham: Ashgate.

Hage, G. (2000), *White Nation: Fantasies of White Supremacy in a Multicultural Society*, London: Routledge.

Hall, S. (2000), 'The multicultural question', in H. Barnor (ed.), *Un/settled Multiculturalisms: Diasporas, Entanglements, Transruptions*, London: Zed Books.

Hallin, D. and Mancini, P. (2004), *Comparing Media Systems: Three Models of Media and Politics*, Cambridge: CUP.

Hartley, J. (1999), *Uses of Television*, London: Routledge.

Iosifidis, P. (2012 [2007]), *Public Television in the Digital Era: Technological Challenges and New Strategies for Europe*, Basingstoke: Palgrave Macmillan.

Iosifidis, P. (2010), 'Reinventing public service communication', *Open Democracy*, 4 May, http://www.opendemocracy.net/ourkingdom/petros-iosifidis/reinventing-public-service-communication. Accessed 10 December 2012.

Isar, Y.R. (2006), 'Cultural diversity', *Theory Culture & Society*, 23:2-3, pp. 372-375.

Larsen, H. (2010), 'Legitimation strategies of public service broadcasters: The divergent rhetoric in Norway and Sweden', *Media, Culture & Society*, 32:2, pp. 267-283.

Lentin, A. and Titley, G. (2011), *The Crises of Multiculturalism: Racism in a Neoliberal Age*, London: Zed Books.

Leurdijk, A. (2006), 'In search of common ground: Strategies of multicultural television producers in Europe', *European Journal of Cultural Studies*, 2: 1, pp. 25–46.

Lievrouw, L. A. (2011), *Alternative and Activist New Media*, Cambridge, UK: Polity.

Lowe, G. F. and Steemers, J. (2012), 'Regaining the initiative for public service media', in G. F. Lowe and J. Steemers (eds), *Regaining the Initiative for Public Service Media: [RIPE@2011]*, Gothenburg: Nordicom, pp. 9–23.

Millwood Hargrave, A. (ed.) (2002), *Multicultural Broadcasting: Concept and Reality*, London: BBC, Broadcasting Standards Commission.

Moe, H. and Syvertsen, T. (2009), 'Researching public broadcasting', in Karin Wahl-Jorgensen and Thomas Hanitzsch (eds), *The Handbook of Journalism Studies*, New York: Routledge.

Murdock, G. (1999), 'Corporate dynamics and broadcasting futures', in H. Mackay and T. O'Sullivan (eds), *The Media Reader: Continuity and Transformation*, London: Sage Publications.

Murdock, G. (2005), 'Building the digital commons: Public broadcasting in the age of the Internet', in G. F. Lowe and P. Jauert (eds), *Cultural Dilemmas in Public Service Broadcasting: RIPE@2005*, Gothenburg: Nordicom.

O'Loughlin, B. (2006), 'The operationalization of the concept cultural diversity in British television policy and governance', *ESRC CRESC Working Paper No. 27*, Milton Kenyes: Open University.

Papathanassopoulos, S. and Negrine, R. M. (2011), *European Media*, Cambridge, UK: Polity.

Pitcher, B. (2009), *The Politics of Multiculturalism*, Basingstoke: Palgrave.

Silverstone, R. (2006), *Media and Morality: On the Rise of the Mediapolis*, Cambridge, UK: Polity.

Srebreny, A. (1999), *Include Me In: Rethinking Ethnicity on Television*, London: Broadcasting Standards Commission.

Stevenson, N. (2003), *Cultural Citizenship, Cosmopolitan Questions*, Maidenhead: Open University Press.

Taylor, C. (1994), *Multiculturalism: Examining the Politics of Recognition*, Princeton: PUP.

Vasta, E. (2007), 'From ethnic minorities to ethnic majority policy: Multiculturalism and the shift to assimilationism in the Netherlands', *Ethnic and Racial Studies*, 30: 5, pp. 713–40.

Section 1

The Rise of Diversity and Transition to Public Service Media: Complementary Perspectives

Chapter 1

Diversity, Broadcasting and the Politics of Representation

Sarita Malik (Brunel University)

Introduction

This chapter addresses issues of representation raised by the shifting emphases on how multiculture should be mediated in contemporary Europe. It foregrounds questions of representation, as a key concept in cultural and media studies, in order to offer a critical overview of the relationship between public service broadcasting, cultural diversity and European societies. One of the main objectives is to consider how lived multiculture is managed and mediated by the broadcasters. Whilst an important dimension of this 'management' is around the area of audio-visual policy frameworks (the dominant approach in current work around diversity and public service broadcasting in Europe (Rumphorst 2004; Freedman 2005), there are important issues of representation that do not relate directly to public policy.

So my interest here is with how the thread of representation runs through two, overlapping areas: first, audience representation (which considers the notion of provision, complex audience involvements with mediated communication and the rise of 'post-national' diasporic TV); and second, textual representation (the ways in which meanings associated with cultural diversity are made on-screen). A third dimension is involved here: the politics of cultural recognition in public communication (pertaining to the idea of how the 'public' of PSB might be defined). Representation is regarded here as a historical, institutional and political process. Media and cultural analysis highlights how, rather than simply reflecting or presenting 'reality', the work of representation constructs 'reality' and, more than that, serves an important role in how social relations develop and in how ideologies are constructed. The various 'ways in' to understanding the meaning of representation, can help us to understand public service broadcasting as a principal signifying system in contemporary society, which actively and continuously depends on the representational process.

The overview presented here considers the broader sociopolitical contexts against which such developments are occurring. Primarily this involves mapping the major European-wide paradigm shift from principles of multiculturalism to social cohesion; and asking what the possible implications are for these various orders of representation – audience developments, textual representations and the politics of cultural recognition. A set of questions begin to emerge here: how have multicultural audiences been implicated in the move away from multiculturalism? What kind of picture of cultural diversity is painted by the public service broadcasters? And what bearing does this have on both the politics of difference and the politics of recognition for Europe's diasporic groups?

Specifically, the chapter will address issues of ethnic minority representation in relation to broader political and economic developments in public service broadcasting since the 1990s. The specific dimension of cultural diversity that will be reflected on will be ethnic minorities, because their case has been especially caught up in the difficulties currently facing public service broadcasters. The relevance of the ethnic minority case study has a wider significance for what we consider the role of public service to be in a diverse Europe. Other chapters in this book take a range of European countries including Denmark, Estonia, Finland, Ireland, the Netherlands, Sweden and Belgium as their national case studies. Although this is a general, thematic chapter which aims to explore some of the overarching themes related to representation, particular reference will be made to the United Kingdom. The rationale for this is that the United Kingdom has typically been at the vanguard of academic debates around the politics of representation and diversity in contemporary Europe (Cottle 2000; Malik, S. 2002). PSB was pioneered in the United Kingdom in the 1920s and has, since then, operated a particularly strong and globally recognized public service framework. Whilst the UK context is discussed here, many of the issues addressed are common ones that are pertinent to the dilemmas currently being faced by other public service broadcasters across Europe (see Malik 2010). This is not to divert attention from the nuanced and national characteristics of the different European public service broadcasters that are dealt with in other parts of the book.

Running parallel to the intensifying Europe-wide retreat from multiculturalism, ethnic minorities have also altered their response to PSB as a form of media governance. This is currently a scenario which indicates the 'autonomous' production and circulation of 'ethnicized' representations targeted at distinct ethnic groups led by cable and satellite systems that have what McQuail in his discussion of the principles of media structure, calls a 'premium on diversity' (McQuail 2010: 224). The textual representations which are offered by these transnational communication outlets appear to flaunt a more culturally intelligent and nuanced mode of representation and address (for example in terms of language, geographical setting and genre). They may also draw on a more diverse set of editorial practices, values and ideologies (see Creeber 2004). But the seeming diversity in provision also holds no guarantees, either that audiences are in turn getting deeper cultural value or an opportunity to position themselves collectively as national citizens. Indeed, diasporic audiences' responses to transnational flows of television across national borders appear far from clear-cut (see Aksoy and Robins [2000] for analysis of Turkish audiences' responses to transnational media in Europe). As we experience the steady erosion of public service broadcasting, this idea of the shared national experience appears to be waning (Tracey 1998).

Mediation of multiculture: A shifting emphasis

Social change and the role of the state in fostering principles of multiculturalism play a significant role in mediated communication, not least in how programme-making and editorial policy is organized in relation to society. Although multiculture is a long-established feature of modern Europe and demographically continues to develop along these lines, multicultural*ism* is also being actively undermined as a normative principle within political and public discourse. Multiculturalism, defined here as both an ideological principle and a practice of addressing cultural diversity through legislation and cultural and social policies, can be made distinct from cultural diversity which is a fact of all societies. If multicultural describes the nature of a society's cultural heterogeneity, multiculturalism refers to 'the strategies and policies adopted to govern or manage the problems of diversity and multiplicity which multi-cultural societies throw up' (Hall 2000: 210). As Europe's streets become more culturally diverse, we have witnessed since the late 1990s a critical shift against the idea of multiculturalism (which had publicly redirected the attention away from the evolving anti-racist politics of the 1970s and 1980s). In its place, a centre-left reconstruction of liberal integrationism and assimilationist-style rhetoric has materialized, aspiring towards an 'absolute citizen' subject based around integration, shared values and citizenship. Kenan Malik suggests the shift away from multiculturalism and towards 'a collective language of citizenship' is important because it

> creates a challenge to the politics of identity and a redefinition of social justice and equality: from the right to be treated the same despite one's cultural and ethnic differences, to the right to be treated differently because of them.
>
> (Malik, K. 2002: 2)

The overtone here is that multiculturalism has gone 'too far' and now requires a redefinition in order to deliver genuine social equality. Kenan Malik's view is reflected in a number of iterative populist European reconstructions which claim that multiculturalism and collective citizenship are incompatible, and renewed public policy concerns around social cohesion. The official turn has been exemplified in, for example, the argument made by Farrukh Dhondy, the UK broadcaster and Channel 4's former Head of Multicultural Programming (1984–97), against what he termed 'the multicultural fifth column' (Dhondy 2001) and in favour of the redirection of state funding towards supporting values of freedom and democracy (see Modood 2007). David Goodhart (2004) has described Britain as 'too diverse' and Trevor Phillips (2005), (former Chair of the Commission for Racial Equality and Chair of the Centre for Equality and Human Rights since 2007) has urged that Britain moves on from the old order of 1980s multicultural policy-making in order to avoid 'sleepwalking our way to segregation' (Phillips 2005). Although the legacy of pre-existing historical trajectories of 'racialization' of belonging in society are apparent (see Malik, S. 2002), these recent reconstructions have tapped into the popular imagination. An alternative and lesser-heard (anti-racist) critique argues that, at worst, multiculturalism has failed to tackle the political realities of racisms (Sivanandan 2006) and, at best, that multicultural policy-making has damaged the race equality agenda.

The media, and especially the right-wing press, has played a formative role in developing and mainstreaming this post-multiculturalist mood with a circuit of headline stories based around 'home-grown terrorists', immigrant 'benefit-cheats' and 'political correctness gone mad'. Meanwhile, popular narratives around 'asylum seekers', 'black gun crime', the 'clash of civilizations' and, most of all, 'the war on terror', have all framed today's mainstream media agenda. One of the facets of mainstream attacks on multiculturalism is the emphasis on cultural difference. The major ideological fear stoked here is that cultural (not social, racial or economic) segregation is problematic (or as Phillips put it, that society is 'becoming more divided by race and religion' and that we are 'eyeing each other over the fences of our differences' [Phillips 2005]). Instances such as rioting in England following the racism habitually directed, not least by the police, at ethnic communities (2001), 'race riots' in France (2005), the UK *Behzti* affair (2004), the *Jyllands-Posten* Muhammad cartoons controversy (2005), the ongoing 'veil debate', the London bombings (2005), the minarets controversy in Switzerland (2009) and the far-right's evolving integration into mainstream politics (culminating in, for example, the British National Party's victories at the European elections in 2009), are all examples that have sustained a preoccupation with publicly evaluating the supposed challenges of living with difference. In 2010, the German Chancellor, Angela Merkel stated that 'the approach [to build] a multicultural [society] and to live side-by-side and to enjoy each other [...] has failed, utterly failed' (Merkel 2010). Subsequently, French Prime Minster Nicolas Sarkozy, on a TF1 French television nationwide broadcast clearly stated that he also considers multiculturalism to be 'a failure' (*CBN News* 2011). In the United Kingdom the current broader political-cultural philosophies around multiculturalism first emerged as part of a broader New Labour politics of citizenship in the 1990s. The UK Prime Minister David Cameron delivered a speech in Munich (2011) where he criticized the 'doctrine of state multiculturalism' for encouraging different cultures to live separate lives and suggested, 'we need a lot less of the passive tolerance of recent years and a much more active, muscular liberalism' (Cameron 2011). The defence of 'social cohesion' has, in practical and rhetorical terms, therefore been mobilized as a populist and popular attack on multiculturalism because of the latter's supposed 'tribalism' and, it is claimed, divisiveness. Such overt condemnations of multiculturalist principles by Merkel, Sarkozy and Cameron would arguably have been inconceivable even a decade before.

The timing of the 'crisis of multiculturalism' across Europe is significant. First, it has been utilized to coincide with the rise of a reinvigorated extreme right in Europe. Cameron's speech, for example, was delivered on the same day as a high-profile English Defence League rally in Luton, England. Both were reported back-to-back in news bulletins during the course of the day. Second, this emergent politics has fed into new exclusionary forms of cultural racism preoccupied with nation, territory and identity. So Cameron's speech was delivered at the 2011 *Munich Security Conference* and combined a comment on radicalization and Islamic extremism with one on multiculturalism. The retreat from multiculturalism, intensified since 9/11, has produced a new discourse of global terrorism and a highly-charged political climate wherever it touches on questions of racial and, increasingly, religious difference.

Representations of British Muslims in the media (Poole 2006) which are indicative of these new forms of cultural racism (Modood 2007) predicated on a discursive turn that mediates, in a Gramscian sense, culturally hegemonic, common-sense responses to 'difference'. And so, it is apparent that contemporary news and documentary editorial directions are increasingly based around these iterative post-multiculturalist themes of the cultural difference of minority lifestyles. When contextualizing media representations, they can be considered as part of a shift from the struggle against racism (apparent for example in the circuit of racialized regimes of representation in the decades spanning the 1950s to the 1980s; see Malik, S. 2002) towards a struggle for religion and culture in contemporary Britain (apparent in representations since the 1990s). For example, the basic media agenda is now less preoccupied with the traditional black versus white diagrammatic seen in earlier sets of race-related reporting than with highlighting discord between those who support a secular state and those who do not. There is a strong pattern of reporting still concerned with issues of race and nation (as in the recent public evaluations of multiculturalism) but overlaid with updated populist narratives conflated with questions of religiosity ('war on terror', 'the enemy within', 'freedom of speech', 'clash of civilizations', 'rise of Islamism', etc.). The news agenda of the public service broadcasters frequently takes its cue from that of the mainstream press, which plays a major public role in these shifts in orientation and in the processes whereby overlapping public identities are constructed and transformed. Many of those who defend the media's focus on Islam and Muslims argue that this is in the public interest, but frequently fail to recognize the role that these same representations can play in stoking fear, amplifying risk and perpetuating the fabled horror of certain religious lifestyles. It is against this unsettled context that we will now turn our attention to PSB.

Audience involvements with mediated communication: Diversity within universality

Issues of representation relate to the notion of provision and complex audience involvements with mediated communication. Public service broadcasting, particularly in western Europe, has traditionally been tied to the ideal of national broadcasting, raising particular issues when we complicate the idea of the national. As the founder of the British Broadcasting Corporation (BBC), John Reith, declared in 1924: 'It is occasionally indicated to us that we are apparently setting out to give the public what we think they need – and not what they want – but few know what they want and very few know what they need (Reith, quoted in Briggs 1961: 238).

Within the context of the British Empire, the tone of Lord Reith's declaration is fitting; a version of Britishness was sanctioned that would elucidate formations of a national identity and be constructed from a white, British perspective. Reithian philosophy has been apparent in the trajectory of public service development and 'national address' over the years. Television from the perspective of ethnic minority communities today has begun to challenge traditional ways of conceptualizing, regulating and running television along national lines as Europe's ethnic minority communities develop their own unique affiliations and points of identification beyond national broadcasting. As delocalization develops, the role of national broadcasting as a kind of 'social glue' that produces the ideological pursuits of national unity and what Raymond Williams has called 'common culture' (1971) has become problematic. PSB's apparently unifying project based around a national public culture and identification is tasked with being entirely inclusive and grappling with the nuances of difference (cultural, racial or otherwise) in a multicultural, if not multicultural*ist*, Europe. At the heart of this ethical dilemma is the question of representation.

In order to acknowledge the historical situatedness of diasporic television in contemporary Europe, it is useful to map the connections between formative models of national televisual address such as the 'multicultural programming' that emerged out of this evolving context of cultural hegemony, and the recent increasingly globalized communications market. Since the 1990s, traditional, national analogue broadcasters that arose in the 1930s (United Kingdom, Germany, France, Poland, Italy), 1940s (Czechoslovakia, West Germany, East Germany) and 1950s (Switzerland, Denmark, the Netherlands, Poland) have had to negotiate their position alongside satellite, cable and digital commercial channels. From the latter, diasporic television has emerged, enabling various 'nationals' to identify with 'the homeland' and build connections amongst and across dispersed regional, national and transnational audiences. For minority audiences, diaspora television has become a powerful mechanism for those sharing common cultural concerns with each other, such as a religion, language or ethnicity, and to defend their collective interests, albeit beyond a national framework. The ways in which these diasporic identities are practised, performed and represented through the medium inevitably raises important cultural and commercial issues for Europe's public service broadcasters who have long legitimated their position in the nation-state as a source of public value.

Cultural diversity functions as a core aspect of the European debate on culture and cultural policy (see Rumphorst 2004). The European concept of cultural diversity and identity is built on two distinct ideas: on the one hand, the diversity of cultures, and, on the other, the assumption of a shared history and commonality. Historically, different (often conflicting) European traditions have existed when it comes to the 'promotion' of cultural diversity (see Bašić-Hrvatin, Thompson and Jusić 2008; also see Frachon and Vargaftig (1995) for a detailed outline of the cultural approaches of different European countries up until the mid-1990s). Diasporic television has therefore become one of the major cultural developments through which we can consider broader European policy objectives such as 'social cohesion', 'European citizenship' and a 'community of values where all the different cultures can flourish' as outlined in the Lisbon strategy and the Model Law on Public Service Broadcasting referenced by the European Broadcasting Union (see Rumphorst 2004). It illustrates European television's shifting role in producing the shared values that democratic culture pursues.

By the 1960s and 1970s in the United Kingdom, it was apparent that various minority groups felt alienated from or misrepresented by the assumptions that customarily underpinned PSB provision based on what the public needs or what the nation constitutes (see Creeber 2004). The primary way in which Britain's ethnic minority communities were catered for was through domestic, terrestrial broadcasters in the shape of 'multicultural programming'. *Apna Hi Ghar Samajhiye* (*Make Yourself at Home*) (BBC, 1965–79) and *Nai Zindagi Naya Jeevan* (*New Life*) (BBC, 1968–82), for example, were early studio discussion and magazine shows with an explicitly integrationalist project helping minorities to settle and adjust to the British way of life. Recognizing diversity within universality was regarded by UK broadcasters as a method of celebrating difference and challenging inequality elsewhere. The United Kingdom frequently helped put these issues on the European agenda. For example, in 1992, 'Public Broadcasting for a Multicultural Europe' (PBME) was launched by BBC Education to formalize the debate with the European Broadcasting Union around the programming and employment policies of selected European broadcasters (see Singh, cited in Frachon and Vargaftig 1995: 60–67).

The early assimilationist and rather paternalistic modes of targeted programming were not exclusive to the United Kingdom. Germany's ZDF launched *Nachbarn, unsere Nachbarn* (*Neighbours, Our Neighbours*) in 1963; Belgium's public French-speaking channel, RTBF, also aired a magazine for immigrants in 1965; and France's FR3 first broadcast the magazine programme *Mosaïque* (*Mosaic*) in 1976 and then *Recontres* (*Meeting*) funded by the Fonds d'Action Sociale (Social Action Fund). Regions with later immigrant communities such as Italy offered more generalist provision, such as *Nonsolonero* (RAI2, 1988–94) a programme about, not for, immigrants (Frachon and Vargaftig 1995: 5). Switzerland's *Temps Présent* and *Tell Quel* launched by TSR in 1969 have exemplified more critical and topical programmes about the immigrant experience in the region. In 1991, the public channels in Hungary, Czechoslovakia and Slovakia launched Romanian-targeted programmes. Even from these few brief examples, it is apparent that most European countries have, at some stage, had some form of multicultural programming. These have either been targeted at immigrants or aimed to address regional diversity, and often functioned as a form of cultural or social intervention to reduce hostility and increase awareness of both migrant and majority communities. Like the United Kingdom, regions such as the Netherlands and Sweden have proclaimed to be multicultural societies and favour positive discrimination for their ethnic minorities. Other countries such as Germany and Austria have also incorporated 'multicultural programming' as a form of public television. By contrast, countries such as France, Belgium or Spain have preferred to work on the principle of individual integration. This divergent politics has been reflected in approaches to commissioning and programming, some (such as the United Kingdom and the Netherlands) placing emphasis on 'cross cultural' formats and others on themes hinged on common aspects of humanity such as love, death, birth and friendship (Leurdijk 2006).

In the United Kingdom, multicultural broadcasting policies (most notably between the 1970s following the Race Relations Acts and the early 1990s) had also included recruitment measures and targets, and specialist departments and slots, designed to explicitly position black and Asian representation on the media agenda. Official industry responses resulted in a range of series such as *Skin* (ITV/LWT, 1980), *Black on Black* (ITV/LWT, 1982–85), *Eastern Eye* (ITV/LWT 1982–85) and *Bandung File* (Channel 4, 1985–89). Additionally, the campaigns of black and Asian cultural workers peaked in the mid-1980s when the focus of anti-racist strategies began to extend from political issues (policing and immigration, for example) to cultural, religious and social ones. Black and Asian groups, such as the independent audio-visual collectives of the 1980s, generated (self-)representational practices and a distinct theory/practice interface within multicultural contexts.

The politics of mainstreaming 'diversity' in PSB

In the years following the UK 1990 Broadcasting Act, the public service case for multicultural programming was undermined by the emerging cultures of commercialism triggered by increasing competition, lighter touch regulation and technological developments. Consequently, the BBC and Channel 4 reformulated their multicultural departments, signalling the beginning of a more mainstream definition of multiculturalism in an attempt to attract bigger audiences. This arguably had serious implications for minority interests. Programmes such as *Goodness Gracious Me* (BBC2, 1998–2001), the British Asian led sketch-comedy series, which 'crossed over' to an 85 per cent-white viewing audience were symptomatic of this drive towards the mainstream. This institutionalized mainstreaming of diversity was also coinciding with the gradual withdrawal from multiculturalism that has been outlined. Minority audiences remained sceptical about such mainstreaming compared to 'majority audiences' (BBC 2002). In 2002, Caroline Thomson, then BBC Director of Public Policy, stated that ethnic minority audiences are

> not connecting with public service broadcasting and all it can offer with its mix of entertainment, education and information. The BBC and other public service broadcasters need to connect with this audience. Just how we make that connection is developing all the time.
>
> (Thompson 2002)

At the 2007 BBC Internal News and Sport Festival, the BBC Deputy Director General, Mark Byford, conceded that, for broadcasters, some people will always be 'unreachable'. He stated, 'If we chase every group with the aim of converting them as an audience, then we could run the risk of losing the core audience we already hold. There will always be some unreachables' (quoted in *The Guardian*, 24 January 2007). The idea that there are some groups who can or cannot be reached by the public service broadcasters is a significant admission in a traditional media culture underpinned by universalist goals.

These discursive shifts within PSB have helped produce an ambivalent response to lived multiculture in which coherent reactions to diverse communities are difficult to pin down. Since the millennium, public service broadcasting policy has shifted towards a more mainstream and less nuanced definition of 'multiculturalism' as 'cultural diversity' and more recently 'creative diversity' (Malik 2013), although there seems considerable ambiguity about the deliverables within these new policy frames. In 2000, for example, a network of UK broadcasters including Channel 4 established the Cultural Diversity Network, designed to promote cultural diversity on- and off-screen. The CDN was relaunched in 2010 after a decade of relative inactivity. In 2011, the Cultural Diversity Network merged with the Broadcasting and Creative Industries Disability Network (BCIDN) announcing 'a new name to reflect the network's remit' (Cultural Diversity Network 2011), the *Creative Diversity Network*. The significance of the literal replacing of 'Cultural' with 'Creative' in this instance is that the network members include all the major UK public service and commercial broadcasters, demonstrating both the current expansiveness of 'creative diversity' and its triumph over cultural diversity within media policy.

Thus the openness of the term 'diversity' is utilized and overlaid with an emphasis on innovation and creativity, which draws parallels with how it tends to operate within creative industries policy at large. It is possible for cultural diversity to be subsumed into the rhetoric of creativity because of the wider creative industries turn that now guides arts and media policy-making. What these 'creative diversity' scripts start to tell us about updated principles of 'public service', branding and accountability is that 'quality' and 'creativity' are now foregrounded over (structural) questions of (in)equality. Human resources becomes more important than content, and a broad sense of diversity is promoted rather than the naming of specific communities. Furthermore, the ubiquitous creative diversity paradigm is shaped by a pro-creative agenda and openly *not* by a politics of recognition of social or cultural difference.

Take as another example the United Kingdom's Channel 4 which, as part of a broader regime of cultural governance, was launched in 1982 with a brief to innovate and cater for minority interests. As the only UK terrestrial channel to have been established with multicultural programming embedded as part of its infrastructure and core practice, the double effect of these social and market transformations can now be identified. The most illustrative consequence of the redistributive project occurred when Channel 4 made the decision in 2002 to close its Multicultural Programmes Department. The channel now repositioned multicultural representations as part of a broader diversity agenda in which ethnic diversity was just one component.

It was suggested that, like British society, Channel 4 had 'moved on' and that the real future of ethnic minority representation was in mainstream programming. In 2001, Michael Jackson, who had been Channel 4's chief executive since 1997, explained the counter-intuitive rationale for the new approach:

Twenty years ago television didn't honestly reflect society. Channel 4 was launched in 1982 to give a voice to those who were underrepresented on the three channels that then existed. In 2001 the 'minorities' of those times have been assimilated into the mainstream of society.

(Jackson 2001)

Once a pioneer in introducing the idea of multiculturalism into the liberal project, the channel now assumed a more customary position, using the language of integration. Of course, in many ways, specialist minority programming did work against public service traditional (Reithian) broadcasting principles of universality. This approach is always in tension with, on the one hand, the struggle for 'recognition' and, on the other, the critique from neo-liberalism that it is both anti-universalistic and represents a drag on the market. It is open to the idea that there is no pay-off from an apparent engagement of political debate into structural questions of redistribution in the economic sphere. It also calls into question the idea that 'difference' can be the basis for effective political agency. However, the rationale given by Jackson was far less theoretical. The closure of the Multicultural Department signalled, for better or worse, the official declaration of post-multiculturalism within UK public service broadcasting.

In March 2008, these assertions were apparently contradicted when Channel 4 announced that as part of its major review of its public service role, it was going to work on

reinvigorating its connection with minority audiences, including appointing a new Head of Diversity, assigning a commissioning editor specific responsibility for multicultural programmes, with a ring-fenced budget and slots at 9pm and 10pm, and doubling the budget for the commissioning team's diversity placement scheme.

(Ofcom 2008: 106)

This fascinating U-turn by Channel 4 can only be regarded as symptomatic of changes in the market, especially if one considers the ensuing output from the department which has been geared towards a very generalist idea of what cultural diversity constitutes. For a channel now under extreme pressure (see Ofcom's second public service broadcasting review in 2008), the rebuilding of its 'connection with minority audiences' is occurring within the framework of an ever-more commercially-oriented media environment.

Channel 4's current public service drive is strategically entwined with its renewed diversity emphasis (which arguably sits at the heart of a public service ethos in which public value is determined). It is an important aspect of the organization's strategy to attract monies in a digital age in which the era of traditional public service broadcasting is fast eroding. Coming back full circle to Reithian ideals of diversity within universality, Channel 4 is now following the path of least resistance by being seen to champion diversity – 'vis-à-vis' creative diversity – and re-establish its brand; a popular manoeuvre and tokenistic gesture for a vulnerable channel needing the protection of public money.

On-screen manoeuvres

As it happened, the demise of specialist multicultural programming in the 2000s did coincide with a more general inclusion of ethnic minority representation in everyday output. The general circuit of representation, from news-readers to soap characters to participants in lifestyle shows, began to give the appearance of a more diverse, multicultural Europe. Strategic policy intervention notwithstanding, this was primarily licensed vis-à-vis genre developments within the medium, with the ways in which 'taste' has altered and specifically, I want to suggest, with the rise of reality and lifestyle programming.

The growth of lifestyle programming in the late 1990s became a turning-point in the relationship between ethnic minorities and television – later to be accelerated by the considerable expansion of the reality television genre. Traditional notions of authored access commonly to be found in the 1970s and 1980s (see Malik, S. 2002) were reinterpreted and updated in the form of docu-soaps, video diaries, makeover and lifestyle shows, giving a highly public platform to a larger range of cultural and social 'types'. The growing commercialization of broadcast media rendered programmes with political campaigning goals less popular with commissioning editors and advertisers than those preoccupied with lifestyle, talk and personal identity which were often associated with tabloid themes such as crime, property, health, celebrity and family. The impact of the evolution of this genre of programming for ethnic minority representation has been significant.

Today's glut of reality TV models from 'talent' shows such as *X Factor* (ITV, 2004–) and *Strictly Come Dancing* (BBC, 2004–) to 'self-improvement' shows like *Celebrity Fit Club* (ITV, 2002–) and *How Clean Is Your House?* (Channel 4, 2003–) to 'lifestyle change' series such as *Wife Swap* (Channel 4, 2003–) and *Supernanny* (Channel 4, 2004–) routinely feature diverse participants from a range of ethnic and social backgrounds. By the late 1990s, the lifestyle genre was thriving and the overall look of public service television had become increasingly pluralistic and 'multiculturalized'. This is also, of course, partly due to wider demographic and cultural forces: in broad terms, an emerging and confident third generation, greater ease for 'new ethnicities' (Hall 1989) and a steadily growing ethnic minority general workforce at certain levels in the media industries. But more intrinsically it is because of the broad-based participation that the new, hybrid formats permitted (Brunsdon 2003: 13). Many of these programmes also have a PSB-friendly educative conceit behind them (Smith 2010). What the genre has helped engineer is a greater visibility and ongoing presence of a range of 'ordinary' social types on our screens. As Graeme Turner argues, this 'demotic turn' (the increasing visibility of the 'ordinary person' in the media) does not necessarily generate social democracy (Turner 2009).

This hyper-visibility of multicultural societies (against the backdrop of 'post-multiculturalism') has produced an interesting dynamic between on- and off-screen contexts. The positioning of ethnic minorities in these programmes is relatively straightforward. Because the reality genre is reasonably unscripted compared with non-reality or narrative television (for example, sitcoms or drama), it largely escapes major accusations of misrepresentation, lack of authenticity or stereotyping; criticisms that television producers, editors and scriptwriters have long wrestled with. This makes the inclusion of ethnic minorities less politically-charged or likely to attract criticism. The reliability of the format has also moved on to other levels of inclusion where cultural, ethnic or religious difference is foregrounded. *Arrange Me a Marriage* (BBC, 2008) in which an Asian presenter uses the principles of modern arranged marriage to matchmake young singles and *Make me a Muslim* (Channel 4, 2007) in which an imam asks non-Muslims to follow Islamic teachings for a few weeks are two such examples. Ethnic contrast provides a twist, cutting through the otherwise formulaic textual approaches deployed in the genre, organized around the predictable narrative pattern of dilemma, transition and transformation. These are all compelling reasons for including a range of ethnic types.

To this degree, reality television has become the most ubiquitous and racially varied form of programming today, with ethnic minorities an important part of the mix; 'cast' in order to be representative of the 'real' lived diversity 'out there'. At the same time, the genre acts as a metaphor for a utopian society in which racial difference does not matter because we have all become assimilated. Referring back to the imaginary 'absolute citizen' that the European populists now covet, we can also identify reality/lifestyle television as a genre that is modelled around such aspirations. So, in reality game shows such as *The Apprentice* (BBC, 2005–) and *I'm a Celebrity Get Me Out of Here* (ITV, 2002–), contestants compete in an apparently 'flat hierarchy' for a prize, be it money, survival, a job or a partner. Symbolically, what underpins the point of the exercise is the desire to change one's life, with personal transformation as the ultimate prize (echoing in fact the narrative trajectory of the immigrant's journey). Here, it is important that reality television neutralizes racial difference, in order to put all contestants on a level playing field, and simulate a world where meritocracy rules; common humanity and sameness are emphasized over difference. On the one hand, this 'colour-blind' approach indicates a certain advance and may offer inspiration for some ethnic minority viewers, because racial power structures appear to be broken; on the other, it offers what is arguably a false sense of achievement or progress. There is a certain irony that these programmes support a widening chasm between those minority groups being publicly and momentarily celebrated on-screen whilst simultaneously being maligned in real, lived contexts and, for that matter, in other spaces of media representation.

The politics of cultural representation in public communication: The case of diasporic television

Alongside these developments in public service representations, more can be said about how diasporic television has become one of the primary ways in which ethnic minority groups now generate media practices and bid for recognition. In the United Kingdom, this was outlined in the Second Public Service Broadcasting Review (2008) led by Ofcom (Britain's media regulator) which reiterated both the ethnic minority turn towards other media outlets and forms and their dissatisfaction with public service provision. In spite of the minority-targeted programming that has now begun to wane, there has been an ongoing criticism that national television has failed to deliver meaningful and culturally 'in touch' representation for minority groups and displayed a particular fascination with certain kinds of topics and themes – asylum, difference and migration (see Georgiou 2010). British Asians were the earliest and most fervent adopters of cable and satellite television and their daily viewing habits indicate a rapidly eroding interest in national public service television, multicultural or otherwise. The growing number of Asian-led and targeted channels such as Zee UK and Europe and Sony Television, mainly transmitting Asian-language music, films and news claim their potential as new spaces of identification for Britain's (and indeed other European) South Asian communities.

Traditional modes of address such as multicultural programming now appear increasingly outmoded in the face of these new 'authentic' forms winning consumer attention. In turn, it is the transnational broadcasting marketplace that has become pivotal in how themes of commonality and the proliferation of difference are being negotiated by a range of broadcasters and audiences (see Karim 2003). In general terms, the old order of multicultural television corresponded with ideas of diversity within the nation-state, 'correcting' mainstream output, a dependence on PSB and strong cultural objectives where the audience is (at least notionally) positioned as national citizen. In contrast, diasporic television relates to diversity beyond the nation-state, an additional resource to PSB and strong commercial objectives where the audience is positioned as individual consumer. In both cases, the idea of the citizen is currently being squeezed out as PSB brands bid for consumer attention.

The emergence of diasporic television has shed light on the critical relationship between two trajectories: one, the threat to traditional public service delivery as it too fights for audience-share; and two, the claims of ethnic minority groups for 'better representation'. Important questions surface here. In what ways are European public service broadcasters responsible for catering for diasporic communities in a transnational marketplace, and to what degree can they afford not to be? What are the potential losses and gains of the free market?

Previously marginalized Europeans, with access, can now tune into foreign television targeted directly at them, and are also able to produce television for the world to see. Take for example Zee TV and Europe (incorporating Zee TV, Zee Music, Zee Cinema and Zee Punjabi) which, by the late 1990s, had a potential audience of 8 million viewers across Europe and an additional 2 million in Britain. This channel alone makes a persuasive case for how new forms of common media culture have become 'de-linked from a singular national reference point' (Aksoy and Robins 2000: 343). Others have been quick to follow suit, such as World TV, which with its self-proclaimed 'South Asian channel bouquet' (including the highly popular Sony Entertainment Television Asia and Star Plus) was rolled out in Continental Europe in 2007 following its success in the United Kingdom. One possible conclusion, as Creeber outlines, is that 'cable and satellite better reflects the complex cultural and national diversities of contemporary Britain and Europe' (Creeber 2004: 33). There is, however, considerable doubt that this transnational marketplace alone can adequately address and represent the entire citizen and consumer interests of Europe's divergent cultural diversity or facilitate democratic participation. There is also the question of regulation (notably Sky and other satellite, cable and digital services are not regulated within the PSB framework of the terrestrial channels in the United Kingdom), underpinned by a more general concern in the area of public communication that as the media and communication environment diversifies, the citizen interest in communication could decline. Ironically perhaps, given the emphasis on the 'absolute citizen' that has emerged in post-multiculturalist public discourse, the precise idea of the 'citizen' remains unformulated in broadcasting policy discourse (see Livingstone, Lunt and Miller 2007). So whilst for some diasporic communities the development of commercial satellite, cable and digital television may actually serve their needs better than a form of PSB developed in relation to the concept of 'bringing the nation together', at the same time there are also problems with leaving the needs of diasporic communities purely in the hands of the free market.

Closing analysis

This chapter has proposed that we have entered a new era characterized by 'post-multiculturalist' and 'post-national' manoeuvres. Whilst this has been clearly articulated in public discourse, for the public service broadcasters there still remains some indecision about abandoning the principles of multiculturalism particularly if public monies are at stake. And yet, in the midst of such uncertainty, Europe's diasporic communities are engaging with new forms of representation that are occurring outside of national, public service frameworks. This is leading to significant alterations in the way ethnic minority media representations are being shaped and in how multiculture is being mediated and recognized.

Public service broadcasters, currently under new sets of pressures, are yet to address adequately the inequity between 'diversity' rhetoric, policy and representation. The tension is exemplified in, and arguably arises from, a concurrent drive towards market liberalization and diversity agendas within public service communication (Freedman 2005). For all this, at the ideological level, evidence of PSB claims to public value have become increasingly necessary as has the requirement for it to facilitate a discourse of critical openness towards group recognition in a media democracy tasked with equality of representation (for example in terms of access and visibility). More than ever, the role of the public service broadcasters are under scrutiny and whilst the debate around its future value is often conducted by itself, it seems that the question of – and for – the public, the citizen and the consumer have never been so urgent. A range of efforts, led by various identity-based groups, to acquire communication rights in the public sphere has coincided with a widespread acceptance from broadcasters that it is impossible for these to be available to all sections of society as a result of changed economic, social and political circumstances.

There are compelling arguments for employing a detailed, comparative approach to multicultural and multi-ethnic presences and themes in past and current European television. The relationship between these diasporic communities and national television, whilst a point of considerable self-examination (reflected in a range of networks and directives), has been a source of ambivalence for the broadcasters when it comes to managing difference, on- and off-screen. (See, for example, Antoni Perotti's tracing of the developments of the Council of Europe's guidelines between 1972 and 1992 [Perotti, cited in Frachon and Vargaftig 1995: 76–87].) In a moment of unsettled negotiation, it remains to be seen how 'local' public service representations will operate alongside global provision and how they will update their formative modes of address targeted at minority diasporic communities.

Importantly, traditional public service national television and new modes of diaspora television do not operate in isolation. National television still carries certain 'responsibilities' for engaging with its diasporic communities, and those same diasporic communities still connect with the traditional alongside the new, picking and mixing their daily diet of television viewing. Moreover, as Aksoy and Robins argue in relation to Turkish communities engaging with satellite television in Germany, they do not simply use these new television forms to reproduce 'Turkishness', but rather to create 'transnational mobilities' which redefine the migrant experience as part of a cultural shift linked to broader, local contexts (Aksoy and Robins 2000). National public service television continues to play a critical role in how the relationship and potential tension between the traditional and the new is played out across Europe's various ethnic minority communities.

My central argument has been that a range of opportunities for representation have been made available to ethnic minorities in addition to public service output. The public service broadcasters are currently fluctuating between and strategically utilizing two positions: the language of 'integration' backed up by mainstreaming strategies of representation; and 'diversity' when it has the potential to cement their public service brand. In both cases, the evidence for meaningful interventions in representations of multicultural European societies is indiscernible. In many ways, the discursive social argument for this may already have been lost to the more forceful economic one. If this is really the case, then beyond the economic determinism, there is also the foremost 'social' consideration of whether this situation also inevitably involves a loss of power by the public with the decline of the citizen emphasis in PSB discourse. Such loss becomes obscured when we consider the force of diasporic television because it is apparently predicated precisely on individual (consumer) choice. The significance of the paradigm shifts that have been described is that even those outlets such as the BBC and Channel 4 (once regarded as pioneering with regards to their relationship with diverse audiences) are now caught up in the current financial difficulties facing PSB, and in the ethical challenges posed by the politics of recognition for the settlement of the relation between a variety of social rights.

The founding principles of public service broadcasting were not based on market share but on providing programmes that large sections of the public often did not actually want to watch. With audience size now as the foremost concern for even non-commercial broadcasters, the question of what viewers are likely to watch dominates how programmes are commissioned, scheduled and marketed. This tends to work against what minority or niche audiences may want or what broadcasters feel they should give them unless it can be easily incorporated into familiar packages such as those that systematize the reality television genre. The present dilemma is premised on how the politics of difference can be recognized and accommodated within a media culture which aspires to 'sameness'. Reality programming might be regarded as an important space here because it demonstrates how market pressures to produce standardized kinds of popular programming do not always have to involve the marginalization of minority representations or the closure of diversity. An inclusion of the 'ordinary' does not guarantee any kind of democratic provision. For example, 'playing up' the sameness of different ethnicities in which racialized differences are 'smoothed out' on-screen, serves a very particular kind of commonality project which as a prevailing textual device raises important questions about how 'reality culture' mediates discourses of race and signs of racial difference in relation to wider culturally assimilationist agendas.

The ambivalence of the broadcast media's approach to ethnic minority representation positions it as deeply imbricated in the struggle between these two principles: multiculturalism on the one hand and equal citizenship on the other. Achieving a representative politics of 'cultural diversity' still remains a highly politicized, contested and complex social process. Public service broadcasting is deeply involved, not just as a key space through which many of these discursive debates have been publicized but, more than that, because it has so far failed to adequately respond to the challenges of representation involved in a diverse Europe, now also characterized as a nation that has turned its back on a liberal multiculturalist ideal.

References

Aksoy, Asu and Robins, Kevin (2000), 'Thinking across spaces: Transnational television from Turkey', *European Journal of Cultural Studies*, 3: 3, pp. 343–65.

Bašić-Hrvatin, Thompson, and Jusić (2008), *Divided They Fall: Public Service Broadcasting in Multiethnic States*, Sarajevo: Mediacentar.

BBC (2002), *Multicultural Broadcasting: Concepts and Reality*, http://www.ofcom.org.uk/static/archive/bsc/plain/pubs.htm. Accessed 15 November 2010.

Briggs, Asa (1961), *The History of Broadcasting in the United Kingdom: Volume 1: The Birth of Broadcasting*, Oxford, UK: OUP.

Brunsdon, Charlotte (2003), 'Lifestyling Britain: The 8–9 slot on British television', *International Journal of Cultural Studies*, 6: 1, pp. 5–23.

Cameron, David (2011), 'PM's speech at Munich Security Conference', 5 February 2011, http://www.number10.gov.uk/news/speeches-and-transcripts/2011/02/pms-speech-at-munich-security-conference-60293. Accessed 14 February 2011.

CBN News (2011), *France's Sarkozy: Multiculturalism has Failed*, http://www.cbn.com/cbnnews/world/2011/February/Frances-Sarkozy-Multiculturalism-Has-Failed/. Accessed 01 October 2013.

Cottle, Simon (2000), *Ethnic Minorities and the Media: Changing Cultural Boundaries*, Buckingham: Open University Press.

Creeber, Glen (2004), '"Hideously white": British television, glocalisation, and national identity', *Television & New Media*, 5: 27, pp. 27–39.

Creative Diversity Network (CDN) (2011), http://www.creativediversitynetwork.org/index.php. Accessed 15 July 2013.

Dhondy, Farrukh (2001), 'Our Islamic fifth column', *City Journal*, 11: 4, http://www.city-journal.org/html/11_4_our_islamic.html. Accessed 28 September 2012.

Frachon, Claire and Vargaftig, Marion (eds) (1995), *European Television: Immigrants and Ethnic Minorities*, London: John Libby.

Freedman, Des (2005), 'Promoting diversity and pluralism in contemporary communication policies in the United States and the United Kingdom', *The International Journal on Media Management*, 7: 1–2, pp. 16–23.

Georgiou, Myria (2010), 'Media representations of diversity: The power of the mediated image', in Alice Bloch and John Solomos (eds), *Race and Ethnicity in the 21ˢᵗ Century*, Basingstoke: Palgrave Macmillan, pp. 166–185.

Goodhart, David (2004), 'Discomfort of strangers', *The Guardian*, 24 February, p.25.

The Guardian (2007), 'Race and class issues dominate BBC conference', 24 January, http://www.theguardian.com/media/2007/jan/24/broadcasting.bbc3. Accessed 30 January 2014.

Hall, Stuart (1989), 'New ethnicities', in Kobena Mercer (ed.), *Black Film, British Cinema*, London: ICA, pp. 27–31.

Hall, Stuart (2000), 'Conclusion: The multi-cultural question', in B. Hesse (ed.), *Un/Settled Multiculturalisms: Diasporas, Entanglements, Transruptions*, London/New York: Zed Books.

Jackson, Michael (2001), 'The fourth way', New Statesman Media Lecture, Banqueting House, Whitehall, 31 October.

Karim, H. Karim (ed.) (2003), *The Media of Diaspora: Mapping the Globe*, London and New York: Routledge.

Leurdijk, Andra (2006), 'In search of common ground: Strategies of multicultural producers in Europe', *European Journal of Cultural Studies*, 9: 1, pp. 25–46.

Livingstone, Sonia, Lunt, Peter and Miller, Laura (2007), 'Citizens, consumers and the citizen-consumer: Articulating the citizen interest in media and communications regulation', *Discourse and Communication*, 1: 1, pp. 63–89.

Malik, Kenan (2002), 'The real value of difference', *Connections*, Winter, http://www.kenanmalik.com/essays/diversity.html. Accessed 1 October 2013.

Malik, Sarita (2002), *Representing Black Britain: Black and Asian Images on Television*, London/New Delhi: Sage.

Malik, Sarita (2010), 'From multicultural programming to diasporic television: Situating the UK in a European context', *Media History*, 16: 1, pp. 123–128.

Malik, Sarita (2013), 'Creative diversity: UK public service broadcasting after multiculturalism', *Popular Communication: The International Journal of Media and Culture*, ll: 3, pp. 227-241.

Mcquail, Denis (2010), *McQuail's Mass Communication Theory*, 6th edn, London/New York: Sage.

Merkel, Angela (2010), 'German multiculturalism has "utterly failed"', http://www.guardian.co.uk/world/2010/oct/17/angela-merkel-german-multiculturalism-failed. Accessed 1 October 2013.

Modood, Tariq (2007), *Multiculturalism*, Cambridge: Polity.

Ofcom (2008), *Second Public Service Broadcasting Review Phase One: The Digital Opportunity*, http://www.ofcom.org.uk/consult/condocs/psb2_1/. Accessed 21 June 2010.

Phillips, Trevor (2005), *After 7/7: Sleepwalking to Segregation*, Speech by Trevor Phillips at the Manchester Council for Community Relations, 22 September 2005. www.humanities.manchester.ac.uk/socialchange/.../sleepwalking.pdf. Accessed 24 September 2012.

Poole, Elizabeth (2006), *Muslims and the News Media*, London: I.B. Tauris.

Rumphorst, Werner (2004), *Public Service Broadcasting in an Enlarging Europe: Contributing to European Policy Objectives*, Speech by W. Rumphorst, Amsterdam, 2 September 2004, http://www.ebu.ch/CMSimages/en/leg_p_psb_wr_300804_tcm6-15161.pdf. Accessed 30 January 2014.

Smith, A. (2010), 'Lifestyle television programmes and the construction of the expert host', *European Journal of Cultural Studies*, 13: 2, pp. 191–201.

Sivanandan, A. (2006), 'Race, terror and civil society', *Race & Class*, 47: 3, pp. 1–8.

Thomson, Caroline (2002), 'The future of public service broadcasting – an international perspective', Speech given at the Broadcast Magazine / Commonwealth Broadcasting Association Conference, 29 January 2002, http://www.bbc.co.uk/pressoffice/speeches/stories/thomsoncarolinecbs.shtml. Accessed 23 January 2011.

Tracey, Michael (1998), *The Decline and Fall of Public Service Broadcasting*, Oxford: OUP.

Turner, Graeme (2009), *Ordinary People and the Media: The Demotic Turn*, London/New Delhi: Sage.

Williams, Raymond (1971), *Culture & Society 1780–1950*, New York: Penguin.

Chapter 2

The Cultural Diversity Turn: Policies, Politics and Influences
at the European Level

Karina Horsti (University of Jyväskylä)

In the early 1990s, Europe experienced a wave of optimism for a borderless continent. The fall of the Berlin Wall became a symbol for the change. This euphoria soon came down as neo-Nazi movements and less organized incidents of xenophobia and racism were reported throughout the continent. Asylum seekers and undocumented migration were securitized. The war in the former Yugoslavia also revealed unhealed wounds of nationalism and ethnic tensions. Nationalist-populist movements emerged in the politics of several European countries. However, the rising xenophobia in the 1990s also resulted in anti-racist projects and sentiments that were expressed at the European level in different types of publicly funded campaigns and in the founding of the European Monitoring Centre on Racism and Xenophobia (EUMC).[1]

This is the sociopolitical background against which the European public service broadcasters in the early 1990s began to articulate their responsibility and role in multicultural societies more clearly. At that time, several initiatives for 'multicultural Europe' were launched as collaborative projects amongst European national media and NGOs (non-governmental organizations) such as Public Broadcasting for a Multicultural Europe,[2] which was a network of public service broadcasters, a university and a migrant organization that produced recommendations for the media in the United Kingdom, the Netherlands and Belgium. Public service broadcasters served as nodal points in these initiatives as they recognized their legal responsibility to 'serve all'.[3] Thus, European public service broadcasting collaboration offers an interesting case to scrutinize what is actually understood about multicultural media policy or cultural diversity media policy. This chapter analyses cultural diversity discourses cultivated in the context of European public service broadcasting collaboration from the 1990s until 2010.

National PSM in Europe very often has a legal responsibility to include ethnic and immigrant minorities into programming as topics and professionals. In addition, the European Broadcasting Union (EBU) states in its policies and regulations that minority inclusion is part of their public service duties. Although there are no legally-binding agreements at the European level of PSB policy concerning ethnic and immigrant minorities, the EBU, NGOs, journalist associations, universities and PSM have carried out projects and conferences which have resulted in recommendations for the media. For instance, the EBU has the Intercultural and Diversity Group that regularly advocates these issues, and in the yearly Prix Europa event, a multicultural prize, TV Iris, is awarded.[4]

I consider this type of collaboration sense-making for the media in a given historical, social and cultural context. Thus, my understanding of policy is broader and more cultural studies-oriented than just equating policy to legislation and regulation. Policy-making requires vocabularies that policy makers and practitioners use to define their policies and goals. It presupposes that problems exist and that these problems should be addressed by PSM. By drafting policies, PSM takes responsibilities for solving such problems. However, as with any discourse, the 'problem definitions' and the vocabularies associated with the policies also both open and close options.[5] They problematize certain issues, and these problematizations make other interpretations invisible or irrelevant. This approach is close to Carol Lee Bacchi's (2009) work on the 'what's the problem represented to be?' approach to policy analysis. She argues that 'it is important to make the "problems" implicit in public policies *explicit*, and to scrutinize them closely' (Bacchi 2009: x). This critical perspective to policy analysis identifies that the strategies for 'promoting multiculturalism and cultural diversity' should be treated critically; they can actually be part of the problem rather than the solution (Ahmed et al. 2006).

The chapter first gives a background to PSB principles, then moves on to analyse how vocabularies and problem definitions in initiatives and collaborative endeavours between PSM, NGOs, universities and associations have changed in the past 20 years in Europe.[6] In the end, I discuss the focus of these initiatives and their idea of disseminating public funding.

Background: Multiculturalism, cultural diversity and the responsibility to 'serve all'

EU funding is a crucial driving force of cultural diversity projects, although there is no binding legal framework regarding the service of new minorities at the EU level. At the European level, cultural diversity is widely and vaguely understood as needed. Sometimes it refers to Europe as a unity of various national identities and languages; sometimes national minority identities such as Sami, Welsh or Catalonian[7] are also recognized as crucial for 'diversity' and 'multiculturalism'. In addition, this notion can include 'immigrant' or 'ethnic' minorities, but they can also be ignored.

EBU membership regulations (EBU n.d.) demand that its members 'provide varied and balanced programming for all sections of the population, including programmes catering for special/minority interests of various sections of the public, irrespective of the ratio of programme cost to audience'. This statement requires a commitment from the broadcasters to include minority rights in programming 'irrespective of the ratio of cost to audience'. However, in its official communications, the EBU remains unclear about the ways in which 'variety' and 'balance' of programming is to be monitored and advanced. The closest attempt to do this at the European level is the *Diversity Toolkit* (FRA 2007) published by the European Agency for Fundamental Rights (FRA) and the EBU.

Public service media in Europe has come up with various strategies to fulfil their legal and democratic principles. In the 1970s up until the 1980s,[8] many broadcasters had addressed the service of ethnic minorities and new immigrant communities either through segregationist or assimilationist paradigms, depending on the more general immigration and integration politics of a country. For instance, Germany adopted the concept of 'guest workers', workers that are in Germany only temporarily and thus are expected to need programming from 'home' (Hargreaves 2002: 212). Other countries like Sweden adopted the concept of 'immigrant' (*invandrare*) and believed that the migrants were in Sweden to stay. This resulted in programming that was assumed to aid integration – or assimilation – into a 'host' society. In the 1980s and 1990s, public service broadcasters in most countries, such as Britain (British Broadcasting Corporation – BBC), the Netherlands (Nederlandse Publieke Stichting – NPS), Ireland (Radio Telifís Éireann – RTÉ) and Sweden (Sveriges Television – SVT), shifted programming to the multicultural paradigm and 'niche' programming for and about ethnic minority communities (Cottle 1998: 300; see also chapters in this volume). Today, such programmes as *Mosaik* (*Mosaic*) (1987–2003) on the Swedish network SVT and the Asian (1965–95) and Afro-Caribbean (1982–95) departments at the British BBC have been closed as the general trend of national policies has shifted from multicultural paradigms to mainstream cultural diversity. Within the Nordic countries, only Norway continues to have an immigrant-specific television programme, *Migrapolis* (1997–). The NRK (Norwegian Broadcasting Corporation) has actually extended the concept to a radio programme in 2005 (see Bjørnsen, this volume), thus taking a different strategy to Denmark, Finland and Sweden.[9] During the past ten years, 'cross-cultural' and 'intercultural' programmes (Leurdijk 2006; Malik 2002: 71) have become a popular format to bring diversity into the mainstream programming. Television shows such as *Goodness Gracious Me* (BBC, 1998–2001) and *De Meiden van Halal (The Girls of Halal)* (NPS, 2005–06)[10] entertain while they introduce and discuss cultures and identities.

The EBU, in its recommendations and reports in the past decade, has discouraged niche programming targeted to immigrant minorities. It considers these programmes to be 'ghettoizing' and accentuating differences rather than inspiring dialogue. This paradigm shift from multicultural niche programming to mainstreaming diversity reflects the wider shift in politics of managing differences in European societies.

For instance, in 2002 an EBU report argued that:

A special obligation to public broadcasters of today's Europe is to reflect our increasingly multi-ethnic and multicultural societies. This must not, on the other hand, take the form of unduly accentuating differences or 'ghettoising' different social and ethnic groups by locking them into 'walled gardens' of programme services, dedicated solely to them.

(EBU 2002: 39)

This example highlights the concerns over multiculturalist media policy that emerged in the new millennium in European policy collaboration. Here, I refer to *multiculturalism* as a policy paradigm that aims to manage and organize difference. Multiculturalism classifies different 'cultural', 'religious' and 'ethnic' groups and recognizes their particularity and rights, particularly in terms of culture and language (Hall 2000: 209–11). Multiculturalism served as a ground to political claims-making on the basis of group identities. However, it is often accused of focusing attention to preserving culture and language and leaving economic and political participation to the background. Whereas multiculturalism talks about groups, *social cohesion*, *integration* and *assimilation* discourses focus on the individual's adaptation to a majority culture (Vasta 2007: 725; Faist 2009: 173), assuming there is a coherent 'culture' and values – a 'standardized pattern' (Ahmed 2000: 96) – into which one should integrate.

Debates on immigration and cultural complexity have intensified in Europe during the past decade. There has been a so-called backlash against the multicultural policies or 'end of multiculturalism' (Back 2007: 133) of the 1980s and 1990s, which was fuelled particularly by terrorist attacks in the United States and Europe at the beginning of the new century. Populist political movements that build their discourses and politics around neo-assimilationist and anti-immigrant or anti-Muslim arguments have risen again in recent years across Europe (see, for example, Vasta 2007; Hervik 2006). In addition, mainstream politicians and parties have taken stronger positions against 'non-integration' and 'illegal immigration'. France and Denmark banned wearing burkhas in public places, Switzerland banned the building of minarets in city centres, and Roma begging and camps have been criminalized in several countries. There is a discourse that considers non-integration as a threat to European societies. Multiculturalism is claimed to be too 'idealistic', and it is argued that separate group rights have actually bred terrorism and gendered and sexual violence. Popular concepts now in European politics and policy-making, also within PSM, are integration and 'social cohesion', which are often interpreted as a demand that minorities accept majority values and traditions.

Anti-racist discourses of the 1990s: Neo-Nazism as a problem

The current public debate and success of populist movements stand in contrast to the early 1990s when, after the fall of communism, European politicians were concerned about racism, neo-Nazis and populist far-right political movements. Anti-racist discourses were expressed at the European level, for instance, in different types of publicly funded campaigns. The Council of Europe (1993) stated in its *Vienna Declaration* in 1993 that the heads of states in Europe are

> alarmed by the present resurgence of racism, xenophobia and anti-Semitism, the development of a climate of intolerance, the increase in acts of violence, notably against migrants and people of immigrant origin, and the degrading treatment and discriminatory practices accompanying them.
>
> (Council of Europe 1993)

Amongst the five points in their plan of action, the Council of Europe in 1993 acknowledged the role of the media in their anti-racist initiatives. The plan of action instructed the committee of ministers to 'request the media professions to report and comment on acts of racism and intolerance factually and responsibly, and to continue to develop professional codes of ethics which reflect these requirements'. Rising journalists' awareness and portrayal of minorities in the media were considered key components in the fight against racism, and the Council of Europe distributed funds to carry out media initiatives. Following the *Vienna Declaration*, the EBU declared in 1994:

> We public service broadcasters, [...] are fully aware of the important role that we have to play in a multiracial, multicultural and multifaith Europe. [...] We, as broadcasters, should ensure that our services defend the equal rights and dignity of all human beings, reject trivialization of violence and act against xenophobia, racism and destructive nationalism. [...] we are concerned at the rise of racism and fascism in Europe and believe it is our duty to combat these attitudes.
>
> (EBU 1994)[11]

Similarly, a booklet of recommendations 'for broadcasting on fair portrayal of ethnic minorities' produced as a European collaboration in 1995, argued for the need of such recommendations as the following:

> Are they [public service broadcasters] inadvertently reinforcing racism, prejudice, and xenophobia through the content of their programmes? These issues are not about special treatment for ethnic minorities but about the professional practice of public service broadcasters – their duty to serve a diverse public and reflect it as accurately and as fairly as possible.
>
> (PBME 1995: 3)

Both the declaration and the booklet take an anti-racist position. They consider rising xenophobia, racism and extreme nationalism as problems that public service broadcasters in particular need to address and take ethical responsibility for. Their position is to combat these 'attitudes'. Both of these examples from the mid-1990s fall into the period when several Council of Europe-funded projects on media and multiculturalism were under way, and most of the initiatives used the discourse of anti-racism and were concerned with rising xenophobia. For instance, in the 1994 and 1995 issues of *Spectrum: The Magazine of Public Broadcasting for a Multicultural Europe*,[12] nearly all articles begin by outlining the situation of rising racism. A good example of this is an article entitled 'A responsibility to respond' that begins with the following sentence: 'As we move towards the 21st century the continuing rise of racism and xenophobia is a matter of great public concern in many countries' (Forde 1995: 17). In addition, titles of stories in the 1994 *Spectrum* issue reflect well the kinds of problems that were considered important: 'The rise of racism in Europe:

The role of school TV'; 'The BOMB IS tikking … ! – A new television co-production between German, Dutch and Austrian broadcasting attempts to challenge the growth of the neo-Nazi movement by getting inside the lives and thoughts of right wing youth in Germany'. However, complexities of addressing and dealing with racism and neo-Nazism in Europe were also acknowledged and discussed at the time. For instance, Europe Singh writes in the editorial of the 1994 issue of *Spectrum* magazine:

> There is no simple formula for the programme or the programming strategy that will tackle racism and xenophobia. […] We have to inform and educate not to moralise and condemn and we have to be critically aware that our programmes are not broadcasting into a vacuum.

In the 1990s, several conferences amongst PSBs and committed journalists and activists produced recommendations and action plans.[13] The main targets in these policies were equal representation of minorities and raising cultural diversity awareness, in addition to the goal of training journalists of minority backgrounds. These training programmes were not organized or funded by public service broadcasters specifically, but were run by NGOs, media educators or professionals with European funding. However, broadcasters participated by taking interns and broadcasting the programmes. The need for recruiting media professionals was acknowledged, but nevertheless, it received much less attention than anti-racist awareness building. One example of a Europe-wide initiative and set of recommendations at the time is the International Federation of Journalists (IFJ) that developed an international strategy to deal with the rising intolerance. Their international media group on racism concluded that the problem of racism should be challenged by (1) producing a manual for European journalists; (2) establishing a media unit for this topic; (3) developing training and education; (4) setting up a European network of media professionals active in this field and representing minority communities; (5) examining the impact of codes of practice; and (6) creating a television project focusing on the role of media in racism (White 1995).

Some of these goals were achieved over the years. *A Diversity Toolkit for Factual Programmes in Public Service Television* was published in 2007. However, it seems that the toolkit became a reality somewhat too late as the discourses have changed. The kinds of discourse it is based on: the focus for ethical recommendations and raising awareness, are no longer popular. I will discuss this argument further in the next section. What have not been realized after the IFJ recommendations in 1995 are methods of examining policy implications or a media-specific European resource centre for multiculturalism. A Dutch NGO, Mira Media,[14] is closest to these IFJ aims, as it has become the nodal point for directing EU-funded projects across Europe. Yet, its position depends on project funding.

It is crucial to understand that anti-racist discourses cultivated in the initiatives of the 1990s also produced interpretations of racism. First, racism in these initiatives was understood to originate from distorted attitudes of some members of European societies, which is typical reasoning in anti-racist campaigning in general (Lentin 2004; Anthias and Lloyd 2002: 7). The word 'some' is crucial here. Although the idea of training implies that 'some' within the PSB institutions have racist ideas and therefore need training, the focus is on the marginal 'some' of the society – that is, the neo-Nazis and 'xenophobes', which are rather unclearly referred to in the texts produced in the initiatives. The responsibility of the broadcasters was then presented to recognize these ideologies in the society and offer balanced and fair reporting. Second, racism is understood to grow out of structural conditions; mainly the lack of representations of cultural differences on-screen and amongst media professionals. However, the aim to recruit more professionals of minority backgrounds and increase their visibility on-screen boils down to individualizing the solution rather than fully addressing institutional and structural issues such as the distribution of decision-making power, distribution of resources, connections to communities and different routines and ways of making programming.

Mainstreaming discourses of the first decade: Non-integration as the problem

The picture that I have described so far of European PSB collaboration looks very different today. The discourses began to change after the turn of the millennium. The EBU does not openly mention racism as a problem any longer, and words like 'racism' and 'xenophobia' have been avoided in European public service broadcasting events of the past decade. What we now find in a variety of initiatives and policy papers in this policy area is, first, concerns that some ethnic minorities and immigrants do not fit into mainstream society and, second, celebration of individual integration into majority values when they do. The concerns of non-integration are particularly focused on Muslim minorities.

For instance, *A Diversity Toolkit* mentions Muslims 27 times, and 13 out of 31 extracts of programmes presented in the DVD that comes with the toolkit are about Islam or Muslims. In addition, Fritz Pleitgen, the director general of the German public service broadcaster WDR and the president of the EBU, addresses the need for the diversity toolkit by referring to 'disturbances in the French suburbs, the Danish cartoon row and terrorist attacks in several European countries' as 'clear warning signals showing us that integration, equal rights and peaceful dialogue between cultures do not happen automatically' (Pleitgen 2007: 8). These events are raised as 'warning signals' of failed (implicitly Muslim) integration. Another example is the yearly Prix Europa Iris that is awarded to the 'best multicultural programme of the year', which offers an opportunity to analyse celebrative discourses in the cultural diversity policy context. Celebrating and accentuating something presupposes a problem. In recent years, themes related to integration have gained more importance in the media prize. Programmes that deal with immigrant roots and diasporic identity, namely themes related to generational differences in families with a history of migration, have been winning the competition after the turn of the millennium. The celebrative discourse in the Prix Iris juries creates a dichotomy between majority tradition ('advanced') and minority tradition ('archaic'). The new country is often celebrated, like in the case of a winning programme in 2007 entitled *0032 Gorcha* (VRT, 2007). The jury reported that the story was of a Kurdish woman, Gorcha, who left Kazakhstan, 'left the whole family and turned away from her Muslim culture, fleeing to Belgium in search of a better future' (Horsti 2009). Celebrating integration and the adoption of 'European values' also presupposes radical differences from 'us' as a problem, and thus, cultural diversity discourses cover only consumable and acceptable differences. Although cultural diversity recognizes transnational and diasporic lives (Faist 2009: 173), the celebratory connotations attached to the term accept only the types of differences that are accommodated in European societies.

As a response to the constructed problem of non-integration, a discourse of cultural diversity has emerged. The policies that are based on the cultural diversity discourse aim to cover a wider scope of differences than multiculturalism. Ethnicity and race are combined with gender, disability, sexuality and sometimes lifestyle. This very broad understanding of cultural diversity claims that as everyone is equally different, no one is specifically different enough to make claims for resources or special rights. Furthermore, cultural diversity discourses promote the mainstreaming of differences. In PSM policy, this means that instead of niche programmes or special resources, differences are to be included throughout programming. The aims of European initiatives began to stress arguments for recruitment and the visibility of talented minority agents in journalism and in entertainment. Using young, culturally diverse talents to make the broadcasters' image more appealing and to broaden PSM audiences to 'ethnic' communities has been celebrated in recent cultural diversity conferences. One such example is the *Diversity Show* conference (2008), which was organized by the Dutch broadcaster NPS for European media producers. It altogether avoided the issues of racism and discrimination that had been so prominent in such collaborations in the 1990s. During the event, only once was racism touched on in references to nationalist populism. Images of right-wing European politicians whose golden days were over by then, such as Jörg Haider of Austria and Jean Le Pen of France, and headlines of political populism were screened in the conference site accompanied by sounds from horror films. This exhibition remained distant and excluded from the other issues discussed at the conference. First, they were images without explanation or discussion, and second, these images do not appear on the DVD that was produced for the event. The conference was unable to discuss racism and discrimination in its celebrative context. The event focused on the visibility of people of minority backgrounds. The main constructed problem at the *Diversity Show* was that people of minority backgrounds are not adequately recruited into European PSM and that they are not visible enough on the screen. There were no claims for specific programming for minorities but for the visibility of minorities throughout programming. The successful examples presented at the conference included Saira Khan, the runner-up for the UK version of the reality TV show *The Apprentice* (BBC, 2005), and a commercially successful public service radio station, FunX (2002–), in the

Netherlands, which started as a response to the fact that young people were no longer listening to public broadcast radio stations. Mezen Dannavi (2008), producer of FunX, argues:

> Authenticity is more important than quality. [...] People were just picked out from the streets. They were true. You get that realness factor. [...] People have cultural surplus, use it. You can teach him how to do it and you can use his surplus. [...] FunX is a success. You can make people socially relevant but also be economically relevant.

In a similar vein, the diversity manager of the Dutch broadcaster NPS, Frans Jennekens, argued at the *Tuning into Diversity* conference in 2010 that 'diversity is a business case, something you can win with' (Jennekens 2010). As a good example of cultural diversity programming, Jennekens mentioned a children's programme called *Het Klokhuis* (*The Core*) (NTR, 1988–) that has a policy of recruiting 'culturally diverse' young people as presenters and incorporating children of minority backgrounds on-screen. He argued that the existing children's-programme formats such as the long-running *Het Klokhuis* do not have to change, but that 'new faces will bring new audiences' (Jennekens 2010).

As these examples show, cultural diversity is presented as a win-win model that does not require changes in the institutional structures or routines. Cultural diversity is a 'surplus' (Dannavi 2008) and a 'business case' (Jennekens 2010). The examples here come from Dutch producers and we could argue that there can be conflicting discourses in other European contexts. However, these examples demonstrate the popular discourses that are explicitly celebrated and admired within European collaborative contexts. They are presented as good practice that others should learn from. Clearly, the Dutch are driving forward cultural diversity discourses and the market-oriented positions as examples for other PSM. Particularly, Nordic PSM endorses the Dutch media as advanced in cultural diversity issues. Ed Klute, the director of the NGO Mira Media, which is the most established agent of European-funded projects, said that 'we (the Dutch) are a little bit ahead of other countries' (Klute 2010).

As the current initiatives are occupied with making cultural diversity more 'visible', we need to ask, how is it possible to show and see diversity? It oftentimes boils down to showing different skin colour or other physical features, sometimes an accent in speech, the kind of difference that for instance Frans Jennekens referred to in his example of *Het Klokhuis*. Sara Ahmed et al. (2006: 43, 72) direct attention in their research on cultural diversity policy-making in education to this very same demand of including those 'who look different'. They argue that this idea keeps institutional whiteness in place. Whiteness is understood here as a normative and invisible[15] rule (Dyer 1997: 45) into which cultural diversity brings colour, but does not change the grammar of how things are managed. In this case, we can extend the idea of whiteness to an idea of white Europeanness, as skin colour is not necessarily the main issue in all European countries when cultural diversity is considered. Regardless, the idea of whiteness allows us to consider the naturalness and invisibility of these institutional norms that cultural diversity is not able – and is not expected or allowed – to question.

Although the commercial discourses and the question of visible diversity prevail in the cultural diversity policy field at large, the NGOs have been pushing forward also a more participatory discourse. The *Tuning into Diversity* conferences (2004 and 2010) that have mainly been organized by Mira Media have set the aim of finding ways of collaboration between civil society and various media 'to make the media more diverse' (Mira Media 2010, author's observation). This approach, which not only understands diversity as a quality *in* media output and recruitment but also as diversity *of* the mediascape, is a rare one in the discourses cultivated in the initiatives of the new millennium. The conference in 2004 drafted a list of recommendations and a European manifesto for supporting community media that was believed to strengthen communication within ethnic minority communities. Furthermore, one of the aims of the Mira Media activities is to generate media competence amongst minority organizations. Ed Klute (2010), the director of Mira Media, refers to increasing multimodality and the changing media landscape when he describes the current media landscape as more 'equal' towards minorities. He stresses the 'responsibility of minorities' to train 'spokespeople who can fight back'. Training minorities and NGOs as well as talented 'culturally diverse' individuals is a strategy the initiatives are taking in their approach to 'think forward'.

Conclusion

In this chapter, I have demonstrated a shift in European collaborative media initiatives with regard to approaches to new immigrant minorities. The vocabulary has shifted from anti-racism to a discourse of cultural diversity that seems to depoliticize differences by overlooking power inequalities and histories of racism. Whereas the policies of the 1990s considered rising racism and xenophobia as problems of European societies, the initiatives of the past ten years have identified non-integration of migrants as the main problem. The vocabulary of the 1990s included words like 'xenophobia', 'racism', 'equality', 'discrimination', 'awareness', 'fairness', 'balance' and 'recommendations'. The vocabulary of the new millennium uses words like 'business sense', 'new audiences', 'talents', 'consulting', 'inclusion' and 'social cohesion'.

The reasons behind this shift in policy language are complex. First, the problem of rising racism was primarily restricted to a focus on neo-Nazi activity, and nationalist-populist politics. Racism was not understood in terms of everyday racism (Essed 1991), institutional racism (Better 2008: 26–27) or educated racism (Ahmed et al. 2006), which would have opened majority society and dominant institutions to criticism. It declared overt racism unacceptable, but this exclusive focus excused society and state from examining racism. Therefore, when the immediate threat of extremist movements in

Europe was contained and the broader polarization between the West and the Muslim world emerged, the problem definition turned its focus to minorities, and the 'non-integrated' and 'radicalized' Other was constructed as a social threat.

Second, policy-making, by definition, involves constant re-writing and re-making. Pragmatically, the same policies and the same vocabularies cannot be repeated, as they become tiring and boring. By the end of the 1990s, racism had accumulated a burden of negative connotations. Cultural diversity, on the contrary, sounded more promising and positive. It does not accuse anyone of being racist, but instead, it embraces everyone. It seems like a true win-win format that all parties can agree on and it makes the adopting institutions, including PSM, look solution-oriented and energetic.

The discursive shift I have discovered in the research material relates to a wider paradigmatic shift in public administration policies, from public administration and regulation to management and entrepreneurialism (Ahmed et al. 2006). Similar to other public-policy fields, also in media policy, the responsibility of inclusion has shifted from PSM institutions to individual journalists who are expected to 'open the mind to other opinions' (Jennekens 2007), to individual migrant activists who are required to train themselves in media logic (Klute 2010) and to 'culturally diverse' talents who are expected to bring in new audiences with their new faces. Thus, the new policies avoid making any organizational or institutional changes or identifying discriminatory practices in the PSM organizations. Instead of that, they dilute organizational responsibility and transfer it to the individual level.

It is necessary to consider some critical dimensions of this discursive change. First, the cultural diversity discourse silences the narrative and history of racism and colonialism. By erasing 'racism', the policy makers end up erasing the ideology of racism and history of white European domination and subordination. Second, the shift directs attention away from discrimination that exists in European societies and media systems. Celebration of cultural diversity in a consumable format dilutes and makes it easier to deny the experiences of discrimination. Third, while the vocabulary has changed, the grammar of media production and media institutions has not necessarily shifted in a more inclusive direction. The 'whiteness' of the organization still exists as the norm into which culturally diverse 'colour' is added, as several studies of the policies and practices of national PSM indicate (see for instance Chapters 6, 7 and 8 in this volume). Fourth, the initiatives are focused on diversity and difference *in* media output. They do not consider that advancing the diversity *of* the media field is important. As Glasser, Awad and Kim (2009: 63) argue, both diversity in journalism and diversity of journalism are crucial for inclusive journalism: 'a decentred democracy includes a communication infrastructure capable of sustaining multiple levels of robust public expression.' Diversity of journalism refers to a structurally mixed system of public communication, including various minority media. Any newsroom can pursue diversity in journalism through recruitment and openness to various perspectives, but no newsroom can achieve diversity of journalism alone. Thus, diversity of journalism promises more than sensitivity to cultural differences.

In the case of European public service media, we can extend Glasser, Awad and Kim's (2009) argument of inclusive journalism to cover other media genres such as fiction and entertainment.

It is very clear that European diversity initiatives focus on diversity *in* media. There is little attention to more profound institutional and social inequalities that shape the framework for media production. Access to education, distribution of public funding, alternative ways of doing media and connecting resources of mainstream and minority media are not seriously addressed in current initiatives related to cultural diversity. Yet, NGOs such as Mira Media in the Netherlands and Cospe in Italy organize media projects that take steps in this direction to find ways of collaboration between media and civil society. However, the real policy silence in European PSM cultural diversity initiatives today is that they are not making efforts to find new public policies that are able to counter the kinds of racism and discrimination that have not disappeared from Europe, but that have taken and are constantly taking new shapes.

References

Ahmed, S. (2000), *Strange Encounters: Embodied Others in Post-Coloniality*, London: Routledge.

Ahmed, S. (2004), 'Declarations of whiteness: The non-performativity of anti-racism', *Borderlands*, 9: 2, http://www.borderlands.net.au/vol3no2_2004/ahmed_declarations.htm. Accessed 25 October 2010.

Ahmed, S., Hunter, S., Kilic, S., Swan, E., and Turner, L. (2006), Race, Diversity and Leadership in the Learning and Skills Sector [Final report], Lancaster: Lancaster University.

Anthias, F. and Lloyd, C. (2002), 'Introduction: Fighting racisms, defining the territory', in F. Anthias and C. Lloyd (eds), *Rethinking Anti-Racisms: From Theory to Practice*, London: Routledge, pp. 1–21.

Bacchi, C. (2009), *Analysing Policy: What's the Problem Represented to be?*, Upper Saddle River, NJ: Pearson Education.

Back, L. (2007), *The Art of Listening*, Oxford: Berg.

Better, S. (2008), *Institutional Racism: A Primer on Theory and Strategies for Social Change*, Lanham: Rowman & Littlefield Publishers.

Bink, S., (2002), *Tuning into Diversity: European Report*, Amsterdam: Dutch Foundation for Ethnic Minorities and Media STOA/Mira Media, www.socsci.kun.nl/maw/cw/jeanm/Binkdive. Accessed 11 October 2010.

Cola, M. (2010), 'Cultural diversity in a "diverse" country: How public service media promote cultural diversity in Switzerland', In ECREA (European Communication Research and Education Association), *3rd European Communication Conference*, Hamburg, Germany, 15 October.

Council of Europe (1993), *Vienna Declaration*, 9 October, Vienna: Council of Europe, https://wcd.coe.int/ViewDoc.jsp?id=621771&Site=COE. Accessed 11 October 2010.

Cottle, S. (1998), 'Making ethnic minority programmes inside the BBC: Professional pragmatics and cultural containment', *Media, Culture & Society*, 20: 2, pp. 295–317.

Dannavi, M. (2008), 'Presentation of FunX Radio', *Diversity Show* (NPS, Netherlands Public Broadcasting), 6 November, Hilversum, the Netherlands.

Dyer, R. (1997), *White*, London: Routledge.

European Broadcasting Union (EBU) (1994), 'EBU declaration on the role of public service broadcasters in a multiracial, multicultural and multifaith Europe', *EBU Television Programme Committee's 66th Meeting*, Geneva, Switzerland, 25–26 October [Repr. *Diffusion EBU 2001/4*, p. 39, Grand-Saconnex: EBU, https://www.ebu.ch/CMSimages/en/publications_automne_2001_tcm6-12444.pdf. Accessed 23 January 2013].

European Broadcasting Union (EBU) (2002), *Media With a Purpose: Public Service Broadcasting in the Digital Era* [report], Digital Strategy Group, European Broadcasting Union, Grand-Saconnex: EBU, http://www.ebu.ch/CMSimages/en/DSG_final_report_E_tcm6-5090.pdf. Accessed 23 January 2013.

European Broadcasting Union (EBU) (n.d.), 'EBU membership regulations', http://www.ebu.ch/departments/legal/activities/leg_membership.php. Accessed 30 September 2008.

Essed, P. (1991), *Understanding Everyday Racism: An Interdisciplinary Theory*, London: Sage.

Fairclough, N. (1995), *Media Discourse*, London: Edward Arnold.

Faist, T. (2009), 'Diversity – a new mode of incorporation?', *Ethnic and Racial Studies*, 32: 1, pp. 171-190.

Forde, G. (1995), 'A responsibility to respond', *Spectrum: The Magazine of Public Broadcasting for a Multicultural Europe*, 3, London: PBME, p. 17.

European Agency for Fundamental Rights (FRA) (ed.) (2007), *A Diversity Toolkit for Factual Programmes in Public Service Television*, Vienna: FRA.

Glasser, T., Awad, I., and Kim, J.W. (2009), 'The claims of multiculturalism and journalism's promise of diversity', *Journal of Communication*, 59: 1, pp. 57–78.

Hall, S. (2009) 'Conclusion: The multicultural question', in B. Hesse (ed.), *Un/settled Multiculturalisms: Diasporas, Entanglements, Transruptions*, London: Zed Books, pp. 209–241.

Hargreaves, A. (2002), 'France', in J. Ter Wal (ed.), *Racism and Cultural Diversity in the Mass Media: An Overview of Research and Examples of Good Practice in the EU Member States, 1995–2000*, Vienna: EUMC/ERCOMER, pp. 203–219.

Hervik, P. (2006), 'The emergence of neo-nationalism in Denmark, 1992–2001', in A. Gingrich and M. Banks (eds), *Neo-Nationalism in Europe and Beyond: Perspectives from Social Anthropology*, Oxford: Berghahn Books, pp. 92–106.

Horsti, K. (2009), 'Anti-racist and multicultural discourses in European public service broadcasting: Celebrating consumable differences in Prix Europa Iris media prize', *Communication, Culture & Critique*, 2: 2, pp. 339–60.

Jauert, P. and Lowe, G. F. (2005), 'Public service broadcasting for social and cultural citizenship: Renewing the enlightenment mission', in G. F. Lowe and P. Jauert (eds), *Cultural Dilemmas in Public Service Broadcasting*, Gothenburg: Nordicom, pp. 9–12.

Jennekens, F. (2007), 'Preface', in FRA (European Agency for Fundamental Rights) (ed.), *A Diversity Tookit for Factual Programmes in Public Service Television*, Vienna: FRA.

Jennekens, F. (2010), 'How diversity is implemented in European media?' [panel contribution, K. Horsti notes], MiM (MiraMedia), *Tuning in to Diversity 2010, Media and Diversity European Conference,* Budapest, Hungary, 25–26 February.

Klute, E. (2010), 'How diversity is implemented in European media?' [panel contribution, K. Horsti notes], MiM (MiraMedia), *Tuning in to Diversity 2010, Media and Diversity European Conference,* Budapest, Hungary, 25–26 February.

Lentin, A. (2004), *Racism & Anti-Racism in Europe*, London: Pluto Press.

Leurdijk, A. (2006), 'In search of common ground: Strategies of multicultural television producers in Europe', *European Journal of Cultural Studies*, 9: 1, pp. 25–46.

Malik, S. (2002), *Representing Black Britain: A History of Black and Asian Images on British Television*, London: Sage.

Mira Media (2004), *Tuning in to Diversity Conference*, Noordwijkerhout, the Netherlands, 23–25 September.

Mira Media (2010), *Tuning in to Diversity 2010, Media and Diversity European Conference*, Budapest, Hungary, 25–26 February.

NPS (Netherlands Public Broadcasting) (2008), *Diversity Show*, Hilversum, the Netherlands, 6 November.

Pleitgen, F. (2007), *Diversity Toolkit for Factual Programmes in Public Service Television*, Vienna: FRA.

Public Broadcasting for a Multicultural Europe (PBME) (1995), *Recommendations for Broadcasting on Fair Portrayal of Ethnic Minorities in European Societies*, London: PBME.

Reisigl, M. and Wodak, R. (2001), *Discourse and Discrimination: Rhetorics of Racism and Antisemitism*, London: Routledge.

Richarson, J. E. (2007), *Analysing Newspapers: An Approach from Critical Discourse Analysis*, New York: Palgrave Macmillan.

Singh, E. (1994), 'Editorial', *Spectrum: The Magazine of Public Broadcasting for a Multicultural Europe*, 2, London: PBME, pp. 5–6.

Vasta, E. (2007), 'Accommodating diversity: Why current critiques of multiculturalism miss the point', *Centre on Migration, Policy and Society Working Papers*, 53, Oxford: University of Oxford.

White, A. (1995), 'The multicultural challenge', *Spectrum: The Magazine of Public Broadcasting for a Multicultural Europe*, 3, London: PBME, p. 16.

Notes

1. Some examples of the anti-racist concerns at high political level in the early 1990s in Europe are the European Commission Against Racism and Intolerance (ECRI), founded by European Commission in 1993, European Monitoring Centre on Racism and Xenophobia (EUMC), founded by the EU in 1997. EUMC became the European Union Agency for Fundamental Rights (FRA) ten years later. This name change illustrates the shift from anti-racism to cultural diversity.

2. A European initiative supported by BBC Education and BBC Television-Equal Opportunities (UK), Belgian radio and television network BRTN (Belgium), Netherlands broadcasting foundation NOS (Netherlands), Dutch Foundation for Ethnic Minorities and Media STOA (Netherlands) and University of Luton (UK) to promote the role of public broadcasting in the development of a multicultural Europe.

3. About the ideology of public service broadcasting in Europe see e.g. Jauert and Lowe (2005).

4. The TV Iris prize originates from 1996 when four national prizes of the Netherlands, Britain, Germany and Belgium merged into one, the Prix Iris. In 2000, this prize joined an acknowledged entity, Prix Europa, and was called Prix Europa Iris between 2000 and 2007 (Horsti 2009).

5. In this work I understand the concept of discourse from the perspective of Critical Discourse Analysis (e.g. Reisigl and Wodak 2001; Fairclough 1995) that refers to discourses as language in use. Crucial is analysis of linguistic character of social and cultural processes and structures in the context of power and historical trajectories (Richardson 2007: 26).

6. Collaboration is approached here as interaction between interested European PSB companies, other media professionals, European agencies and NGOs like Media in the Netherlands that lobby for minority rights and run various projects on diversity. The European Commission, the European Union and the Council of Europe have been important funding bodies for the realization of these initiatives and projects. The research material consists of publications produced between 1994 and 2010 (see the list of references) and participant observation at two European events where PSBs and NGOs have shared 'good practices' and discussed the role of various media in multicultural European societies. The first event *Diversity Show* was organized by the Dutch PSB NPS in Hilversum, the Netherlands, 6 November 2008 and the second one, *Tuning in to Diversity 2010* by a Dutch NGO, Mira Media, together with other partners, 25–26 February 2010.

7. Marta Cola (2010) analyses that the Swiss cultural diversity policies focus on the national linguistic minority issues rather than new immigrant minorities.

8. As early as the 1980s there were some European collaborative projects such as the conferences of a research project called *The Role of Information in the Realisation*

of the Human Rights of Migrant Workers in Tampere in 1983 and Lausanne in 1988. In addition, the Council of Europe organized a conference titled *Migrants, Media and Cultural Diversity* in Noordwijkerhout in 1988. All these conferences produced recommendations and plans of action and brought together academics, media professionals, migrant organizations and journalists' associations. These earlier conferences, particularly the one in Noordwijkerhout, generated ideas and networks for the activism that took off in the 1990s (Bink 2002).

9. Denmark never had a specific niche programme like Finland, Sweden and Norway.

10. *Goodness Gracious Me* is a radio (BBC Radio 4, 1996–98) sketch and a TV comedy (BBC 2, 1998–2001) which played with stereotypes of the British and the Indian. *Meiden van Halal* (NPS, 2005, 2006) is a Dutch show that featured three hijab-wearing Muslim sisters as hosts. This programme inspired the Swedish SVT in its *Halal-TV* show in 2008.

11. The declaration adopted by the EBU television programme committee at its 66th meeting in Geneva on 25 and 26 October 1994. Declaration reprinted in Diffusion *Diffusion EBU 2001/4*, https://www.ebu.ch/CMSimages/en/publications_automne_2001_tcm6-12444.pdf. Accessed 9 October 2007.

12. The two issues (*Spectrum* 1994 and 1995) have been studied here as examples of the discourses circulated in the 1990s among European PSB collaborations.

13. Examples of conferences: *Media and Minorities*, Utrecht, 1991 serves as an example of the early collaboration when BBC representatives were invited to the Netherlands to present their actions and good practices as an example for Dutch future policies. The conference presented ideas for the Dutch parliament; *Public Broadcasting for a Multicultural Europe*, Noordwijkerhout, 1992 was a pioneering conference between the Dutch and British PSBs, academics and NGOs that set the frame for future broader European collaboration; the second PBME conference, Solingen, 1994 and the final PBME conference, Strasbourg, 1995; other conferences in Amsterdam, 1995; Strasbourg, 1995; Hilversum, 1998; Cologne, 1999; and Berlin, 2000 (Bink 2002).

14. Mira Media is an independent cooperative body founded in 1986 by the major national migrant organizations in the Netherlands.

15. Sara Ahmed (2004) points out that whiteness is invisible to those who inhabit it, but those who are positioned 'non-white' see whiteness everywhere.

Chapter 3

Public Service Media and Cultural Diversity: European
Regulatory and Governance Frameworks

Tarlach McGonagle (University of Amsterdam)

Introduction[1]

By virtue of their core philosophy, mandate and typical status in most countries, public service broadcasters are ideally suited to act as vectors for the promotion of cultural diversity. They are equally well-suited to provide shared forums in which a range of different cultures can interact, be explored and, indeed, contested. Notwithstanding the difficulties involved in defining the notion of cultural diversity, various promotional strategies may viably be employed by PSBs. Such strategies include the safeguarding of access for discrete cultural groups to editorial, production and other structures and processes. They could also include measures to ensure that programming and other related services targeting culturally diverse audiences correspond to the audiences' actual needs and preferences – in qualitative and quantitative terms. In doing so, relevant approaches should seek to balance the needs and preferences of discrete societal groups against the needs and preferences of a more complex societal whole.

The emergence of new technological and communicative possibilities and paradigms has prompted conceptual and terminological shifts within the European audio-visual sector. PSBs are nowadays expected to operate across an array of technological platforms in order to perpetuate their traditional position of prominence in a rapidly changing and already highly diversified mediascape. This is evidenced by an increasing tendency to frame relevant regulatory discussions in terms of public service *media* (as opposed to *broadcasting* in the traditional sense of the word), *value(s)* and *governance*.

The existing European regulatory framework for public service broadcasting/media is extensive and spans legal and policy instruments emanating primarily from the European Union and the Council of Europe, but also including standard-setting measures from other intergovernmental organizations (IGOs) such as UNESCO (United Nations Educational, Scientific and Cultural Organization) and, to a lesser extent, the Organization for Security and Co-operation in Europe (OSCE). Even within the European Union and the Council of Europe, differences of focus and emphasis may readily be detected across the most salient instruments. They engage with the issues highlighted in the preceding paragraphs to varying extents.

The principal aim of this chapter is to present a panorama of regulatory instruments applicable at the European level and to assess their overall coherence. The significance of selected examples of divergence in the broader regulatory approach will be explained and evaluated accordingly.

PSB/M and cultural diversity: The European regulatory framework

At the European level, public service broadcasting – or media – is/are regulated by both the European Union and the Council of Europe. Relevant regulation focuses on various aspects of PSM, including its mission, independence, organization, financing, and programming and services. In the field of audio-visual regulation and policy, the relationship between the European Union and the Council of Europe tends to oscillate from constructive and synergic cooperation to inter-institutional tensions and trade-offs. In respect of PSB/M, however, interaction between both organizations tends to involve a predictable fidelity to their own approaches while acknowledging the relevance of the other.

European Union

The European Union's regulatory framework for PSB is characterized by its economic and cultural emphases, resting as it does on two main pillars: financing (including State aid and competition law issues) and cultural aspects. It is little more than a framework: the Protocol to the Treaty of Amsterdam on the system of public broadcasting in the member states recognizes that it is largely for member states to confer, design and organize the remit for PSB in their own countries. This is because 'the system of public broadcasting in the member states is directly related to the democratic, social and cultural needs of each society and to the need to preserve media pluralism' (EU 1997). The Protocol also sets out that State funding for PSB must be tied to the fulfilment of the broadcasters' public service remit.

The importance of PSB, including in a technologically reconfigured media environment, was set out expansively in a Resolution concerning public service broadcasting adopted by the Council of the European Union in 1999. The Resolution notes that 'in view of [PSB's] cultural, social and democratic functions which it discharges for the common good, [it] has a vital significance for ensuring democracy, pluralism, social cohesion, cultural and linguistic diversity' (Council of the European U 1999: Recital (B)). It continues by 'stressing that the increased diversification of the programmes on offer in the new media environment reinforces the importance of the comprehensive mission of public service broadcasters' (Recital (C)). In consequence, it positively encourages PSB to branch out into new media services and to exploit the potential of the new technological opportunities on offer in furtherance of their mandate.

The European Union's main regulatory instrument dealing with the audio-visual media – the Audiovisual Media Services Directive (2010) – does not contain any *substantive* provisions dealing *specifically* with PSM. The only specific reference in the Directive to PSM is *preambular*: Recital 13. It recalls that the Council's 1999 Resolution on public service broadcasting 'reaffirmed that the fulfilment of the mission of public service broadcasting requires that it continue to benefit from technological progress'. As such, it does not make any new claims and, as Karol Jakubowicz has noted, there was no formal need to include this Recital in the Directive at all. The Recital can therefore be seen as a political or symbolic response to concerns expressed during the drafting process that increased choice and competition among online audio-visual media services would erode the traditional role of public service media as general mediators of culture (Jakubowicz 2010: 196).

Two main reasons explain the absence of specific references to PSM in the Directive. First, as has already been seen, key EU texts have deliberately and formally shifted the regulation of PSM to the national level. Second, the Directive applies to all audio-visual media services; it does not differentiate between different types of audio-visual media, such as PSM, commercial, community and transnational media. Rather, the most important distinctions made by the Directive are between linear and non-linear audio-visual media services (i.e. so-called 'push' and 'pull' delivery models for audio-visual content, respectively), on the one hand; and audio-visual media services and commercial communications (i.e. television advertising, sponsorship, teleshopping and product placement), on the other.

The Directive contains a number of provisions designed to promote (independent) European productions, and thereby strengthen a sense of European identity (European Parliament and Council 2010; in particular Articles 13, 16 and 17). Article 13 involves a rather vague commitment for States to ensure that on-demand audio-visual media services adopt measures to promote the production of and access to European works. Articles 16 and 17 involve transmission and investment requirements for (traditional/ linear) broadcasters. Non-European productions – a source of cultural diversity, neutrally-defined – are not covered by these promotional provisions. Moreover, the objective of stimulating cultural creativity in the European audio-visual sector has been alloyed by the objective of increasing the competitiveness of the European audio-visual industry in response to US hegemony (McGonagle 2008: 208). These critical observations prompt the conclusion that the objectives behind relevant provisions in the Directive are not to embrace cultural diversity for intrinsic reasons, but to promote a Eurocentric version of cultural diversity for a mixture of economic and political reasons (McGonagle 2008).

Before concluding this section, it is useful to return to – and briefly discuss – the two main pillars of the European Union's regulatory framework for PSB: financing and cultural aspects of PSB. The financing regime for PSM is governed by the Treaty on the Functioning of the European Union['s] provisions on competition in the internal market and State aid (in particular, Articles 106–08) and the European Commission's 2009 'Communication on the application of State-aid rules to public service broadcasting'. It allows States to define the public service remit, and to provide for the financing and general organization of the public broadcasting sector, in a manner that would give due recognition to relevant national specificities. All of this is, however, subject to the important proviso that any measures adopted for the financing of public service broadcasters will have to conform to certain standards of transparency in order to allow for the assessment of the proportionality of such measures.

The cultural pillar, a crucial counterbalance to the financing pillar, is bolstered by a number of statements of commitment to cultural diversity in the Treaty on European Union (Article 3[3]); the Treaty on the Functioning of the European Union (Article 167) and the Charter of Fundamental Rights of the European Union (Article 22) (EU 2008, 2010a, 2010b). Taken together, these provisions oblige the European Union to respect cultural diversity and to contribute to the flowering of the cultures of the Member States. The cultural pillar has also consistently been supported and strengthened by the European Parliament (EP). Over the years, various EP Resolutions (EP 1996, 2002, 2006, 2008, 2010) have tended to emphasize:

- The importance of the cultural dimension to broadcasting in general and PSB in particular.
- The importance of broadcasting, including PSB, as a means of sustaining a sense of European identity.
- The importance of PSB for the European dual system of broadcasting and therefore for pluralism in the European audio-visual sector.
- The continued importance of PSM in an online environment and the need for PSM to maximize opportunities for the exploitation of new media technologies.

The relevance of UNESCO standards to PSM and cultural diversity was adverted to in the introduction to this chapter. While the UNESCO Convention on the Protection and Promotion of the Diversity of Cultural Expressions (UNESCO 2005) has, of course, an autonomous legal existence of its own, it is important to mention it in the EU context as well because the European Union acceded to the Convention in December 2006. It is therefore legally-binding on all EU member states. Among the measures the Convention envisages that States Parties may undertake in order to protect and promote the diversity of cultural expressions in their own territories are: 'measures aimed at enhancing diversity of the media, including through public service broadcasting' (Article 6[2][h]). This is the Convention's only explicit reference to PSB/M, but a number of its provisions, including other measures that States Parties could usefully adopt to foster the diversity of cultural expressions, are implicitly relevant.

The regulatory picture that has been sketched in the foregoing paragraphs shows that it is largely for EU member states to define and develop the remit of PSB in their own countries and that they may finance PSB as long as a certain number of procedural and other criteria are met. In the overall EU approach to PSB, financing issues have tended to dominate, which can largely be explained by the traditional, core internal-market objectives of the European Union. That dominance has, however, been offset by the EP's backing for the cultural cause and, significantly, explicit recognition of the importance of relevant Council of Europe standards on PSB. Finally, EU regulatory texts strongly and consistently encourage the continuation and development of PSB activities on new media platforms.

Council of Europe

Various Council of Europe treaties serve to promote cultural diversity; the present analysis will concentrate on the European Convention on Human Rights, the European Convention on Transfrontier Television, the European Charter for Regional or Minority Languages and the Framework Convention for the Protection of National Minorities. These treaties are meaningfully supplemented by a variety of other 'standard-setting' initiatives, which are not treaty-based, by different bodies of the Council of Europe, in particular its Committee of Ministers and Parliamentary Assembly. Although those standard-setting initiatives are not legally-binding on Council of Europe Member States, they are nevertheless meaningful because they provide valuable guidance for national policy makers and they are routinely used as reference points by European regulatory texts that are legally-binding on States. In this section, the treaty-based and other general standard-setting initiatives will be considered in turn.

European Convention on Human Rights

The European Convention on Human Rights (Council of Europe 1950, hereafter ECHR) does not explicitly provide for the protection of cultural rights as such or for the promotion of cultural diversity. An initiative proposing to draft an additional protocol to supplement the ECHR in the cultural field in the 1990s never came to fruition (for an overview of the process, see Thornberry and Estébanez 2004: 203–06). Nevertheless, cultural rights and cultural diversity enjoy de facto protection under the Convention. That is because cultural rights comprise a range of different rights, such as the rights to non-discrimination/equality, freedom of expression, participation in public affairs, enjoyment of a particular way of life, association, religion and education. These rights are also prerequisites for enabling cultural diversity, and none more so than the right to freedom of expression, which is enshrined in Article 10, ECHR.

Article 10(1), ECHR, sets out the right to freedom of expression as a compound right comprising three main elements: the right to hold opinions; the right to receive information and ideas; and the right to impart information and ideas without interference by public authority and regardless of frontiers. Article 10(2) enumerates a number of grounds (e.g. national security, the protection of the reputation or rights of others, etc.), based on which the right may legitimately be restricted, provided that the restrictions are prescribed by law and are necessary in a democratic society or, in other words, correspond to a 'pressing social need'.

In its seminal ruling in *Handyside v. the United Kingdom* (a case involving restrictions on the right to freedom of expression in order to protect morals), the European Court of Human Rights (ECtHRs) affirmed that freedom of expression

is applicable not only to 'information' or 'ideas' that are favourably received or regarded as inoffensive or as a matter of indifference, but also to those that offend, shock or disturb the State or any sector of the population. Such are the demands of that pluralism, tolerance and broadmindedness without which there would be no democratic society.

(ECtHRs 1976: para. 49)

The *Handyside* judgment recognizes that in democratic society, space has to be created and sustained for public discussion and debate. However, democratic society is not without its rough edges and pluralist public debate necessarily involves disagreement and confrontation between opposing viewpoints. Such disagreement and confrontation – even when expressed in strong terms (because Article 10 protects not only the substance of information and ideas, but also the form in which they are conveyed) – ordinarily come within the scope of the protection offered by Article 10. The deliberative space set out by *Handyside* is crucial for the articulation, communication, affirmation and contestation of differing cultural experiences and perspectives. As such, it is crucial for sustaining cultural diversity in pluralist democratic societies.

Cultural diversity and societal pluralism are contiguous concepts and they enjoy a symbiotic relationship. The ECtHRs regards pluralism as 'indissociable from a democratic society' (ECtHRs 1993a). It has considered the nature of societal pluralism on numerous occasions, emphasizing the importance of different rights for safeguarding that pluralism. It has repeatedly found that pluralism demands a certain balancing of majority/minority interests and the democratic accommodation of the latter (ECtHRs 1981; 2004).

In order to operationalize the principle of pluralism, the Court has explored its implications for the media and other forums for public debate and intergroup communication (McGonagle 2011a: 429-75). The Court has consistently held that the State is the 'ultimate guarantor' of the principle of pluralism, especially 'in relation to audio-visual media, whose programmes are often broadcast very widely' (ECtHRs 1993b: para. 38). This important finding suggests that States authorities have a positive obligation to uphold pluralism in the (audio-visual) media sector. It is an approach that is informed by a powerful democratic rationale that prioritizes inclusive participation in public affairs: 'groups and individuals outside the mainstream [must be able] to contribute to the public debate by disseminating information and ideas on matters of general public interest' (ECtHRs 2005: para. 89).

In *Manole & Others v. Moldova*, a case involving governmental interference in the operations of the public service broadcaster, the Court spelt out in detail what the State's role as the ultimate guarantor of pluralism in the audio-visual sector entails, including relevant positive obligations (particularly in respect of PSB) (ECtHRs 2009). The Court considered that, 'in the field of audiovisual broadcasting', the State is under a duty 'to ensure', amongst other things, that the public has access through television and radio to impartial and accurate information and a range of opinion and comment, reflecting inter alia the diversity of political outlook within the country (ECtHRs 2009: para. 100).

Another relevant principle from the Court's settled case-law is that all sections of the public must be able to receive a wide range of information and ideas. The Court's judgment in the case, *Khurshid Mustafa & Tarzibachi v. Sweden*, illustrates this principle and prises it open in a way that favours cultural diversity (ECtHRs 2008). The Court acknowledged that it was of 'particular importance' for the applicants, as an immigrant family from Iraq living in Sweden, to be able to receive a wide range of information (i.e. not just political and social news, but also 'cultural expressions and pure entertainment') from their country of origin in order to be able to maintain contact with their native culture and language (para. 44). It found that the applicants

> might have been able to obtain certain news through foreign newspapers and radio programmes, but these sources of information only cover parts of what is available via television broadcasts and cannot in any way be equated with the latter.
>
> (ECtHRs 2008: para. 45)

Thus, the Court recognizes that the mere existence of other expressive or informational opportunities is not sufficient: they must also be viable opportunities in the sense that they are suited to the expressive or informational purpose of the individual or group concerned. An important upshot of this finding is that the availability of culturally diverse content in other media does not remove the need for culturally diverse content in the audio-visual sector.

The implications for PSM and cultural diversity of the case-law surveyed above can be summarized briefly as follows. The scope of the right to freedom of expression is shaped by the principles of pluralism, tolerance and broadmindedness that characterize democratic society. This entails an acceptance that diversity is important for society as a whole and that all groups in society should have opportunities to receive and impart information and ideas of all kinds, including of a cultural nature, via the (audio-visual) media. States have a positive obligation to uphold pluralism in the audio-visual sector and a particular role has been identified for PSB (which depend on a certain amount of State support) in that connection. These principles provide an important legal basis for relevant standard-setting and policy-making by other branches of the Council of Europe, exercises which typically seek to elaborate on and operationalize these principles (see further, below).

Besides the European Convention on Human Rights, the relationship between freedom of expression and cultural diversity is palpable in other Council of Europe treaties.

European Convention on Transfrontier Television

The main purpose of the European Convention on Transfrontier Television (Council of Europe 1989, hereafter ECTT) is to 'facilitate, among the Parties, the transfrontier transmission and the retransmission of television programme services' (Article 1) and thereby advance the general objectives of the Council of Europe, including freedom of expression and information, pluralism, cultural development, etc. (Council of Europe 1989, Preamble). Until 2007, the ECTT was (informally) aligned with the European Union's Television without Frontiers Directive – the forerunner to the Audiovisual Media Services Directive. The alignment was intended to ensure a broadly consistent regulatory framework for the European audio-visual space (Krebber 2002). Since the adoption of the Audiovisual Media Services Directive in 2007, the ECTT has been left in the slipstream of technological and regulatory change in Europe.

Article 10 of the ECTT is entitled 'Cultural objectives', but like comparable provisions in the European Union's Audiovisual Media Services Directive, its focus is also Eurocentric and does not explicitly embrace the promotion of cultural diversity per se. Rather, it seeks to promote European works/production by requiring broadcasters to devote the majority proportion of their transmission time to European works (Article 10[1]) and to get States to 'look together for the most appropriate instruments and procedures to support, without discrimination between broadcasters, the activity and development of European production, particularly in countries with a low audiovisual production capacity or restricted language area' (Article 10[3]). As such, its contribution to the promotion of cultural diversity is limited and specifically European. This contribution is likely to decrease further because the ECTT faces an uncertain (political) future. The revision and modernization of the ECTT, partly to bring it into line with the European Union's Audiovisual Media Services Directive, was formally discontinued in 2011.[2] As a result, although the Convention – with its now outdated focus on only 'linear' broadcasting and broadcasting services – remains in force, it has lost much of its erstwhile relevance for European-level media regulation.

European Charter for Regional or Minority Languages

The Preamble to the European Charter for Regional or Minority Languages (Council of Europe 1992, hereafter ECRML) acknowledges that

> the protection and promotion of regional or minority languages in the different countries and regions of Europe represent an important contribution to the building of a Europe based on the principles of democracy and cultural diversity within the framework of national sovereignty and territorial integrity.
>
> (Council of Europe 1992: Recital 7)

Article 11, ECRML, entitled 'Media', sets out a range of specific undertakings to which States can commit in order to promote the use of regional or minority languages in different types of media. The undertakings involve varying degrees of onerousness and the choice between them offers States a lot of flexibility to determine the precise focus and extent of their commitments in respect of the media. For example, Article 11(3) is noteworthy for addressing an often underappreciated factor in the promotion of cultural diversity in the media sector. It offers States the possibility to undertake to ensure that the interests of the users of regional or minority languages are represented or taken into account within such bodies as may be established in accordance with the law with responsibility for guaranteeing the freedom and pluralism of the media.

(Council of Europe 1992)

Article 12, ECRML, is entitled, 'Cultural activities and facilities', and it comprises a list of possible measures to be taken by States Parties with a view to enhancing cultural activities and facilities in regional or minority languages. Among the activities and facilities listed are libraries, cultural centres, vernacular forms of cultural expression and the use of new technologies. Thus, the exploitation of new media technologies is expressly envisaged for the development of cultural activities and facilities (see further, Moring and Dunbar 2008).

Framework Convention for the Protection of National Minorities

Whereas the title of the Framework Convention for the Protection of National Minorities (Council of Europe 1995, hereafter FCNM) may suggest a certain narrowness of focus, it actually addresses many issues concerning society as a whole, and not only persons belonging to national minorities. It pursues its central objective – the protection of national minorities – in a complex, majority-minority dialectic. In other words, it strives to assure the protection of national minorities within the broader context of pluralist society. A couple of provisions of the FCNM explicate the strong linkage between the goals of promoting tolerance, intergroup understanding and cultural diversity, and in particular, the instrumental importance of the media in respect of each goal:

The Parties shall encourage a spirit of tolerance and intercultural dialogue and take effective measures to promote mutual respect and understanding and co-operation among all persons living on their territory, irrespective of those persons' ethnic, cultural, linguistic or religious identity, in particular in the fields of education, culture and the media.

(Council of Europe 1995: Article 6[1])

In the framework of their legal systems, the Parties shall adopt adequate measures in order to facilitate access to the media for persons belonging to national minorities and in order to promote tolerance and permit cultural pluralism.

(Article 9[4])

In practice, the monitoring of the FCNM involves the examination of behavioural and structural media regulation at national and sub-national levels. It also takes account of functional differences between different types of media, e.g. public service, community and commercial, each of which can contribute to the goal of promoting cultural diversity in different ways. The Advisory Committee therefore monitors the calibration of prescriptions (e.g. broadcasting quota and percentages of programming budgets) of particular types of content, such as that produced by or for minorities, including in their own languages. It also monitors the allocation of timeslots for the same, with a view to determining whether they are long enough, frequent enough and scheduled at appropriate times. Subtitling and dubbing practices are also routinely monitored on account of their potential for making content accessible to a wider audience comprising varied linguistic backgrounds.

Non-treaty-based standards

Alongside the Council of Europe's treaty-based standard-setting work, described in the previous section, a host of relevant standard-setting texts have also been adopted by various bodies of the Council, most notably its Committee of Ministers. These texts are not legally-binding on the member states of the Council of Europe, but they are of political importance. They often map out ongoing or anticipated developments in relation to freedom of expression and the media at European and national levels. As such, they are regarded as an important means of supplementing relevant treaty law and of ensuring the effective realization of the right to freedom of expression throughout Europe (Council of Europe CM 2010; McGonagle 2011b: 1–4).

The Council of Europe's approach to PSB is predominantly shaped by standard-setting texts adopted by its Committee of Ministers and Parliamentary Assembly, which are the organization's decision-making and deliberative bodies, respectively. Some texts explicitly address different aspects of PSB, whereas others are indirectly or incidentally significant. Taken together, they constitute an expansive corpus of standard-setting texts that are detailed and varied in their focuses and emphases. Cross-referencing increases their overall coherence and the flexibility to engage with emerging issues or introduce new ones (e.g. most recently, PSM governance) increases their dynamism. They are clearly more than the mere sum of their parts, and are listed in the references at the end of this chapter.

Committee of Ministers

Broadly speaking, these texts show recurrent concern for issues such as PSB's:

- Remit (including its cultural components);
- Editorial independence;
- Financial independence and security;
- Contribution to democracy and society;
- Contribution to media pluralism;
- Online presence and activities.

The texts do not attempt to set out an exhaustive definition of PSB, but key definitional elements have been synthesized in the CM's 2007 Recommendation on the remit of public service broadcasting in the information society (Council of Europe CM 2007a). It portrays PSB as:

- A reference point for all members of the public, offering universal access;
- A factor for social cohesion and integration of all individuals, groups and communities;
- A source of impartial and independent information and comment, and of innovatory and varied content which complies with high ethical and quality standards;
- A forum for pluralistic public discussion and a means of promoting broader democratic participation of individuals;
- An active contributor to audio-visual creation and production and greater appreciation and dissemination of the diversity of national and European cultural heritage.

The promotion of cultural diversity is widely regarded as a general objective of PSB, both in academic writings (Barendt 1993; Born and Prosser 2001; Mendel 2011) and in normative standards (Council of Europe CM 2006: Preamble; 2003: Preamble; 2000: para. 2.5). The above-mentioned characteristics speak to PSB's ability to advance cultural diversity through the provision of culturally diverse content; the facilitation of culturally diverse communication; and the creation of governance structures that encourage culturally diverse participation. The specific roles that PSB can play in fostering cultural diversity have been teased out in more detailed fashion in various standard-setting texts. For instance, the CM's Recommendation on the remit of public service media in the information society emphasizes that:

> In their programming and content, public service media should reflect the increasingly multi-ethnic and multicultural societies in which they operate, protecting the cultural heritage of different minorities and communities, providing possibilities for cultural expression and exchange, and promoting closer integration, without obliterating cultural diversity at the national level.
>
> (Council of Europe CM 2007a: para. 23)

Furthermore, PSM 'should promote respect for cultural diversity, while simultaneously introducing the audience to the cultures of other peoples around the world' (para. 24). Cultural diversity is clearly understood here in an open, inclusive way – there is no question of the notion being restricted to European cultural diversity, as in the prescriptions for the promotion of European audio-visual works in the European Union's Audiovisual Media Services Directive or in the Council of Europe's ECTT.

The foregoing section has sketched the main European-level regulatory points of reference for PSM and the promotion of cultural diversity. There is a multiplicity of relevant texts, which vary in status (legally-binding/political) and some of which are formally related to one another, some informally and some not at all. All of this means that it can be difficult to see the proverbial wood for the trees. The actual overall coherence of these texts can therefore be difficult to discern. Significant dot-joining and explanation are called for and the foregoing section aimed to contribute to those processes. Having set out the relevant European regulatory and policy framework, the focus will now shift to new developments within that framework.

Emergent emphases in European regulation and policy

Current regulatory and policy approaches to PSB are placing increasing emphasis on the role of PSM in a reconfigured mediascape; public service value (of the Internet); and public service media governance. Each of these emergent issues will now be addressed in turn.

The role of PSM in a reconfigured mediascape

The fate of PSB has been described as that of 'an institution born in one age, seeking to survive in one which is utterly different' (Tracey 1998: 10). In a similar vein, Karol Jakubowicz has observed that PSB is currently in a state of transition, but that 'there was hardly a time in the eight decades of PSB's existence when it was not "in transition"' (Jakubowicz 2007a: 116). He describes the challenges constantly faced by PSB as being 'at once conceptual and contextual': different understandings of the role of PSB and the fact that 'changing contexts of PSB operation have always affected the shape, nature and objectives of that media institution and positioned it in society and on the media scene in a variety of ways' (Jakubowicz 2007a: 116). He explains that the current state of transition has been triggered by technological, market-related and sociocultural trends (2007a: 120). Similarly, other experts have identified the 'main contextual drivers stimulating PSB to become PSM' as 'digitization, globalization, convergence, fragmentation, individualization and a paramount market logic' (d'Haenens, Sousa and Hultén 2011: 196).

How PSB engages with these new trends will largely determine its future, but its engagement must also remain within relevant parameters set by EU law, e.g. rules and guidelines governing State funding for PSB and the relationship between such funding and PSB mandates. Broadcasting technologies are becoming inexorably digitized and converged. If PSB is to retain its previous (or even current) level of influence in this new technological environment, it is imperative that it develops into an effective player across diverse media formats. This underscores the need to develop 'content strategies' aimed at 'remedying market failure and offering public value, in a world of rampant commercialism, fragmentation, time and place shifting' (d'Haenens, Sousa and Hultén 2011: 213).

It is noteworthy that since 2007, the Council of Europe generally, and its Committee of Ministers in particular, has been referring more consistently to 'public service media' instead of public service broadcasting. This is a clear acknowledgement that other media platforms are increasingly being used to pursue public service objectives (see further, in this connection: Ofcom 2007). Further recognition of that trend is provided by a subsequent Recommendation adopted by the Committee of Ministers – on measures to promote the public service value of the Internet (Council of Europe CM 2007b). Moreover, PSM should

- Have a distinct place in the new media ecosystem;
- Be equipped to provide high-quality and innovative content and services in the digital environment, and
- Be able to resort to relevant tools (for example to facilitate interaction and engagement) (Council of Europe CM 2011: para. 82).

Calls for increased general PSB exploitation of new technological opportunities are also increasingly being linked to the specific goal of promoting cultural diversity. For example, again in its Recommendation on the remit of public service media in the information society, the CM stated:

Public service media should play a particular role in the promotion of cultural diversity and identity, including through new communication services and platforms. To this end, public service media should continue to invest in new, original content production, made in formats suitable for the new communication services. They should support the creation and production of domestic audiovisual works reflecting as well local and regional characteristics.

(Council of Europe CM 2007a: para. 19)

It is important to note the erstwhile reluctance of PSB to embrace new technologies – partly, perhaps, due to limited financial means and for reasons of organizational culture, but also for fear of overstepping its mandate and thereby inviting sanctions based on unfair competition/impermissible State aid. This reluctance has long since been overcome and replaced with enthusiastic engagement. The enormous shift in mindsets and practice was undoubtedly precipitated by the European Union and the Council of Europe's repeated, emphatic affirmations that PSB are to make maximum use of the new technological opportunities at their disposal for the discharge of their mandate. Once this Rubicon had been crossed, new regulatory and policy terrain could finally be explored in a purposeful manner.

Public service value
The CM's Recommendation on measures to promote the public service value of the Internet, picks up on the theme of public service, specifically in an online context. Its central objective is to prompt States authorities, where appropriate in cooperation with all interested parties, to take all necessary measures to promote the public service value of the Internet, inter alia by 'upholding human rights, democracy and the rule of law [...]

and promoting social cohesion, respect for cultural diversity and trust' in respect of the Internet and other information and communications technologies (ICTs) (Council of Europe CM 2007b: p. 2). States authorities are expected to draw on the guidelines appended to the Recommendation in their efforts to realize its central objective. The guidelines have five main focuses: human rights and democracy; access; openness; diversity; and security. Section I, 'Human rights and democracy', stresses the importance of values and interests such as 'pluralism, cultural and linguistic diversity'. Section IV, 'Diversity', strives for equitable and universal involvement in the development of Internet and ICT content. As such, it encourages: developing a cultural dimension to digital content production, including by public service media; preserving the digital heritage; participation in 'the creation, modification and remixing of interactive content'; measures for the production and distribution of user- and community-generated content; capacity-building for local and Indigenous content on the Internet; multilingualism on the Internet.

The CM's Declaration on a European Policy for New Information Technologies (Council of Europe 1999) also engages in a detailed way with the specific potential of new media technologies for stimulating cultural diversity. The most relevant section of the Declaration, section (iv) concerning diversity of content and language, includes the following aims:

- To encourage the development of a wide range of communication and information networks, as well as the diversity of content and language, so as to foster political pluralism, cultural diversity and sustainable development;
- To promote the full use by all, including minorities, of the opportunities for exchange of opinion and self-expression offered by the new information technologies;
- To acknowledge the usefulness of these technologies in enabling all European countries and regions to express their cultural identities;
- To encourage the provision of cultural, educational and other products and services in an appropriate variety of languages and to promote the greatest possible diversity of these products and services (Council of Europe CM 1999).

These examples of engagement with the specificities of new media technologies and the identification of how those technologies can serve the goal of promoting cultural diversity are welcome. They represent a significant step forward from numerous generalized affirmations of the potential of new media technologies for promoting cultural diversity (which, while welcome in their own right, offered little practical guidance as to how they actually promoted the goal) (Council of Europe CM 2000: Preamble and para. 2.3; Council of Europe CM 2005: Section 3; Council of Europe CM 1999: Preamble). Although their focus is on new media technologies generally, their specific resonance for PSM's goal to promote cultural diversity is clear.

Public service media governance

The concepts of media regulation and media governance are often distinguished. Media regulation focuses on the operation of specific (often legally-binding) tools that are deployed on the media to achieve established policy goals. Media governance, on the other hand, refers to the sum total of mechanisms, centralized and dispersed, that aim to organize media systems according to the resolution of media policy debates (Meier 2011: 159). Denis McQuail describes media governance as

> the overall set of laws, regulations, rules and conventions which serve the purposes of control in the general interest, including that of the media industries. Governance refers to a process in which a range of different actors co-operate for different purposes, with actors drawn from market and civil society institutions as well as from government.
>
> (McQuail 2010: 232)

Whatever the preferred working definition, it is important to note that media regulation increasingly provides for, and encourages, different forms of media governance.

It has been noted that 'from a societal point of view, governance is seen as a possibility for civil society to gain or to consolidate some (new) forms of participation in political processes and decisions' (Meier 2011: 158). Governance is often associated with regulatory bodies, but it can also apply to specific media institutions or entities, e.g. PSM. In such a context, Raymond Williams has suggested that if

> we can make a further distinction between 'public service' of a traditional kind, controlled by appointed central authorities, and 'public service' of a new kind, controlled democratically by local communities and by those who work in the institutions, a new range of social possibility will have been opened.
>
> (Williams 2003: 153)

This points towards the more democratic, participatory model of media governance elaborated by Karol Jakubowicz: 'representative participatory communicative democracy' (Jakubowicz 1996: 145). This involves the application of principles of participatory democracy to broadcasting (structures). The basic idea is that while not every individual member of a group can actually broadcast, the organizational structures of the broadcasting entity should strive to facilitate maximum participation by all members in influencing policies and decisions and fixing goals.

At the European regulatory/policy level, the topic of public service media governance was broached in the CM's Recommendation on a new notion of media, which stated that PSM 'should, ideally, involve the public in its governance structures' (Council of Europe CM 2011: para. 81). This paved the way for much more explicit and detailed engagement with the topic shortly afterwards, in the CM's Declaration (2012a) and Recommendation

(2012b), both titled 'Public Service Media Governance'. The Declaration proposes a broad definition of 'governance' that includes the following elements:

- The legal frameworks through which the State ensures an appropriate balance between the independence and accountability of public service media;
- The regulations and practices through which public service media ensure that their processes and culture are the most appropriate to fulfil their remit and best serve the public interest;
- An active and meaningful dialogue with its wider stakeholders including new levels of interaction, engagement and participation (Council of Europe CM 2012a: para. 11).

The relevance of PSM governance to the advancement of cultural diversity had earlier been acknowledged in the CM's Recommendation on a new notion of media:

> The new ecosystem offers an unprecedented opportunity to incorporate diversity into media governance, in particular as regards gender balanced participation in the production, editorial and distribution processes. The same is true as regards various ethnic and religious groups. This will be a key factor in ensuring balanced representation and coverage by media and in combating stereotypes in respect of all constituent groups of society.
>
> (Council of Europe CM 2011: para. 83)

The new emphasis that the Council of Europe is placing on media and PSM governance can be seen as a significant policy development. The European Court of Human Rights has developed firm principles on participation in public debate *via* the media; recent CM standard-setting texts emphasize the need for participation *in* the media. The importance of the distinction between participation in and through the media has been captured well by Nico Carpentier (2011: 66–70; see also Grünangerl, Trappel and Wenzel 2012). He explains that participation in the media implies 'participation in the production of media output (content-related participation) and in media organizational decision-making (structural participation)', which enhances the potential for members of different groups in society to influence how they are represented in the media (Carpentier 2011: 68). Self-representation and empowerment are strengthened through participation in the media.

Conclusion

Over the years, public service broadcasting has had to contend with sustained challenges to its *raison d'être* from various quarters. In the face of such challenges, it has demonstrated considerable resilience, both as an ideology and as an institution. It currently faces the challenge of consolidating its presence in an online environment, arguably its biggest challenge yet. The process of consolidation necessarily includes the expansion of PSB's key services across a multiplicity of platforms, to include an optimal blend of general, thematic and personalized services for a diverse and diversified audience or users.

Central to the challenge of consolidation is the need for PSM to continue to promote cultural diversity in ways that are appropriate and effective in the altered technological environment. Due to the increasingly interactive nature of the Internet, new possibilities for the promotion of cultural diversity have arisen. The focus no longer needs to be exclusively on strategies for PSM's output to cater for the varying informational needs and interests of various societal groups. Rather, a revised focus should give pride of place to promoting the participation of as diverse a range of societal groups as possible in PSM's production and organizational structures and processes. This shift of focus reflects a deeper conceptual shift – one that perceives cultural diversity not only as a result, but as a process.

It has been argued that the 'story of public broadcasting is thus the story of our times, a weave of institutional decay and transformation, emerging powerful technologies and their consequences, shifting sociologies and forms of life' (Tracey 1998: 277). If PSM is to remain *our* story of *our* times, then inclusive, participatory approaches to PSM governance may well offer the best chance of ensuring that the narrative is a shared one.

References

Barendt, E. (1993), *Broadcasting Law: A Comparative Study*, Oxford: Clarendon Press.

Bens, E. de (ed.) (2007), *Media Between Culture and Commerce*, Bristol/Chicago: Intellect.

Born, G. and Prosser, T. (2001), 'Culture and Consumerism: Citizenship, Public Service Broadcasting and the BBC's Fair Trading Obligations', *The Modern Law Review*, 64: 5, pp. 657–87.

Carpentier, N. (2011), *Media and Participation: A Site of Ideological-Democratic Struggle*, Bristol/Chicago: Intellect.

Council of Europe, Conventions

(1995) Framework Convention for the Protection of National Minorities [1 February] ETS 157.

(1992) European Charter for Regional or Minority Languages [2 November] ETS 148.

(1998) European Convention on Transfrontier Television [5 May 1989] ETS 132, as amended [1 October] ETS 171.

(1950) Convention on the Protection of Human Rights and Fundamental Freedoms (ECHR) [4 November] ETS 5.

Council of Europe, Committee of Ministers (CM)

(2012a) Declaration on public service media governance [15 February].

(2012b) Recommendation CM/Rec (2012)1 on public service media governance [15 February].

(2011) Recommendation CM/Rec (2011)7 on a new notion of media [21 September].

(2010) Declaration on measures to promote the respect of Article 10 of the European Convention on Human Rights [13 January].

(2007a) Recommendation Rec(2007)3 on the remit of public service media in the information society [31 January].

(2007b) Recommendation CM/Rec(2007)16 on measures to promote the public service value of the Internet [7 November].

(2006) Declaration on the guarantee of the independence of public service broadcasting in the member states [27 September].

(2005) Declaration on human rights and the rule of law in the information society [13 May].

(2003) Recommendation Rec(2003)9 on measures to promote the democratic and social contribution of digital broadcasting [28 May].

(2000) Declaration on cultural diversity [7 December].

(1999) Declaration on a European policy for new information technologies [7 May].

European Court of Human Rights (ECtHRs)

(2009) *Manole and Others v. Moldova*, no. 13936/02, ECHR 2009 (extracts).

(2008) *Khurshid Mustafa and Tarzibachi v. Sweden*, no. 23883/06, 16 December 2008.

(2005) *Steel and Morris v. the United Kingdom*, no. 68416/01, ECHR 2005-II.

(2004) *Gorzelik and Others v. Poland* [GC], no. 44158/98, ECHR 2004-I.

(1993a) *Kokkinakis v. Greece*, 25 May 1993, Series A no. 260-A.

(1993b) *Informationsverein Lentia and Others v. Austria*, 24 November 1993, Series A no. 276.

(1981) *Young, James and Webster v. the United Kingdom*, 13 August 1981, Series A no. 44.

(1976) *Handyside v. the United Kingdom*, 7 December 1976, Series A no. 24.

European Union (EU)

(2010a) Treaty on the Functioning of the European Union [consolidated version], OJ C 83, 30.3.2010, p. 47.

(2010b) Charter of Fundamental Rights of the European Union [Nice, 7 December 2000, as adapted], OJ C 83, 30.3.2010, p. 89.

(2008) Treaty on European Union [consolidated version], OJ C115, 9.5.2008, p. 13.

(1997) Protocol to the Treaty of Amsterdam on the system of public broadcasting in the Member States [Amsterdam, 2 October], OJ C 340, 10.11.1997, p. 109.

Council of the European Union

(1999) Resolution of the Council and of the Representatives of the Governments of the Member States concerning public service broadcasting [25 January], OJ C 30, 5.2.1999, p. 1.

European Commission
(2009) Communication on the application of State aid rules to public service broadcasting [2 July], OJ C 257, 27.10.2009, p. 1.

European Parliament and Council
(2010) Directive 2010/13/EU of the European Parliament and of the Council on the coordination of certain provisions laid down by law, regulation or administrative action in member states concerning the provision of audiovisual media services (codified version) [10 March], OJ L 95, 15.4.2010, p. 1.

European Parliament (EP)
(2010) Resolution on public service broadcasting in the digital era: The future of the dual system [25 November], OJ C 99 E, 3.4.2012, p. 50.

(2008) Resolution on concentration and pluralism in the media in the EU [25 September], OJ C 8 E, 14.1.2010, p.85.

(2006) Resolution on the transition from analogue to digital broadcasting: an opportunity for European audiovisual policy and cultural diversity? [27 April], OJ C 296 E, 6.12.2006, p. 120.

(2002) Resolution on media concentration [20 November], OJ C 25 E, 29.1.2004, p. 205.

(1996) Resolution on the role of public service television in a multi-media society [19 September], OJ C 320, 28.10.1996, p. 180.

Grünangerl, M., Trappel, J. and Wenzel, C. (2012), 'Public value and participation of civil society – a case for public service or community media?', *kommunikation.media*, 1, April, pp. 1–32.

Haenens, L. d', Sousa, H. and Hultén, O. (2011), 'From public service broadcasting to public service media', in J. Trappel, W. A. Meier, L. d'Haenens, J. Steamer and B. Thomass (eds), *Media in Europe Today*, Bristol/Chicago: Intellect, pp. 187–218.

Jakubowicz, K. (2010), 'From PSB to PSM: A new promise for public service provision in the information society', in B. Klimkiewicz (ed.), *Media Freedom and Pluralism: Media Policy Challenges in the Enlarged Europe*, Budapest/New York: Central European University Press, pp. 193–227.

Jakubowicz, K. (2007a), 'Public service broadcasting: A pawn on an ideological chessboard', in E. De Bens (ed.), *Media Between Culture and Commerce*, pp. 115–41.

Jakubowicz, K. (2007b), 'Looking to the future', in E. De Bens (ed.), *Media Between Culture and Commerce*, pp. 179–95.

Jakubowicz, K. (2007c), 'Media governance structures in Europe', in E. De Bens (ed.), *Media Between Culture and Commerce*, pp. 197–224.

Jakubowicz, K. (1996) 'Access to the media and democratic communication: Theory and practice in Central and Eastern Europe', in A. Sajó (ed.), *Rights of Access to the Media*, The Hague: Kluwer Law International, pp. 139–63.

Krebber, D. (2002), *Europeanisation of Regulatory Television Policy: The Decision-making Process of the Television without Frontiers Directives from 1989 & 1997*, Baden-Baden: Nomos Verlagsgesellschaft.

McGonagle, T. (2011a), *Minority Rights, Freedom of Expression and of the Media: Dynamics and Dilemmas*, 44, School of Human Rights Research Series, Antwerp: Intersentia.

McGonagle, T. (2011b), 'Introduction', in S. Nikoltchev and T. McGonagle (eds), *Freedom of Expression and the Media: Standard-setting by the Council of Europe, (I) Committee of Ministers – IRIS Themes*, Strasbourg: European Audiovisual Observatory, pp. 1–4.

McGonagle, T. (2008), 'The quota quandary: An assessment of Articles 4–6 of the Television without Frontiers Directive', in D. Ward (ed.), *The European Union and the Culture Industries: Regulation and the Public Interest*, Aldershot: Ashgate, pp. 187–212.

McQuail, D. (2010), *McQuail's Mass Communication Theory*, 6th edn, LA: Sage.

Meier, W. A. (2011), 'From media regulation to democratic media governance', in J. Trappel, W. A. Meier, L. d'Haenens, J. Steamer and B. Thomass (eds.), *Media in Europe Today*, Bristol/Chicago: Intellect, pp. 155–66.

Mendel, T. (2011), *Public Service Broadcasting: A Comparative Legal Survey*, 2nd edn, Paris: UNESCO.

Moring, T. and Dunbar, R. (2008), *The European Charter for Regional or Minority Languages and the Media*, Strasbourg: Council of Europe Publishing.

Ofcom (2007), *A New Approach to Public Service Content in the Digital Media Age: The Potential Role of the Public Service Publisher*, Discussion Paper, 24 January [Summary of responses, 13 June 2007].

Thornberry, P., Estébanez, M. A. M. (2004), *Minority Rights in Europe*, Strasbourg: Council of Europe Publishing.

Tracey, M. (1998), *The Decline and Fall of Public Service Broadcasting*, Oxford/New York: OUP.

UNESCO (United Nations Educational, Scientific and Cultural Organization) (2005) Convention on the Protection and Promotion of the Diversity of Cultural Expressions [20 October], 33rd Session of the General Conference of UNESCO.

Williams, R. (2003), *Television: Technology and Cultural Form*, London/New York: Routledge.

Notes

1. This chapter draws from and builds on relevant sections of McGonagle (2011a).
2. For details, see: Council of Europe Press Release, 'Transfrontier television: The revision of the Convention discontinued', 4 February 2011, http://www.coe.int/t/dghl/standardsetting/media/T-TT/default_en.asp. Accessed 10 October 2013.

Section 2

Policies, Practices and Future Directions: National Case Studies

Chapter 4

Between Diversity and Pluriformity:
The 'New Style' of Dutch Public Broadcasting

Isabel Awad and Jiska Engelbert (Erasmus University, Rotterdam)

Introduction

In late August 2010 – together with the programming for its new season – the Dutch public broadcaster, NPO, announced a 'new style' and an accompanying logo: an orange ampersand. A video on NPO's website shows that the ampersand was formed in the overlap of the 'P', the public (*publieke*), and the 'O', the broadcaster (*omroep*). Orange, in the Netherlands, is the colour of the royal house, of the national football team and of 'all occasions on which national identity wants to be celebrated' (Schnabel 2007: 34). With an orange ampersand then, NPO wanted to represent both its fit into and its capacity to unify Dutch society. The broadcaster's connecting or integrating (*verbinden*) power derives from its effort to bring together all opinions, to include everybody, according to the chair of NPO's directory board, Henk Hagoort (2010). Significantly, Hagoort's introduction of the broadcaster's new style underscored both the urgent need for such a bonding force in the Netherlands – 'a country where disunion and polarization increase'[1] – and the particular aptness of NPO to fulfil this role:

> The unique Dutch broadcasting establishment with broadcasting associations and task organizations guarantees that the public broadcasting can offer quality and pluriformity. With the colorfulness of its programmes, in which as many Dutch people as possible recognize themselves, the public broadcaster is present always & everywhere; it is of & for everyone.
>
> (Hagoort 2010)

Particularly relevant in Hagoort's words is the conceptualization of the public broadcasting system's mission as a combination of difference (i.e. various broadcasting associations, pluriformity, colourfulness) and unity. The *uniqueness* of the Dutch system – traditionally based not on one, but on several broadcasters – refers to the former rather than to the latter. However, Hagoort suggests that the system can maintain this uniqueness and, at the same time, strengthen its power to unify Dutch society. The way in which this mission combines difference and unity, and its presentation not only as new, but also as urgent, turn it into a useful entry into the theme of this chapter, namely, the Dutch public broadcaster's struggle to (re)define and justify its position vis-à-vis the current political climate in the Netherlands, one marked by scepticism against state institutions and by calls to restrict immigration and to assimilate cultural differences. More specifically, the chapter examines how cultural diversity is being (re)conceptualized in the public broadcaster's struggle to reposition itself within this political context. Although cultural diversity has been in the broadcaster's agenda for decades, the new style stresses a specific, and relatively recent, take on this issue. What cultural diversity actually means in Dutch public radio, television and Internet today can only be understood in relation to how the public broadcaster interprets and reacts to broader political forces.

Arguably, the interplay between political power, public broadcasting and cultural diversity had never been as visible in the Netherlands as since 2010, under the right-wing Freedom and Responsibility government. The government – a coalition of liberals (VVD: Volkspartij voor Vrijheid en Democratie) and Christian-democrats (CDA: Christen-Democratisch Appèl) – was appointed in mid-October 2010, after four months of tense negotiations. Since it was a minority coalition (with less than 50 per cent of the seats in parliament), its actual power to govern depended on a commitment of support (or 'tolerance') from a third party, the populist Freedom Party (Partij voor de Vrijheid, henceforth PVV).[2] Founded in 2004 and almost single-handedly controlled by Geert Wilders, the PVV grew from 9 to 24 parliamentary seats in the 2010 general elections. Based on this negotiating power, it signed the 'agreement of tolerance' (*gedoogakkoord*) with the governing coalition, which, as a result, was nicknamed the 'Wilders-cabinet'.

Wilders's influence on the government – or at least his strong affinity with the VVD–CDA coalition – was also clearly visible in the coalition's 'Freedom and Responsibility' ruling agreement. The agreement reflected not only the most prominent issue in Wilders's political agenda, that is, its anti-Islam and anti-immigration position, but also his party's other priority of reducing bureaucracy and thus its attack on most public institutions, including public service broadcasting. Specifically, the cabinet's agreement announced a budget cut of more than 25 per cent for this institution, as an effort to reduce government expenditures and to make the broadcaster more 'efficient, open and governable' (VVD–CDA 2010: 33; see also Boston Consulting Group 2011). More concrete policy proposals based on this agreement underscored the need to simplify and consolidate the public broadcasting system (Ministerie voor Onderwijs, Wetenschap en Cultuur (Ministry of Education, Culture and Media) 2011).

The scrutinizing of public service broadcasting is also emblematic of Wilders's broader anti-establishment and overall populist approach. Characteristic of that approach is an aversion to institutions that, according to Wilders, propagate leftist interests and perspectives. The PVV's 2010 election manifesto 'The Agenda of Hope and Optimism', for example, systematically termed NPO the 'state broadcaster' and argued that the different broadcasting organizations that exist in the Netherlands 'pretend to represent a color, but are in fact as leftist as each other' (PVV 2010: 33). As a whole, the public broadcasting system was considered part of the 'leftist elite', accused by Wilders of having led to a 'multicultural nightmare', where 'Henk and Ingrid are paying for Ali and Fatima' (PVV 2010: 7, 5). Within this logic, then, the public service broadcaster was implicated in the charge that Dutch public institutions systematically privilege the voices of 'Ali and

Fatima' – that is, the voices of non-western immigrants, and more specifically Muslims – at the expense of the perspective of 'Henk and Ingrid', the white and non-immigrant working and middle classes.

Despite Wilders's specific influence on the government coalition, however, 'Freedom and Responsibility' should not be read as a revolutionary turn in Dutch politics. As it will become clearer below, this was rather the consolidation of major political developments of the last decades. Consequently, this chapter's effort to interpret the Dutch public broadcaster's new style and its connection to concrete cultural diversity initiatives and programming necessarily takes a historical perspective. More specifically, the chapter traces three parallel developments in policy since the mid-1990s: (1) the move from multiculturalism to assimilation in the politics of ethnic diversity and immigration, (2) the restructuring of public broadcasting in the face of social, economic and commercial transformations, and (3) how these two developments interact in the public broadcasting system's approach to cultural diversity. Based on these historical developments, the chapter then underscores the specificity of the broadcaster's most recent approach to cultural diversity. It explains how this approach evolved in contraposition to a tradition of (ideological) 'pluriformity' in Dutch public broadcasting. It argues that while difference among dominant ideological perspectives is valued and even promoted, (ethnic) minority-based difference is being depoliticized and assimilated.

Minorities and immigration policies: From multiculturalism to assimilation

The Dutch approach to ethnic diversity and immigration from the early 1980s to the mid-1990s has received different interpretations among academics. For some authors, the approach reflected an extraordinary commitment to multiculturalism. Thus, Joppke (2007: 5; see also Sniderman and Hagendoorn 2007) argues that

> [s]ince the early 1980s, the Netherlands had pursued Europe's most prominent and proudly exhibited multiculturalism policy, which envisaged 'emancipation' for designated 'ethnic minorities,' but within their own state supported ethnic infrastructures, including ethnic school, ethnic hospitals and ethnic media.

The policy Joppke refers to is the Minorities Policy of 1983 (*Minderhedennota*), which aimed at strengthening minority groups and their cultural identity. According to the most common interpretation, this policy was based on the principle of 'integration with preservation of own identity', in the sense that group ties were assumed to facilitate minority groups' emancipation and their effective integration in Dutch political life (Carle 2006; Fermin, Kjellstrand and Entzinger 2005; Sniderman and Hagendoorn 2007; Uitermark, Rossi and van Houtum 2005). More sceptical views, in contrast, argue that multiculturalism in the Netherlands was always limited. According to Vasta (2007: 727), for example, the Dutch model did not succeed in countering the country's 'institutional discrimination based on a denied history and culture of racism'. Vink (2007), in turn, explains that the Minorities Policy supported minorities' group cohesion not for multicultural and emancipatory purposes, but in order to facilitate their expected return to their home countries.

Despite the different views on whether the Netherlands of the 1980s exposed a model of strong or limited multiculturalism, there is some kind of agreement on what happened after that. In the last decades, the country has allegedly positioned itself at the forefront of Europe's growing apprehension towards ethnic diversity and toughening immigration policies, what Joppke (2004) calls, the 'retreat of multiculturalism'. This process started in the mid-1990s, was translated into a first law in 1998 – when the Minorities Policy was replaced by the Law on Civic Integration for Newcomers – and became a major issue in public debate in the early 2000s. Like its predecessor, the Law on Civic Integration for Newcomers focused on 'non-Western immigrants'.[3] However, in contrast to the previous policy, the 1998 legislation distrusted group identities. It treated immigrants as individuals (not collectively) and obliged them to take Dutch language and civic lessons (Joppke 2004; Kofman 2005). Further reforms and a new Law on Civic Integration in 2006 have become even stricter. Potential non-western immigrants are now required to pass a basic Dutch language and culture test in their own countries in order to be eligible to immigrate. Once in the Netherlands, they have to cover the costs of the language and civic lessons on their own and to pass stricter tests than before. Moreover, the VVD–CDA coalition agreement proposes that those who fail the integration test lose their provisional residence permit (VVD–CDA 2010; see also Ministerie van Binnenlandse Zaken en Koninkrijksrelaties (Ministry of Interior and Kingdom Relations) 2011).

In 2000, an opinion piece in the leading quality Dutch newspaper *NRC Handelsblad* entitled 'The Multicultural Drama' stirred intense debate on this issue. The article, written by historian and Dutch Labour Party member Paul Scheffer, argued that the Dutch approach to immigration had failed because it had helped create a segregated society, with a large 'ethnic underclass' and 'few sources of unity'. Scheffer's main concern were Muslim minority groups – whose 'cultural differences [...] do not lend themselves to concession, compromise or buying off' – and his solution was a model of integration that would presuppose minorities' cultural assimilation: 'Let's start by taking our [i.e. the dominant Dutch] language, legal culture and history a lot more seriously' (Scheffer 2000; see Entzinger 2006; Vasta 2007).

Since 2000, Scheffer's initially controversial statements have flooded the mainstream of Dutch politics. Particularly important in this move were the September 11 attacks in New York in 2001 and, in the Netherlands, the murder of two prominent anti-Muslim voices: politician Pim Fortuyn, killed by an animal rights and environmental activist in 2002; and film-maker Theo van Gogh, assassinated by a Muslim fundamentalist in 2004. Moreover, a series of newly formed far-right political parties have capitalized on the populist sentiment, by adopting the critique of Islam, the restriction of immigration and the protection of a traditional Dutch identity at the core of their political agenda. Fortuyn's own political party (List Pim Fortuyn) was followed by Rita Verdonk's Proud of the Netherlands party and by Geert Wilders's Freedom Party. Even if typically short lived, these parties' popularity and electoral successes have forced other political actors and institutions to engage with their far-right political agenda. A rather extreme, but relevant case is the PVV's 2010 'agreement of tolerance' with the governing coalition, discussed earlier.

In sum, not only the notion of a 'multicultural drama', but also the identification of Islam as the main source of the problem and of assimilation as the way out have became increasingly prevalent in Dutch policy and public debate. Significantly, this is also the case in discussions about the role of public broadcasting. Indeed, it is in this political context that the sense of urgency in NPO's new (integrating) style should be understood. According to NPO's head, in the quote cited above, the Netherlands, is 'a country where disunion and polarization increase' (Hagoort 2010).

Restructuring of public broadcasting: The ambiguous legacy of pillarization

Since the 1990s, roughly in parallel to the above changes in minority and immigration policy, the Dutch government has been forced to 'restructure and "reinvent" its broadcasting policy' (Bardoel 2003: 83). Important changes in society, as well as in technology and media economics have gradually eroded the unique foundations of the Dutch public broadcasting system. Furthermore, these changes have been used to justify a redefinition of relations, first, among the system's different components and, second, between the system and the public.

The Radio Law of 1928, the first effort to regulate broadcasting in the Netherlands, established a *pluriform*[4] as opposed to a national public broadcaster. Pluriformity, in this context, meant that radio and later television broadcasting would be controlled by and serve as 'mouthpieces' for the four social 'pillars' that structured the rest of Dutch society (Commissie Publieke Omroep 1996). Thus, associations of Catholic, Protestant, socialist and liberal listeners and viewers established separate broadcasting associations, which produced and financed their own programmes. They were allocated airtime in the radio and television public channels according to the size of their membership. This public organization of private associations was designed as a fair basis for the distribution of limited resources (the electromagnetic spectrum) among the different constituencies of Dutch society, while a separate 'task-broadcaster', NOS (Nederlandse Omroep Stichting), was in charge of the production of news programmes for all segments of the population.

Until the 1960s, then, the Dutch broadcasting system derived its legitimacy from the associations' close connection with their membership base (Bardoel 2003). However, the system, and with it, its sources of legitimation, have changed since then. On the one hand, the country's traditional pillars do not contain citizens' alliances and interests anymore (Dekker and Ester 1996). On the other hand, liberalization and deregulation of media markets have opened the doors to new players within and outside the public broadcasting system. Most notably, in the Netherlands – like in most of Europe – the end of the 1980s and beginning of the 1990s marked the end of the old monopoly of public broadcasting (Bardoel 2003; Brants and Bardoel 2003). This was also the beginning of the dominance of a commercial logic, in which public broadcasting is under increasing threat, involved in what Jakubowicz (2003: 147) calls 'a life-or-death struggle' (see also: Brants, Hermes, and van Zoonen 1998; McQuail and Siune 1998).

Important policy changes in public broadcasting since the 1990s have thus been meant to account for the competition of commercial broadcasting as well as for the erosion of the system's association-based support. A key instrument in the consolidation of these changes was the 2000 Concession Law (Bardoel 2003). The law contained two related measures, with particularly important consequences for understanding the public broadcaster's current situation and how it accommodates cultural diversity. The first measure affected the broadcasting system's general structure. NOS, which until then had operated as both the system's coordinating agency and a task broadcaster in charge of current events and other special programming, lost its coordinating function. A new organization, NPO was created to assume this function. The new law turned NPO into the legal representation, and thus the single concession holder, of the overall broadcasting system (Bardoel 2003). The result was a stronger and more centralized administration, as well as new guarantees for independence in news production.

A second important measure of the 2000 Concession Law implied a shift in the way in which the broadcasters relate to the public. As suggested above, traditionally broadcasters' 'accountability and responsiveness [had been] organized through the member-based structure of the different institutions' (Brants and Bardoel 2008). By 2000, there was consensus within broadcasting and policy circles that the traditional approach could not secure the public broadcaster's accountability in the twenty-first century, where 'bureaucratization of organizations and professionalism of journalists [had] gradually replaced active participation of citizens' (Bardoel 2003: 83). The broadcaster committed itself to be more transparent by, for example, making public a yearly financial report and engaging in public debate (Bardoel and d'Haenens 2004; Brants and Bardoel 2008). Furthermore, the Concession Law established a system of 'Assessment Commissions' composed by independent experts and assigned to assess the broadcasters' performance every five years. The commission's report is relevant, among other things, for maintaining (or not) existing broadcasters and incorporating new ones into the system (Bardoel 2003).

The main question is no longer that of who has the 'right' to broadcasting time based upon membership figures and representativeness. The main question now is what

Dutch society can expect. A broadcasting corporation's achieved and prospective accomplishments determine whether it will receive more broadcasting time.

(C. P. M. Van der Haak, cited in Bardoel and d'Haenens 2004)

By creating NPO and privileging performance over membership, the Concession Law of 2000 undermined the pillarized structure of the Dutch public broadcasting system. Hence, the law was seen as a 'step in the transformation process of public broadcasting from a specific, national tradition towards a European future' (Bardoel 2003: 84). However, because the transformation is not complete, the Dutch broadcasting system is somehow caught in-between the 'national tradition' and the 'European future'. Thus, NPO, whose role has been strengthened since 2000, coexists with 20 broadcasting associations.[5] Moreover, while it is often considered – not in the least by the broadcasting organizations themselves – as limiting the power of the broadcasters, NPO is bound by its task to coordinate and not shape or affect the activities and programming of individual broadcasters (see Brants and Bardoel 2008).

Likewise, even though the 2000 Concession Law forced the broadcasting associations to reconfigure their relationship with the public and to focus on performance over membership, it maintained the reference to pluriformity 'as the heritage of the Dutch broadcasting tradition and to the importance of stimulating national culture' (Bardoel 2003: 84).[6] The law complicated the relationship between broadcasters and the public further, by referring as well 'to a new role public broadcasting should play, as a forum in a multicultural information society for which support from the young and from migrants is essential' (Bardoel 2003: 84). The challenge for the public broadcaster, then, is to figure out what pluriformity means and how to implement it in ways that resonate with the now depillarized Dutch society and that contribute to a national culture. On top of that, it has to find ways to be pluriform and multicultural at the same time. As explained below – and already suggested in Hagoort's announcement of a new style – in its attempt to fulfil this double task, the broadcaster relies on complex and apparently contradictory strategies.

Overall, an uncomfortable position of the Dutch public broadcasting system in relation to its pillarized origins, makes it particularly vulnerable. It suffers, first, from the same crisis of legitimation of public service broadcasting in other European countries, where the general notion of publicly funded media is under attack (Bardoel 2003; Bardoel and d'Haenens 2008; NPO 2010; Trappel et al. 2011). But in the Dutch case, the crisis of legitimation is double since 'the specificities of Dutch broadcasting policies and their traditional legitimation' are also under attack (Bardoel 2003: 88; see also Bardoel and d'Haenens 2004). This means that even if the basic question of 'Why spend public money on public broadcasting?' is satisfactorily answered, the survival of public broadcasting (as we know it) in the Netherlands also depends on its ability to respond to an increasing number of voices that ask: 'Why pay for multiple public broadcasters?' (see, for example, Dake et al. 2010).

Ethnic diversity in public broadcasting: Mainstreaming the margins

The Minorities Policy of 1983 underscored the importance of minority-targeted media for minorities' social integration in the Netherlands, as well as 'their own cultural experience and development' (cited in Schakenbos and Marsman 1988: 56). The public broadcasting system's coordinator, NOS, had the special responsibility to turn this principle into concrete policies and programmes. NOS did this through a 'follow-up policy' that acknowledged the 'vital role' of radio and television for both minority groups and 'Dutch people'. Media's *vital role* was described in terms of 'the promotion of participation in society, the mutual adaptation and acceptance of all social groups in this country, [and] the defiance of discrimination' (NOS Vervolgnota, cited in Schakenbos and Marsman 1988: 56). Furthermore, these policy goals were linked to 'the provision of programming focused on information and education (also in one's own language) and on increasing one's own identity and cultural exchange' (NOS Vervolgnota, as cited in Schakenbos and Marsman 1988: 56). As a result, special radio and television programmes were created to address different migrant groups. For the most part, the programmes were produced by members of these groups themselves, in languages other than Dutch (though, in some cases, with Dutch subtitles), and they focused on Dutch and international news as well as on music. A significant number of these programmes were transmitted by NOS (Leurdijk 2004; Schakenbos and Marsman 1988).

Since this early formulation of NOS's policy on minority-targeted programmes, there have been significant changes in the public broadcaster's understanding and handling of cultural diversity. To start with, three successive reorganizations within the broadcaster's structure have transferred NOS's ethnic diversity responsibilities to other institutions. First, in 1995, a new public broadcaster, NPS (Nederlandse Programma Stichting), took over NOS's programming obligations with respect to ethnic minorities, as well as those related to culture and children. Second, in 2002, together with the rest of NOS's administrative functions, NPO became responsible for the design and monitoring of the broadcasting system's general diversity policies. Finally, in late 2010, NPS merged with two other task-broadcasters (both dedicated to education) as a measure to save costs. The three together became NTR (NPS, Teleac, RVU). These structural changes have been coupled with changes in what counts as multicultural or minority content in public radio and television.

By law, multicultural programming was one of NPS's – and is now NTR's – special tasks. Moreover, when NPS was created in 1995, it had to meet specific quotas in this area: 20 per cent in its television schedule and 25 per cent in its radio schedule. That same year, brand-new NPS organized a special congress to discuss 'the dilemmas of the broadcaster in a diverse society' (Van der Wal 1995) and what its minority programming should look like. Media policy makers, researchers and producers at the congress criticized NOS's targeted-programming tradition as old-fashioned, narrow-minded and ineffective in both attracting ethnic minorities and contributing to their integration (Algemeen

Dagblad 1995; Leurdijk 2004). They advocated, instead, for programmes that would 'offer a better reflection of the multicultural society' (Leurdijk 2004: 128). Eventually, this led to a transformation that has been described as a move 'from the margins to the mainstream' (Leurdijk 2008) or 'from exclusivity to inclusiveness' (Bink 2006) in Dutch public broadcasting's cultural diversity policy. The old policy approach is labelled 'exclusive' or 'marginal' because it prescribed separate radio and television programmes for different ethnic minority groups. The new policy, in contrast, is considered 'inclusive' or 'mainstream' because it stipulates *cross*-cultural or *inter*-cultural programmes targeted at both minority and mainstream audiences at the same time (Awad and Roth in 2011; Leurdijk 2006).

A more concrete way to understand the difference between the public broadcaster's approach to cultural diversity in the 1980s and today is to consider specific programmes. This is what Frans Jennekens – Head of Diversity at NTR and Chairman of the Intercultural and Diversity Group of the European Public Broadcasting Union – does when he uses the formula 'from *Passport* to *Raymann is laat*' (Jennekens, personal communication, 24 November 2010). *Passport* and *Raymann is laat* (*Raymann is late*) are emblematic 'multicultural' television programmes from each of the two periods. The first was produced by the public broadcaster between 1975 and 1992, with the aim of empowering immigrants and contributing to their integration (Leurdijk 2004). Popular among so-called foreign-workers, *Passport* introduced them – in Spanish, Turkish, Serbo-Croatian, Italian, Portuguese or Morrocan Arabic – to key aspects of Dutch society and institutions, while also covering events from their home country (Bink and Serkei 2009; Breimer 1995). The contrast with *Raymann is laat*, which has been airing since 2001, is telling. The latter is a Dutch-language, late-night entertainment show, with an expensive budget and a large audience of minority as well as mainstream viewers. The humour and playfulness with which Suriname Dutch stand-up comedian Jörgen Raymann addresses common prejudices against his own community have turned the show into one of NTR's most successful efforts to underscore 'the funny side of diversity' (Jennekens 2010: 18).

The so-called 'mainstreaming' strategy successfully followed by programmes such as *Raymann is laat* is also at the core of other recent diversity initiatives of the Dutch public broadcasting system. Probably the single most visible among these was the 2008 European Broadcasting Union's diversity conference, which was organized by NPO and NPS in collaboration with other European broadcasting organizations. The congress, called *The Diversity Show: Diversity as a Creative Opportunity*, was held in the biggest TV studio of the Dutch public broadcaster and brought together some 600 participants from different European countries (NPS 2009). The full-day programme showcased successful multicultural programmes and included well-known television personalities: it was conducted by Pakistani British television presenter Saira Khan (author of the self-help book *P.U.S.H. for Success* [2006]) and by Jörgen Raymann and it started with a keynote from African American marketing consultant, bestselling author and Oprah Winfrey's partner, Stedman Graham.

Another example of the mainstreaming logic of recent diversity initiatives in the Dutch public broadcasting system is the 'Diversity Incentives Programme' for which NPO reserved 1 million Euros in 2010. On a competitive basis, broadcasters could apply for funds to increase the representation of ethnic minorities in existing programmes. Priority was given to 'popular, high-impact' radio and television programmes that could reach a wide audience 'in order to maximize progress and visibility' (NPO 2009: 1). Moreover, the funds could not be spent in hiring new people or bringing in new content, but had to be used for training the current staff and for incorporating more diverse guests and experts. The idea was not to change the direction of the programmes, but to 'mainstream diversity', according to a policy advisor from NPO's Media and Financial Policy Department (Y. Staal, personal communication, 22 November 2010). To explain how the incentives plan worked in practice, Jennekens mentioned a well-known current affairs television programme, which not only expanded its network of minority guests, but also recorded a 'mirror' version, replacing the usual staff with ethnic minorities. This mirror version was not broadcasted, but was used to convince the producers themselves of the viability of working with 'different people' (Jennekens, personal communication, 24 November 2010).

Political and apolitical differences

The mainstreaming of diversity is justified in descriptive, as opposed to normative terms. This means that diversity is seen as necessary in order to make programmes that reflect society as it is, not that aim at changing it. In the words of NTR's head of diversity: 'Diversity [in public broadcasting] is not the answer to solve racism and discrimination. It is about making people aware that the country is diverse' (Jennekens, personal communication, 24 November 2010). According to Jennekens, the days in which public broadcasting was treated as 'a political instrument', and was thus expected to produce 'service programmes', such as *Passport*, are over. Diversity in public broadcasting in the Netherlands today, he argues, aims at innovation and at attracting larger audiences, an approach commonly summarized – by Jennekens and others – as 'the business case for diversity' (Jennekens, personal communication, 24 November 2010; see Awad 2008).

The apolitical rhetoric associated with the business case for diversity in Dutch public broadcasting helps accommodate ethnic diversity to the other policy changes described above: the anti-immigrant and assimilationist policies, on the one hand, and the restructuring of public broadcasting, on the other. With respect to the first, the commercial justification defines diversity as non-threatening even to the most outspoken opponents of multiculturalism. 'Not even Geert Wilders would be negative about a Moroccan businessman with many employees', explains Jennekens (personal communication, 24 November 2010). In *The Diversity Show*, for example, questions of racism and discrimination were exceptional, while the emphasis was put on successful multicultural programmes and minority celebrities, such as Jörgen Raymann, Saira Khan and Stedman Graham. The NPS itself described *The Diversity Show* as a turning point for the European Broadcasting Union in this respect: 'Whereas earlier conferences would typically stagnate in the problems of diversity, the NPO/NPS congress focused especially on diversity's opportunities and potential, all of which was presented in an inspiring setting' (NPS 2009: 9). In this way, the business case for diversity privileges what Horsti (2009) calls 'consumable differences'. It neglects 'structural aspects of racism and power relations in society' and thus avoids representations that could challenge the status quo (Horsti 2009: 356). By limiting diversity to cultural differences that fit into mainstream social norms and structures, this approach is also assimilationist: in broadcasting – like in other spheres of society – inclusion is an opportunity offered to well-adjusted (minority) individuals. As it is particularly evident in the Diversity incentives programme, diversity is welcome to the extent that it does not threaten to significantly change the programmes or the people who are in charge of them.

Similarly, the business case for diversity responds to the restructuring of public broadcasting of the last decades. As explained above, the Dutch broadcasting system has been compelled to adopt a commercial logic and to redefine its relationship with the audience in ways that have moved it away from the old pillarized model and closer to a (centralized) European one. Not only the broad market appeal of the new multicultural programmes, but also their apolitical character resonates with this shift. As observed by Leurdijk (2006: 25), broadcasting professionals can see diversity as a threat to the quality and objectivity of their job 'if political objectives such as "promoting multiculturalism" or "introducing minority perspectives" were to take precedence over professional standards'. Within the Dutch system, this would definitely be the case for professionals who work in the two task-broadcasters: NOS, dedicated to news; and NTR, dedicated to education, current events, youth, culture and diversity. Task-broadcasters have legally defined tasks, which they have to fulfil in an unbiased and independent way, addressing all Dutch people. As stressed in the press release announcing the start of NTR in 2010, what makes NTR essentially different from other broadcasting organizations is that it provides 'a reliable and objective interpretation of the events of yesterday, today and tomorrow' (NTR 2010).

Significantly, NTR (and formerly NPS) is responsible not only for *Raymann is laat*, but for most multicultural programming in Dutch public media today. Diversity initiatives and programmes are largely concentrated in NTR for reasons grounded on the specific organization of the Dutch public broadcasting system. First, NTR has the special status of task broadcaster and one of its tasks is to focus on cultural diversity. Second, NTR is responsive to NPO's policies and guidelines in ways that the broadcasting associations are not. As mentioned above, broadcasting associations are autonomous in content decisions. In contrast to other European public broadcasting systems, then, 'NPO cannot set centralized targets' (Jennekens, personal communication, 24 November 2010). A third and more complex reason is that broadcasting associations are compelled to give priority to pluriformity over diversity. While dictionary definitions may equate one with the other, a crucial difference between pluriformity and diversity persists in the

Dutch system. Pluriformity, on the one hand, is what justifies the existence of multiple broadcasters within the Dutch broadcasting system. It refers to the ideological differences that were the basis for Dutch pillarization (among Catholics, Protestants, socialists and liberals), although today these differences are generally reduced to left and right politics (see Sterk 2010). Diversity, on the other hand, is the term used for non-traditional cultural differences associated with immigrant groups. Thus, for example, while Catholic or right-wing views may contribute to 'pluriformity', Muslim or Moroccan Dutch views are most commonly considered 'diverse'. How should a Catholic or a right-wing broadcaster, to use these examples, secure its particular (plurifom) profile, while extending the representation of Muslim and/or Moroccan Dutch views?

The tension between pluriformity and diversity has intensified in recent years, as the Dutch public broadcasting system – like other public and cultural institutions – has been accused of leaning to the left (Sterk 2010). Notably, some of the accusations come from inside the system. Thus, in 2008, the chair of NPO's directory board, Henk Hagoort (previously in charge of the Evangelical broadcaster) coined the phrase 'three times *Volkskrant*' to critically characterize the public broadcaster's current affairs programmes. The *Volkskrant* is a quality newspaper with a high-income, well-educated readership (Bakker and Scholten 2009) and known as the most leftist of all large national newspapers. The public broadcaster, and in particular its current affairs programmes, should also reach *Telegraaf* readers, argued Hagoort (Trouw 2008), making reference to another national newspaper – in this case a tabloid broadsheet with the largest circulation in the Netherlands – which, according to Hagoort himself, resonates with Wilders's voters (Trouw 2008). It is in relation to this criticism that one should understand the public broadcaster's introduction of the *Uitgesproken* (Outspoken) programmes in its 2010–11 'new style' season, for example. *Uitgesproken* was a 30 minutes-long prime-time programme, used daily by different broadcasters, to *outspokenly* interpret and comment on current affairs from their particular politico-ideological perspectives.[7] Likewise, the 'three times *Volkskrant*' complaint coincided with the acceptance of two new right-wing organizations into the Dutch broadcasting system: WNL (Wakker Nederland), an initiative of the *Telegraaf* newspaper (WNL 2010), and Powned, born out of a popular anti-establishment weblog called *Geen Stijl* (No Style), also linked to the Telegraaf Media Group.

Conclusion

The notions of diversity and pluriformity in Dutch public broadcasting reflect an important hierarchy of differences that exists in Dutch society today. To use common Dutch terminology, pluriformity and diversity refer to *autochthonous* and *non-autochthonous* differences.[8] Non-autochthonous differences are associated with immigrant groups, most notably people from Turkish, Moroccan, Suriname and Antillean descent. These are differences that need to be neutralized and assimilated. They are acknowledged only at a superficial or 'ornamental' level (Lugones and Price 1995: 105), detached from the political-ideological underpinnings that could challenge (and not just *colour*) the public broadcasting system. Autochthonous differences, in contrast, are being encouraged as part of the system's key politico-ideological resources. Tellingly, both strategies – diversity and pluriformity – operate in the same direction; they both reinforce a common and dominant definition of Dutchness. Indeed, a quote from Bardoel (2003: 84) cited earlier referred to pluriformity as important for 'stimulating national culture', while this chapter has argued that that same 'national' culture is being protected from 'foreign' cultures through the mainstreaming of cultural diversity.

However, it would be unwarranted to argue that it is the public broadcaster's aim to defend a dominant notion of Dutch culture or, even less, to support the agenda of right-wing political parties. What is apparent in the broadcaster's changing approach to diversity and in the contrast between diversity and pluriformity is the system's own struggle to legitimize, and thus secure, its own place in Dutch society. Diversity and pluriformity are some of the ways in which the broadcaster confronts what was described earlier as a double crisis of legitimation. In other words, the broadcaster's specific conceptualization of diversity and pluriformity reflects the need to answer the two questions mentioned above: why spend money on public broadcasting? And why pay for multiple broadcasters? In this process, the public broadcaster is compelled to address the most pressing and increasingly powerful voices posing these sorts of questions in the Netherlands today, the same voices who call for reducing the state, restricting immigration and assimilating cultural differences. Thus, it makes sense to answer the first and more general question by arguing that the broadcaster can play a key bonding role in times of 'disunion and polarization' (Hagoort 2010). Following an apparently contradictory, but congruent logic, it also makes sense for the broadcaster to answer the second question and justify its peculiar structure by reinforcing certain kinds of politico-ideological differences among its different components. Both answers, it is worth underscoring, are brought together in the new style that the Dutch public broadcaster claimed for itself and that served as the entry point to this chapter.

References

Awad, I. (2008), 'Cultural diversity in the news media: A democratic or a commercial need?', *Javnost – The Public*, 15: 4, pp. 55–72.

Awad, I. and Roth, A. (2011), 'From minority to cross-cultural programs: Dutch media policy and the politics of integration', *International Communication Gazette*, 73: 5, pp. 400–18.

Bakker, P. and Scholten, O. (2009), *Communicatiekaart van Nederland: Overzicht van Media en Communicatie/Communication Map of the Netherlands: Overview of Media and Communication*, 7th edn, Amsterdam: Kluwer.

Bardoel, J. (2003), 'Back to the public? Assessing public broadcasting in the Netherlands', *Javnost – The Public*, 10: 3, pp. 81–96.

Bardoel, J. and Brants, K. (2003), 'From ritual to reality: Public broadcasters and social responsibility in the Netherlands', in G. F. Lowe and T. Hujanen (eds), *Broadcasting and Convergence: New Articulations of the Public Service Remit*, Göteborg: Nordicom, pp. 167–85.

Bardoel, J. and d'Haenens, L. (2004), 'Media meet the citizen: Beyond market mechanisms and government regulations', *European Journal of Communication*, 19: 2, pp. 165–94.

Bardoel, J. and d'Haenens, L. (2008), 'Reinventing public service broadcasting in Europe: Prospects, promises and problems', *Media, Culture & Society*, 30: 3, pp. 337–55.

Bink, S. (2006), *Nearly 25 Years of Media and Minorities Policy in the Netherlands: From Exclusivity to Inclusiveness*, Utrecht: Mira Media, http://www.docstoc.com/docs/146206451/Paper-Antwerpen-Susan-Bink. Accessed 8 October 2013.

Bink, S. and Serkei, C. (2009), *Verbinden of Polariseren: Over de Multiculturele Kwaliteit van de Media in Nederland/Connect or Polarize: On the Multicultural Quality of the Media in the Netherlands*, The Hague: SDU Uitgevers.

Boston Consulting Group (2011), *Tussenrapportage Efficiëntieonderzoek Landelijke Publieke Omroep/Efficiency Study of the National Public Broadcaster. Interim Report*, Hilversum: Boston Consulting Group, http://www.rijksoverheid.nl/documenten-en-publicaties/rapporten/2011/06/23/tussenrapportage-efficientieonderzoek-landelijke-publieke-omroep.html. Accessed 25 June 2011.

Brants, K., Hermes, J. and van Zoonen, L. (eds) (1998), *The Media in Question: Popular Cultures and Public Interests*, London: Sage.

Brants, K. and Bardoel, J. (2008), 'Death duties: Kelly, Fortuyn and their challenge to media governance', *European Journal of Communication*, 23: 4, pp. 471–89.

Breimer, J. (1995), 'Dertig jaar minderhedenprogramma's'/'Thirty years of minority programming', in G. Van der Wal (ed.), *Gemengde Berichten: De Dilemma's van de Omroep in een Plurale Samenleving/Mixed Messages: The Dilemmas of the Broadcaster in a Diverse Society*, Hilversum: NPS, pp. 35–40.

Carle, R. (2006), 'Demise of Dutch multiculturalism', *Society*, 43: 3, pp. 68–74.

Commissie Publieke Omroep (1996), *Terug naar het Publiek: Rapport van de Commissie Publieke Omroep/Back to the Public: Report from the Commission Public Broadcaster*, The Hague: Ministry of Education, Culture and Science, http://www.icce.rug.nl/~soundscapes/DATABASES/TNP/Terug_naar_het_publiek.shtml. Accessed 20 November 2010.

Dake, A., 's-Gravesande, A., Haasbroek, N., Kalkman, K. and Wildenberg, I. (2010), *Nederlandse Publieke Omroep: Nieuwe Stijl/Dutch Public Broadcaster: New Style*. The Hague: Workgroup APO/Werkgroep Andere Publieke Omroep, http://www.anderepubliekeomroep.eu/sites/default/files/DOCS/30078_Notitie-publieke-omroep-c.pdf. Accessed 8 October 2013.

Dekker, P. and Ester, P. (1996), 'Depillarization, deconfessionalization, and de-ideologization: Empirical trends in Dutch society 1958–1992', *Review of Religious Research*, 37: 4, pp. 325–41.

Entzinger, H. (2006), 'Changing the rules while the game is on: From multiculturalism to assimilation in the Netherlands', in Y. M. Bodemann and G. Yurdakul (eds), *Migration, Citizenship, Ethnos: Incorporation Regimes in Germany, Western Europe and North America*, New York: Palgrave MacMillan, pp. 121–44.

Fermin, A., Kjellstrand, S. and Entzinger, H. (2005), *Study on Immigration, Integration and Social Cohesion* [Final report], Brussels: European Commission, DG Employment, Social Affairs & Inclusion, http://igitur-archive.library.uu.nl/fss/2007-0227-200324/fermin_05_study_on_immigration.pdf. Accessed 20 October 2008.

Hagoort, H. (2010), *Publieke Omroep Ziet Verbinden als Kerntaak/Public Broadcaster Sees Connecting as Core Task*, Hilversum: NPO, http://www.publiekeomroep.nl/artikelen/publieke-omroep-ziet-verbinden-als-kerntaak. Accessed 28 October 2010.

Hallin, D. and Mancini, P. (2004), *Comparing Media Systems*, Cambridge: CUP.

Horsti, K. (2009), 'Anti-racist and multicultural discourses in European public service broadcasting: Celebrating consumable differences in Prix Europa Iris media prize', *Communication, Culture & Critique*, 2: 3, pp. 339–60.

Jakubowicz, K. (2003), 'Bringing public service broadcasting to account', in G. F. Lowe and T. Hujanen (eds), *Broadcasting and Convergence: New Articulations of the Public Service Remit*, Göteborg: Nordicom, pp. 147–65.

Jennekens, F. (2010), *The Funny Side of Diversity, EBU Report: Public Media Delivering on Diversity*, pp. 18–19, Geneve: EBU (European Broadcasting Union), http://www.ebu.ch/en/union/under_banners/Cultural_Diversity_2010.php. Accessed 20 December 2010.

Joppke, C. (2004), 'The retreat of multiculturalism in the liberal state: Theory and policy', *The British Journal of Sociology*, 55: 2, pp. 237–57.

Joppke, C. (2007), 'Beyond national models: Civic integration policies for immigrants in Western Europe', *West European Politics*, 30: 1, pp. 1–22.

Kofman, E. (2005), 'Citizenship, migration and the reassertion of national identity', *Citizenship Studies*, 9: 5, pp. 453–67.

Leurdijk, A. (2004), 'De eerste zwarte talkshow op de Nederlandse televisie'/'The first black talkshow in Dutch television', in R. Buikema and M. Meijer (eds), *Kunsten in Beweging 1980–2000/Cultures in Motion 1980–2000*, The Hague: SDU Uitgevers, pp. 113–33.

Leurdijk, A. (2006), 'In search of common ground: Strategies of multicultural television producers in Europe', *European Journal of Cultural Studies*, 9: 1, pp. 25–46.

Leurdijk, A. (2008), *Van Marge naar Mainstream: Essay over Mediabeleid en Culturele Diversiteit 1999–2008/From the Margin to the Mainstream: Essay on Media Policy and Cultural Diversity 1999–2008*, The Hague: Ministerie van Onderwijs, Cultuur & Wetenschap, http://www.minocw.nl/documenten/10197a.pdf. Accessed 26 October 2008.

Lugones, M. and Price, J. (1995), 'Dominant culture: El deseo por un alma pobre (The desire for an impoverished soul)', in D. A. Harris (ed.), *Multiculturalism from the Margins*, Westport, CT: Bergin & Garvey, pp. 103–27.

Maas, Jonathan (2008), 'Alle kijkers serieus nemen', *Trouw*, 16 October, http://www.trouw. nl/achtergrond/deverdieping/article1879297.ece/_rsquo_Alle_kijkers_serieus_ nemen_rsquo___.html. Accessed 12 December 2010.

McQuail, D. and Siune, K. (eds) (1998), *Media Policy: Convergence, Concentration, and Commerce*, Thousand Oaks, CA: Sage.

Ministerie van Binnenlandse Zaken en Koninkrijksrelaties (2011), *Integratie, Binding, Burgerschap/Integration, Binding, Citizenship*, The Hague: Ministry of Interior and Kingdom Relations, http://www.rijksoverheid.nl/documenten-en-publicaties/ notas/2011/06/16/integratienota.html. Accessed 10 October 2013.

Ministerie van Onderwijs, Cultuur en Wetenschap (2011), *Uitwerking Regeerakkoord Onderdeel Media/Implementation Coalition Agreement Section Media*, The Hague: Ministry of Education, Culture and Science, http://www.rijksoverheid.nl/ onderwerpen/omroepen/documenten-en-publicaties/kamerstukken/2011/06/17/ uitwerking-regeerakkoord-onderdeel-media.html. Accessed 27 June 2011.

Nederlandse Publieke Omroep (NPO) (2009), *Diversity Incentive Programme*, NPO: Hilversum [Available from the authors].

Nederlandse Publieke Omroep (NPO) (2010), *Concessiebeleidsplan 2010–2016: Verbinden, Verrijken, Verrassen/Concession Policy 2010–2016: Connect, Enrich, Surprise*, Hilversum: NPO, http://corporate.publiekeomroep.nl/page/organisatie/ verantwoording. Accessed 18 November 2010.

Nederlandse Programma Stichting (NPS) (2009), *Jaarverslag 2008/Yearly Report 2008*. Hilversum: NPS, http://www.nps.nl/page/jaarverslag#archief. Accessed 2 January 2011.

Nederlandse Programma Stichting (NPS) (2010), *Jaarverslag 2009/Yearly Report 2009*. Hilversum: NPS, http://www.nps.nl/page/jaarverslag. Accessed 18 November 2010.

NTR (2010), *Persbericht Lancering NTR/Press Release Launch NTR*, 1 July, http://www. ntr.nl/static/docs/Persbericht-lancering-NTR.pdf. Accessed 12 December 2010.

Partij voor de Vrijheid (PVV) (2010), *De Agenda van Hoop en Optimisme: Een Tijd om te Kiezen: PVV 2010–2015/The Agenda of Hope and Optimism: A Time to Choose: PVV 2010–2015*, Hilversum: PVV, http://www.pvv.nl/images/stories/Webversie_ VerkiezingsProgrammaPVV.pdf. Accessed 10 October 2013.

Schakenbos, E. and Marsman, G. (1988), *Migranten en de Media/Migrants and the Media*, Nijmegen: Masusa.

Scheffer, P. (2000), 'Het multiculturele drama'/'The multicultural drama', *NRC Handelsblad*, 29 January, http://www.nrc.nl/W2/Lab/Multicultureel/scheffer.html. Accessed 15 January 2010.

Schnabel, P. (2007), 'Modern monarchism: From "Vivat oraenge" to "Long live the queen"', in D. J. Elzinga (ed.), *The Dutch Constitutional Monarchy in a Changing Europe*, Alphen aan den Rijn: Kluwer, pp. 35–36.

Sniderman, P. M. and Hagendoorn, L. (2007), *When Ways of Life Collide: Multiculturalism and its Discontents in the Netherlands*, Princeton, NJ: PUP.

Sterk, G. (2010), 'Weinig culturele diversiteit bij publieke omroep in tv-seizoen'/'Little cultural diversity in the public broadcaster's tv season', *Wereldjournalisten/World Journalists*, 14 September, http://www.wereldjournalisten.nl/artikel/2010/09/14/a/. Accessed 12 December 2010.

Trappel, J., Meier, W. A., d'Haenens, L., Steemers, J. and Thomass, B. (eds) (2011), *Media in Europe Today*, Bristol: Intellect.

Uitermark, J., Rossi, U. and van Houtum, H. (2005), 'Reinventing multiculturalism: Urban citizenship and the negotiation of ethnic diversity in Amsterdam', *International Journal of Urban and Regional Research*, 29: 3, pp. 622–40.

Van der Wal, G. (ed.) (1995), *Gemengde Berichten: De Dilemma's van de Omroep in een Plurale Samenleving/Mixed Messages: The Dilemmas of the Broadcaster in a Diverse Society*, Hilversum: NPS.

Vasta, E. (2007), 'From ethnic minorities to ethnic majority policy: Multiculturalism and the shift to assimilationism in the Netherlands', *Ethnic and Racial Studies*, 30: 5, pp. 113–40.

Vink, M. P. (2007), 'Dutch "multiculturalism" beyond the pillarisation myth', *Political Studies Review*, 5: pp. 337–350.

VVD–CDA (2010), *Vrijheid en Verantwoordelijkheid: Regeerakkoord VVD–CDA/ Freedom and Responsibility: Coalition Agreement VVD-CDA*, http://www. kabinetsformatie2010.nl/Actueel/Pers_en_nieuwsberichten/2010/oktober/ Opstelten_biedt_eindverslag_aan. Accessed 20 October 2010.

WNL (Wakker Nederland) (2010), 'Over WNL', http://www.omroepwnl.nl/wnl/over-wnl. Accessed 13 January 2011.

Notes

1. Quotes from Dutch-language documents have been translated by the authors.
2. Whereas the term 'gedogen' (to tolerate) has been traditionally associated with a politics of tolerance in relation to soft drugs and prostitution in the Netherlands, it has been officially used since 2010 to refer to the Freedom Party's relationship to the VVD-CDA coalition.
3. The Dutch population statistics distinguishes minority groups on the basis of origin in terms of country/region. The strictest integration measures affect non-western immigrants. These are people from Turkey, Latin America, Africa and Asia, with the exception of Japan and Indonesia.
4. Pluriformity (*pluriformiteit*) is sometimes translated as diversity, though there is a different Dutch word for that (*diversiteit*). In relation to media systems, pluriformity could also be equated with the notion of external pluralism (Hallin and Mancini

2004). However, this chapter purposely uses the term pluriformity to capture its specific connotations in the Dutch broadcasting system, that is, its origins in pillarization and its current interpretation in terms of left-right politics

5. In early 2011, the Dutch broadcasting system included ten large associations, seven religious organizations and two non-member based broadcasters, created for the execution of specific programmatic tasks: NOS is in charge of newscasts and NTR of programming focused on information, education and culture.

6. A policy document released in mid-June 2011 and announcing major budget cuts for public broadcasting reconsidered the relevance of membership once more. The Minister of Education, Culture and Media wanted to reinforce the relevance of membership for the allocation of airtime (Ministerie voor Onderwijs, Wetenschap en Cultuur (Ministry of Education, Culture and Media) 2011: 21).

7. In early 2011, three versions of the programme were on-air: *Uitgesproken VARA*, from the socialist broadcaster; *Uitgesproken EO*, from the evangelical broadcaster; and *Uitgesproken WNL*, from one of the broadcasters linked to the Telegraaf Media Group.

8. The official terminology in the Netherlands distinguishes between *autochtonen* for people from Dutch descent, and either western or non-western *allochtonen*, for immigrants and their children. In popular discourse the term *allochtonen* is mainly used to refer to immigrants from Surinam, Turkey, the Antilles and Morocco, and their descendents.

Chapter 5

Struggling With Multiculturalism? Cultural Diversity In
Flemish Public Broadcasting Policies and Programmes

Alexander Dhoest (University of Antwerp)

Introduction

Flanders, the Dutch-speaking northern part of Belgium, presents an interesting case for the analysis of ethnic and cultural diversity in public service broadcasting. On the one hand, it is a region with a long history of struggles around cultural identity within the Belgian multilingual context. On the other hand, it has always been and still is a stronghold of PSB, as the VRT (Vlaamse Radio en Televisie) has been the market leader most of its history. In these contexts, cultural diversity has become a prominent but touchy issue over the past decades, legislators, broadcasters and researchers hesitantly adding it to their agendas.

This chapter will discuss the struggles to adequately deal with ethnic and cultural diversity in Flemish public broadcasting. To start, it will briefly introduce the Flemish national, ethno-cultural and media context, which is necessary to understand the specificities of the Flemish case. Then, this chapter will take a closer look at the policies and instruments used to increase (awareness of) ethnic and cultural diversity in public broadcasting in the 2000s, drawing on policy documents, research reports and interviews. It will also discuss some of the programmes dealing with cultural diversity, documenting their attempts to cater for different (ethnic majority and minority) audiences and tastes. To conclude, this chapter will discuss the outcomes of these policies and actions, drawing on research on representations and reception processes, and it will take a look at the future, discussing the latest policy changes.

Throughout this account, reference will be made to problems and tensions which are familiar from international literature but which get a particular 'national' slant in the Flemish context. The point is not that any of these issues are unique to Flanders, but rather that each national context makes for particular inflections of problems facing Northern European countries in the early twenty-first century. A central, underlying challenge is that of devising sound and effective policies to deal with cultural diversity at a time when the former model of multiculturalism is criticized from different sides.

National, ethnic and conceptual contexts

Like many European nation-states, Belgium has been internally culturally diverse from its independence in 1830. Beside a small German-language community, it consists of Flanders, the northern Dutch-language community, and Wallonia, the southern French-language community. This has led to a complex institutional history, with a gradual shift from a unitary to a federal state and constant tensions between the two main language groups. In the nineteenth and early twentieth centuries, Flanders was the weaker region demographically, economically, politically and culturally, but from the mid-twentieth century the balance tilted and Flanders became the driving force behind several state reforms. While it is now a strong and self-confident region, Flemish policies still betray the former underdog position in their fierce defence of Flemish language and culture.

The gradual political emancipation of Flanders was guided by nationalism and supported by the concomitant search for and construction of Flemish identity, in which language, history, culture and national character occupied a central position. As all nationalist movements, the 'Flemish Movement' supported the idea of a homogeneous and coherent nation, a discursively constructed 'us' which was contrasted to 'them', in particular the French-language Walloons. This emerging Flemish (sub-)national identification may explain why twentieth-century Flanders had a harder time dealing with ethnic and cultural diversity than French-language Wallonia, which identified less as a (sub-)nation and was strongly oriented towards France.

Belgium, like most European countries, has a long history of migration. While immigrants mostly came from neighbouring countries until the 1920s, from then on Belgian policies of labour migration started recruiting in eastern and southern Europe. From the 1960s, a great number of immigrants came from Morocco and Turkey. The active recruitment of unskilled labour migrants ceased in the 1970s as a consequence of the economic crisis, but since then there has been continuing labour migration from EU countries as well as family and marital migration from non-EU countries (CGKR 2009: 13–14).

Discussions about the 'problems' of the Belgian and Flemish multi-ethnic society mostly concern the latter non-EU groups. These were initially called 'guest workers', which encapsulated the idea – shared by policy makers and migrants – of temporality. Partly for this reason, not until 1989 were policies developed to guide their integration in Belgian society (CGKR 2009: 13). While earlier generations of EU migrants have gradually integrated into Belgium (through naturalization, mixed marriages, etc.), the later groups are still strongly rooted in their culture and country of origin. Combined with limited Dutch-language skills, low levels of schooling and high unemployment, these cultural divisions coincide with social and economical divisions which were only gradually and hesitantly tackled through the emergent policies of the 1990s. These focused on social integration and officially adhered to the Anglo-Saxon model of multiculturalism and respect for cultural diversity, but were actually quite assimilationist and ethnocentric, focusing on homogeneity rather than acceptance of diversity (Loobuyck and Jacobs 2006). The concept of multiculturalism was only introduced quite late and half-heartedly in Flanders, which has always struggled to position itself vis-à-vis this concept.

Two further factors complicate the picture. First, the extreme right party Vlaams Blok (renamed Vlaams Belang in 2004 after a conviction for racism) gained a massive following from the late 1980s. It combined Flemish nationalism and ethnocentrism with blatant xenophobia, primarily targeting non-European ethnic minorities and deliberately capitalizing on the cultural and economic fears of the Flemish people (Billiet 2006). It illustrates the specific national context for diversity politics in Flanders: both external (the French-language Walloons) and internal (former migrants) 'out' groups are seen (by some) as a threat to Flemish self-dependence and prosperity. The Vlaams Belang put ethnicity on the agenda but simultaneously hijacked the theme, so other parties were reluctant to take a stance because they feared to lose voters to this populist party. The Vlaams Belang was never part of government and their visions were never translated into policies, but they dominated the debate on these issues. As a result, Flemish policies dealing with ethnic diversity were never very progressive, particularly in comparison to the Netherlands, the guiding country in this respect. Moreover, in the aftermath of 9/11 the (perceived) growing rift between ethnic groups was catapulted back on the public agenda, leading to an increasingly polarized social debate focusing on Islam.

Processes of policy-making were further complicated by the terminological quicksand surrounding the issue. Official statistics only take into account the nationality of the Belgian population, so they do not provide accurate information on ethnic minorities, only on 'foreigners' (people with a foreign nationality living in Belgium). The growing number of naturalized former immigrants thus disappears from the statistics: while in 2008 8.57% of the inhabitants of Belgium were foreigners, the total population of foreign origin was estimated at approximately 15%. Moreover, although 67% of the foreigners living in Belgium were EU citizens, public discourse about ethnic minorities mostly refers to Moroccans and Turks, the largest groups of non-EU foreigners (ADWA 2008; CGKR 2008).

There is an ongoing struggle to adequately define and name these groups. As indicated by Verhaeghe (2010), in the 1960s and 1970s the terms 'foreigner' and 'guest worker' were used, referring to the foreign nationality and the temporary stay of migrants. In the 1980s, as the more permanent nature of their presence in Belgium became clear, the term 'migrant' was used. From the 1990s, the term 'allochtoon' (literally 'from another country') was taken over from the Netherlands to better include the second and third generations of ethnic minorities. While in principle, the term included everyone with foreign origins, in practice it was mostly used to refer to people of non-European descent, in particular from Morocco and Turkey. Moreover, there is some confusion as to who exactly is 'allochtoon': although it officially only refers to people born abroad or having at least one parent born abroad, in practice later generations are equally designated with the term, even after they acquired the Belgian nationality. More fundamentally, the term is used in opposition to 'autochtoon', which refers to ethnic Flemish people, so it installs a fixed binary opposition, reducing ethnic 'others' to essentialist notions of ethnicity and cultural identity (Verhaeghe 2010). Although the term is increasingly criticized, it is not completely relinquished as it is an important tool to develop focused policies for the groups it refers to, which are indeed disenfranchised in terms of education, employment and income. Moreover, there is no widely accepted alternative, although there are some emerging candidates, in particular hyphenated labels such as 'new Belgians' or 'new Flemings', 'Moroccan Belgians' and 'Turkish Flemings'.

These Flemish conceptual struggles are not unique and they illustrate problems inherent in the very definition of ethnicity and the concept of multiculturalism building upon it. Defining ethnic groups implies creating borders between groups, assuming homogeneity within and differences with the outside. Ethnicity is based on discursive processes referring to language, religion, culture, origins, history, etc. As discursive constructs, ethnicities are temporary and changeable but they are seen as natural, fixed and eternal and they are, indeed, very real in their consequences. In this way, definitions of ethnicity as they are used in everyday life carry echoes of racism, replacing the idea of biologically fixed differences with the idea of culturally determined borders. This rigid definition of ethnicity is criticized as 'new racism': it focuses on group difference rather than inferiority but still presents a fixed and static view on groups (Cottle 2000; van Dijk 2000). Instead, contemporary notions of ethnic identity stress its hybridity, changeability, fluidity and dynamism, within a broader model of identities as multi-dimensional, layered, multiple and intersectional (e.g. Ross and Playdon 2001; Ross 2004; Gillespie 2007).

Multiculturalism, in its stress on the acceptance of cultural and ethnic difference, encapsulates many of the problems mentioned above. It builds on 'romantic' notions of inborn (pseudo-racial) cultural differences, not only defending but also fixing them. Its focus on the preservation of cultural authenticity suggests that transformation is impossible and it considers minorities as homogeneous. Internal differences within cultural communities are neglected and different cultural communities are opposed to each other, thus undermining rather than stimulating dialogue (Malik 2007). In its stress on the particularity of cultures, the ideology of multiculturalism opposes any idea of universalism and of universal principles like equality and social justice (Malik 2002). This criticism of multiculturalism and the concomitant debates on national identity and ethnic diversity (for a critical account, see Lentin and Titley [2011] and Kundnani [2012]) are only starting to seep into the Flemish debate, which remains stuck in fixed notions of ethnic opposition. Also, Flanders lacks the breadth and depth of public discussions on national history, identity and multi-ethnicity as witnessed in Britain (for instance in the Parekh report; see Weedon 2004) and the Netherlands (WRR 2007). Thus, at this time Flanders is doubly struggling with multiculturalism: on the one hand catching up with the abovementioned developments in thinking about ethnic and cultural identity, while on the other hand – echoing Angela Merkel's comments in the German context – noting the 'failure' of multicultural policies in a society where integrationist ideas and policies are gaining ground.

Public broadcasting policies and actions

The national, ethnic and conceptual contexts sketched above help to explain the specific history and nature of Flemish public broadcasting. From the start in 1953, television was integrated in the public broadcasting institution NIR/INR, which had a television monopoly. Although this was a unitary Belgian institution, from the very beginning television was organized separately for Flanders and the French community. Consecutive legislations and reorganizations confirmed this split, which was completed in 1977. This means that Belgium does not have one 'national' broadcaster covering the whole region, nor do the Flemish- and French-language broadcasters have any obligation towards the other regions and their languages and cultures. Early Flemish public broadcasting was heavily inspired by the European ideal of public service as exemplified by the British Broadcasting Corporation (BBC), from which it adopted its cultural-pedagogical policies aiming to educate and enlighten the viewers. It was also strongly driven by cultural nationalism, defending and stimulating Flemish culture and language (Van den Bulck 2001). In terms of programming, Flemish television has always been very 'monocultural', focusing on the 'own' history and culture and promulgating Flemish identity (Dhoest 2004). Arguably, television played an important role in the discursive construction of Flemish identity which accompanied its political emancipation as described above. As elsewhere in Europe, this national 'imagined community' was predominantly and seemingly self-evidently white (Morley 2004).

After the liberalization of the broadcasting market, from 1989 VTM (Vlaamse Televisie Maatschappij) became the main competitor of the public broadcaster, then called BRT (Belgische Radio en Televisie) and renamed BRTN (Nederlandse Radio- en Televisieuitzendingen in België) in 1991. From the start, this Flemish-owned commercial channel had tremendous success, with market shares starting at 27% and rising above 38% in the 1990s, well above the public channels' ratings which dropped to an all time low of 22.6% in 1995 (Saeys 2007; Bauwens 2007). After a few years of crisis, from the mid-1990s the public broadcaster was radically reorganized and renamed VRT (Vlaamse Radio en Televisieomroep) in 1997. Public broadcasting is now run as a genuine company with a CEO, guided by five-year management agreements with government. These contracts contain detailed objectives to be met by the public broadcaster, the first agreement (1997–2001) focusing in particular on ratings and audience reach, as detailed in measurable 'performance indicators'. The ensuing market-oriented policies lead to a gradual rise of the ratings for the public broadcaster, who managed to regain market leadership since 2002. In 2010, VRT's main channel Eén was market leader with a share of 34.4%, the main commercial channel VTM only reaching 23.1% (source: CIM Audimetrie).

After the VRT had regained its market position, new questions arose concerning the specificity of the public broadcaster. These were reflected in the subsequent management agreements, which more strongly stressed public broadcasting duties such as quality and diversity. For instance, in its description of the public broadcasting remit, the second management agreement (2002–06) stated: 'The VRT has an important role to play in the further development of the identity and diversity of Flemish culture' (art. 1 §3).[1] However, in this agreement diversity was still primarily defined in terms of programme and audience diversity. The third management agreement (2007–11) still stressed the importance of 'Flemish cultural identity', but it also more explicitly dealt with diversity, stating that the VRT has to be there for all people in Flanders, including minorities (art.

1 §4). This management agreement contained an entire article dealing with diversity policies (art. 31), stating that the VRT had to take action to ensure diversity in terms of representation ('The total offer of the VRT attempts to correctly reflect the diversity in Flemish society') and employment ('The VRT strives towards a staff that is as diverse as possible') (art. 31 §2). Reference was also made to existing initiatives that had to be continued: the Diversity Charter, the Diversity Cell and the Diversity Barometer.

The Diversity Charter was signed in 2003 and signalled the official start of cultural diversity policies in the VRT. It was the product of the growing awareness of ethnic diversity issues from the late 1990s and it built upon earlier VRT actions concerning equal gender opportunities (De Ridder 2006). The Diversity Charter stated that the VRT wanted to be a 'reflection of the diversity in Flemish society, both in its programmes and in its staff', opposing discrimination and guaranteeing equal opportunities. It juxtaposed – and therefore saw no contradiction between – issues of identity and diversity, wanting

> to play an important role in the further development of the identity and diversity of Flemish society and to contribute to the social cohesion and integration of all individuals, groups and communities, with a democratic and tolerant society as its aim.
>
> (VRT 2003)

Against the closed sense of identity proposed by the Vlaams Belang, it defended an open and inclusive definition of Flemish identity. It aimed for the representation of 'members of ethnic-cultural minorities' in programmes, with special attention to 'reporting about allochtones', as well as a staff 'that is as diversified as possible'. The goal was, ultimately, to 'create bridges between individuals, groups and communities, to contribute to a harmonious, pluralist and tolerant society where everyone can feel at home' (VRT 2003). In its stress on social integration, the Diversity Charter clearly signalled a move away from ideas of multiculturalism as merely juxtaposing different cultures, a tendency noted across Europe by Leurdijk (2006). The Diversity Charter also illustrates how, at least in its written policies, the public broadcaster adhered to notions of social responsibility and inclusivity. As will be developed below, the main problem was how to implement these quite vague principles in everyday broadcasting practices.

When the Diversity Charter was signed, the VRT also initiated its Diversity Cell, consisting of two staff members supporting diversity from within the institution. On the one hand, they stimulated programme diversity, for instance by giving advice to programme makers on issues of representation, raising awareness and increasing diversity competency by organizing workshops and discussion sessions, and creating a network of (ethnic) minority contacts. On the other hand, they organized different activities to attract ethnic minority staff, such as 'snuffeldagen' (literally 'sniffing days') where ethnic minority students from the last year of secondary school could meet media people and do some radio or television work. They also offered paid internships, in which minority group members (including people with a handicap) got to know the media and possibly could get a long-term contract. Overall, the aim was for the VRT to accurately reflect Flanders, both on and behind the screen (De Clercq 2010; De Ceuleneer 2011).

Reviewing the initiatives up to 2010, there is reason for pessimism. The issue was only really put on the agenda in the early 2000s and while the VRT was clearly sympathetic – and in this way completely contradicts the Vlaams Belang ideal of a 'closed' Flanders – by the end of the decade there still was a lot of work to do in terms of consciousness raising and effective policy-making. External actors such as the Minority Forum ('Minderhedenforum'), an organization uniting and representing associations of ethnic-cultural minorities,[2] the minority media monitoring and lobby forum *Trefmedia* [3] and KifKif, the ethnic minority organization and media watchdog, [4] helped to keep the issue on the agenda. While there were some positive changes, Katleen De Ridder from the Minority Forum remained quite pessimistic. In 2008, in an overview of 15 years of action for minorities and media, she lamented the extremely poor representation of ethnic minorities in journalism (mentioning overall figures of less than 1%) and the lack of coherent policies, the VRT still being the only medium with diversity policies (De Ridder 2008).

Programmes and problems

In order to better understand how the VRT translated its good intentions into action, it is worth taking a closer look at some programmes explicitly addressing cultural diversity. Overall, there have not been all that many programmes 'about' cultural diversity. One early example from the 1980s was *Babel*, which was explicitly oriented towards different ethnic minorities which it addressed in their own language, in an attempt to contribute to their integration in Belgian society (Devriendt 2008). Apart from the 'ghettoization' this kind of programme implies, according to Geert De Clercq who used to work for the VRT Diversity Cell it also poses the practical problem that if you have a programme for one community, you have to have one for all communities (De Clercq 2010). For similar reasons, the plans in 2002 to create an ethnic minority broadcaster were quickly dismissed (De Ridder 2008). *Babel* was followed by *Couleur Locale* (1992–95), a more inclusive 'multicultural magazine' in Dutch, oriented towards a broad audience and celebrating cultural diversity, illustrating the broader shift from assimilationist and integrationist policies in the 1980s to multicultural and anti-racist paradigms in the 1990s, as noted by Horsti and Hultén (2011).

After these early efforts, the idea was to integrate diversity in different programmes, in line with the general change in strategies observed across Europe by Leurdijk (2006). She notes how 'ghetto' programmes increasingly gave way to programmes simultaneously addressing majority and minority audiences, looking for commonalities rather than differences. However, in Flanders the issue mostly disappeared from the agenda until the early 2000s when the Diversity Charter created a better climate for diversity. From then on, the core objective was inclusivity, portraying ethnic minorities in programmes aimed at a broad, general audience and thus (again) supporting integration. However, the term 'integration' is not explicitly used, for as De Clercq stresses, the VRT does not see itself as an 'educator' anymore, unlike some other European public broadcasters. Instead, the VRT now wants to show how living together in diversity is possible, without necessarily drawing attention to the issue. As elsewhere, the term 'multiculturalism' has lost currency, the preferred term now being 'interculturality' (De Ceuleneer 2011). Similarly, the problematic term 'allochtoon' is used as little as possible and more specific terms (e.g. Turkish Belgians) or 'ethnic cultural minority' are favoured, although the latter does not have an adjective in Dutch so 'allochtoon' remains the pragmatic choice to refer to the totality of non-European ethnic minorities. Guidelines about such terminological matters can be found in the *Deontological Pocket Book* available to VRT journalists. The general recommendation is to not overly stress ones ethnic background, but also not to hide it (VRT n.d.).

Since the early 2000s, several programmes have made an effort to include ethnic minorities, in different ways. *Thuis*, the VRT soap which has been on-screen since 1995, first introduced the Moroccan plumber Mo and later added several other ethnic minority characters like Mo's daughter Aïsha, the Moroccan medicine student Youssef and the Polish plumber Waldek. While some of these characters have since disappeared, Mo has become one of the core characters in *Thuis*. He was introduced as a very nice and likeable character, a clear counter-stereotype, but he was perceived as a boring character with limited dramatic potential, among others by an ethnic minority viewer panel (Devriendt 2008). Introducing his more modern daughter allowed the exploration of generational issues, which made Mo more human but also – to some – too 'old fashioned'. While Mo illustrates how hard (not to say: impossible) it is to get isolated ethnic minority characters right, he is a laudable and noted presence in Flemish prime-time, which is generally white (Dhoest and Simons 2009). This effort is appreciated by ethnic minority audiences, *Thuis* getting the Integration Prize from the Belgian Turkish Union in 2007.

A similar but less structural ethnic minority presence in VRT fiction was Birsen, one of the two protagonists in the equal opportunities telenovela *Emma* (2007). She was an ambitious young Turkish woman trying to make a media career, much to the dislike of her old-fashioned husband. While her family context allowed for more exploration of differences within one ethnic minority community in Belgium, Birsen did remain a 'singleton', the term used by Geraghty (1991: 141–44) to refer to black characters introduced in storylines about black issues. The (preferred) strategy of incorporation, where ethnic minority characters are represented as part of the community, is still rare in Flemish television fiction.

In non-fiction, information programmes made an effort to incorporate more ethnic minority members as specialists or 'man/woman in the street'. While their presence in entertainment programmes (reality TV, game and quiz shows, etc.) is still very limited, some soft information programmes do better. In the documentary series *Moslima's* (2007), four very different Muslim women (ranging from conservative to progressive) were interviewed about core themes in their religion. While well-intentioned, this programme meant to clarify Islamic concepts for Flemish viewers while ethnic minority viewers were disappointed with their framing as radically different 'others' (Van den Bulck and Broos 2009). Similar criticisms were heard about the documentary series *De weg naar Mekka* (*The Way to Mecca*, 2008), in which presenter Jan Leyers travels to Mecca and on his way shows the many faces of Islam. While the programme was lauded by some as a more complex representation of Islam, questioning its strong link with terrorism, to others (in particular Muslims) it showed a problematic 'outside' view on religion (De Clercq 2010). Another documentary format was *0032* (2007), dealing with people who had recently arrived in Belgium, often asylum seekers. By not merely focusing on the 'usual suspects' (Turks and Moroccans) and by presenting a wide range of nationalities and life stories, this touching programme was very effective in supporting the notion of diversity in Flanders and it won the Prix Europa Iris Award for best multicultural programme.

The above account clearly illustrates the move from integrationist to multicultural to inclusive programming. In different ways and with varying success, recent programmes have tried to show diversity at the heart of Flemish society. However, besides these programmes, ethnic diversity remains largely absent from Flemish television and the few programmes that explicitly deal with ethnic diversity are well-intentioned but still problematical, in their unwitting confirmation of a binary division between the 'autochthonous' and 'allochthonous' populations which are often treated as two homogeneous and opposed groups. There are simply too few ethnic minority characters or people on-screen for them not to carry a heavy burden of representation. They have to be perfect and to represent all the diversity within a particular community, which is necessarily doomed to fail. In this respect, Flanders has some catching up to do in order to get in line with contemporary thinking about complex, changeable, 'intersectional' identities.

Monitoring and assessing on-screen diversity

The scarcity of ethnic minority representations on-screen becomes more tangible when we turn to the final instrument mentioned in the 2007–11 management agreement, the Diversity Barometer or Monitor. This research was first executed in 2004 by the VRT research department, which carried out a quantitative content analysis of television representations of 'colour' on public and commercial Flemish channels for one constructed week (VRT Studiedienst 2004). The main criterion, here, is visibility (not presence) of ethnic minorities, based on skin colour and cultural markers of ethnic difference. However problematic (in methodological terms) and pseudo-racist (reducing ethnicity to skin colour) such a system may seem, it is indeed a good way to 'measure' perceptible ethnic diversity. The study was repeated in 2007 and 2009, thus offering insights into the results of the policies mentioned above (VRT Studiedienst 2007; 2010).

Comparing the three studies, it becomes clear that Flemish television at the end of the 2000s was still predominantly white, with only 13.4% of 'coloured' persons across all channels in 2009. Sadly, the public channels (which are the only ones supported by diversity policies) generally scored lower than average: 4.5% on youth channel Ketnet and 8.8% on the generalist channel Eén, as opposed to a high 19.4% on the second channel Canvas. Looking at non-fiction, in 2009 9.8% of all speaking persons on Eén were coloured, which is lower than the average for all Flemish channels (13.2%) and lower than the measurement for Eén in 2007 (17.4%) and even 2004 (10.7%). To put it differently: after a few years of explicit diversity policies, in 2007 it seemed like Eén was getting more diverse, but this improvement had completely disappeared in 2009. Similarly, looking at fiction, in 2009 the percentage of 'coloured' persons (5.5%) on the biggest channel Eén was lower than average (13.7%) and than its initial measurement in 2004 (7.7%).

These figures are dramatic – and indeed, the VRT chose not to communicate them publicly – but we should qualify them. The comparison with private channels is misleading, because particularly the smaller commercial channels are 'coloured' simply because they import a lot of American TV fiction with a strong African American presence. If we only consider programmes produced in Flanders, or set in Belgium, or characters speaking Dutch, the public broadcaster as a whole does consistently better than the private channels. This, however, discloses another problem: across all channels, most 'coloured' people on Flemish TV appear in imported programmes, do not live in Belgium and do not speak Dutch, so the average of 13.4% is misleading. The actual overall representation of Flanders is even less diverse than this study suggests. Moreover, in non-fiction on the public channels 'coloured' people are more likely to appear in information programmes than in entertainment, so inclusion remains a challenge in everyday genres like entertainment and fiction. In news programmes, 'coloured' people are more likely to appear in items on criminality than white people, which is consistent with earlier findings (e.g. d'Haenens and Koeman 2005; Wal, d'Haenens and Koeman 2005). This is also confirmed by a study comparing public and commercial newscasts before and after the Diversity Charter, and finding few differences or improvements (Van den Bulck and Broos 2011).

While this kind of content analysis is a blunt measuring instrument, not taking into account the context and meaning of representations, it is part of a long tradition of research on racial and ethnic representations which has helped to identify problematic patterns. Thus, American content analyses over the past decades have effectively supported calls for more racially diverse representations in fiction (Mastro and Greenberg 2000). However, to fully understand the meaning of representations, it is necessary also to study their reception. For instance, in 2003 the representation of ethnic minorities in Dutch news and current affairs programmes was evaluated by a viewer panel, which criticized their stereotypical and one-sided nature (Sterk 2006). A second viewer panel assessed Dutch television drama and found that almost 18% of the characters were of ethnic minority origins (as opposed to approximately 10% in Dutch society), while their portrayal was all but negative. Nevertheless, the panel members were not happy with the way cultural difference was erased from their portrayal in fiction and they found it hard to identify with the few ethnic minority characters carrying the 'burden of representation' (Sterk 2006). In short: positive representations on-screen do not necessarily lead to more contented viewers.

In Flanders, more research has been done on media ownership and use than on processes of reception, most of this latter research focusing on Moroccan and Turkish adolescents. Devroe, Driesen and Saeys (2005) found that these groups have access to TV equal to Flemish adolescents and that Moroccans consume a lot of Flemish television, but that Turkish adolescents tend to prefer Turkish television. According to d'Haenens et al. (2004), this is partly due to discontentment about their representation in Flemish media. For Turkish youngsters in the Low Countries, in particular, television is a way to keep in touch or 'bond' with the homeland (Peeters and d'Haenens 2005). News seems to be particularly important for ethnic minority youth, but they are generally dissatisfied with their representation in the Flemish news (Devroe, Driessens and Verstraeten 2010). Similarly, Van den Bulck and Broos (2009) found that Muslim women are not happy with the way they are 'framed' in the abovementioned documentary *Moslima's*. Finally, Dhoest (2009) found an equal discontentment with representations in Flemish fiction and soaps, despite the attempts at positive representation by the public broadcaster. Ironically, the smaller commercial channels scheduling a lot of imported fiction are more popular with (younger) ethnic minority viewers than the public channels, so the attempts of the latter to be inclusive are lost on most ethnic minority viewers.

Discussion and conclusion

Reflecting on the totality of VRT actions concerning ethnic and cultural diversity up to 2010, we can observe that the initiatives mentioned above, although laudable in principle, came quite late, particularly in comparison to the two countries which inspired them, the United Kingdom and the Netherlands. The BBC has a long tradition of equal opportunities policies, Scannell (1996) situating the start of British public service cultural pluralism in 1977. In the Netherlands, a federation of immigrant organizations started with media actions in 1981 (Sterk 2006). Moreover, the Flemish initiatives so far were relatively small-scale and they were not translated into concrete, structural actions throughout the organization. The initiatives developed by the Diversity Cell were well-intentioned but not very effective. According to the former staff member of the Diversity Cell, stronger support from higher management as well as more binding commitments would be necessary to get clearer results (De Clercq 2010).

However, partly as a result of the dramatic results of the 2009 Diversity Monitor, things have started to move at the time of writing (2011). Together with the newly appointed Diversity Cell responsible Geertje De Ceuleneer (since September 2010), from spring 2011 General Director of Production Lena De Meerleer is charged with the implementation of diversity actions, thus providing more central and weighty support within the organization. All departments now have a high-ranking diversity project coordinator making concrete plans. In 2010 the VRT already defined some measurable targets for on-screen diversity, for instance 12% of 'coloured' people in its own programmes on Eén (Debackere and Dumon 2010). These objectives were clearly communicated, among others in the briefings for new programmes (De Ceuleneer 2011). Subsequently, the new Management Agreement (2012–16) was signed and it gives diversity a more central position in the organization. Among other things, it formulates a target of 5% of 'new Flemings' in the total TV production, a yearly monitoring of on-screen diversity and a yearly study into the audience reach among new Flemings. The 2011 Diversity Monitor (VRT Studiedienst 2011) already indicates some improvements: ethnic-cultural diversity across all VRT channels rising to 13.5%, increasing on all channels for both fiction and non-fiction (apart from fiction on the main channel Eén, further lowering to 5%).

In terms of HR policies, the initiatives up to 2010 have also been too small-scale and non-committal. As positive discrimination is legally forbidden in Belgium, positive action is used to attain a stronger ethnic minority presence in the VRT staff. Information on ethnicity is not known to the personnel department, so in 2008 and 2010 an internal survey was circulated among the VRT staff. For 2010, based on 1,327 returned questionnaires (a response rate of about 47%) the ethnic minority presence was estimated at 2.3%, higher than the 2.15% in 2008 but still below the internal objective of 2.5% (De Clercq 2010; De Ceuleneer 2011). This figure is also well below the Flemish government objective of 4%, which is justified by referring to the high share of higher education jobs in the VRT, where ethnic minorities are generally under-represented due to lower average levels of schooling. In this light, one could say that the problematic situation in the VRT (both on and behind the screen) is an accurate but worrying reflection of the actual marginal position of ethnic minorities in Flemish society. The 2012–16 Management Agreement is more ambitious and less ambiguous, enforcing a target of 2.5% 'new Flemish' staff by 2012 and 4% by the end of 2014.

While one could argue that the VRT should make a stronger effort to hire ethnic minority staff, it is indeed harder to find ethnic minority candidates for many broadcasting jobs. The first generation of non-European migrants mostly came to Belgium to work in blue-collar jobs. The second and third generations, if they are successful at school, prefer to do 'serious' (and high-income) jobs, so the media are not a very attractive (nor respected) profession for many (De Clercq 2010). For instance, there is a marked lack of ethnic minority actors, so the VRT co-organized an actor training course for eight months in 2006. While some participants were able to get bit parts in VRT fiction afterwards, this one-time effort did not lead to a clear shift in the ethnic minority presence on Flemish television. Quite often, foreign (Dutch) actors play ethnic minority parts in Flemish fiction. One exception was *Rwina* (2008), a comedy sketch show written and performed by young ethnic minority actors. While it was brave to schedule their efforts in prime-time on the first channel, the quality of the show and the performances was problematic – echoing Ross' (2004: 95) comment that programmes dealing with social issues have to be good television in the first place. From 2011, a more large-scale campaign is used to stimulate ethnic minority students to take media studies degrees, using the slogan 'Colour your media!', thus investing in future diversity among the VRT staff (De Ceuleneer 2011).

To conclude, we could say that the presence of ethnic minorities in Flemish public broadcasting is problematic but not hopeless. More and more (mostly young) articulate ethnic minority members speak up in public debate and in the media. Isolated ethnic minority media figures, like the Moroccan Flemish *Thuis* actor Nouredinne Farihi (playing Mo) and commercial broadcaster VTM's Turkish Flemish news anchor Faruk Özgunes, have a great symbolic impact. Although the introductory account may suggest otherwise, the problem is not Flemish nationalism, for despite its strong focus on Flanders the public broadcaster is known (and criticized by the Right) as quite a progressive institution. At least in terms of policies, the VRT is (or tries to be) inclusive, so the intentions are clearly good. Still, the results are limited so far. Besides the lack of a clear awareness of its own 'whiteness' within the institution, the main obstacle – particularly in times of economic crisis – seems to be the underlying social inequality on the level of schooling and employment, which needs to be addressed in order for cultural and media initiatives to truly take root.

References

Algemene Directie Werkgelegenheid en Arbeidsmarkt (ADWA) (2008), *De Immigratie in België: Aantallen, Stromen en Arbeidsmarkt: Verslag 2007 (Immigration in Belgium: Numbers, Streams and Labour Market: Report 2007)*, Brussels: FOD Werkgelegenheid, Arbeid en Sociaal Overleg.

Bauwens, J. (2007), 'De openbare televisie en haar kijkers: Oude liefde roest niet' (Public television and its viewers: Old love doesn't rust), in A. Dhoest and H. Van den Bulck (eds), *Publieke Televisie in Vlaanderen: Een Geschiedenis (Public Television in Flanders: A History)*, Ghent: Academia Press, pp. 91–124.

Billiet, J. (2006), 'Attitudes towards ethnic minorities in Flanders: Changes between 1989 and 2003 and a comparison with the Netherlands', in L. d'Haenens, M. Hooghe, D. Vanheule and H. Gezduci (eds), *'New' Citizens, New Policies? Developments in Diversity Policy in Canada and Flanders*, Ghent: Academia Press, pp. 34–56.

Centrum voor Gelijkheid van Kansen en voor Racismebestrijding (CGKR) (2009), *Ben ik een Migrant? De Geschiedenis van onze Migraties (Am I a Migrant? The History of our Migrations)*, Brussels: CGKR.

Cottle, S. (2000), 'Introduction: Media research and ethnic minorities: Mapping the field', in S. Cottle (ed.), *Ethnic Minorities and the Media: Changing Cultural Boundaries*, Buckingham: Open University Press, pp. 1–30.

Debackere, J. and Dumon, P. (2010), 'Openbare omroep streeft naar meer vrouwen en allochtonen op het scherm' (Public broadcaster strives towards more women and ethnic minorities on screen), *De Morgen*, 20 November, p. 14.

De Clercq, G. (2010), 'Head of Diversity Unit' [interview by A. Dhoest, Brussels], 9 July.

De Ceuleneer, G. (2011), 'Head of Diversity Unit' [interview by A. Dhoest, Brussels], 26 April.

De Ridder, K. (2006), *Bouwstenen VI: Diverse Media en Evenwichtige Beeldvorming/Building Blocks VI: Diverse Media and Balanced Representation*, Brussels: Minderhedenforum, http://www.minderhedenforum.be/documents/bouwstenenmedia.pdf. Accessed 31 May 2010.

De Ridder, K. (2008), *Kroniek: 15 Jaar Actie voor Minderheden en Media/Chronicle: 15 Years of Action for Minorities and Media*, Brussels: Minderhedenforum, http://www.minderhedenforum.be/2media/minderhedenforum-noodaancoherentbeleidvoordiversiteitindemedia.htm. Accessed 31 May 2010.

Devroe, I., Driesen, D. and Saeys, F. (2005), *Beschikbaarheid en Gebruik van Traditionele en Nieuwe Media bij Allochtone Jongeren in Vlaanderen /Availability and Use of Traditional and New Media Among Allochtonous Youngsters in Flanders*, U.A. (University of Antwerp) and L.U.C. (University Center Limburg): Steunpunt Gelijkekansenbeleid.

d'Haenens, L. and Koeman, J. (2005), 'De blinde vlek in het nieuws: Multiculturaliteit in de Nederlandse en Vlaamse televisieberichtgeving'/'The blind spot in the news: Multiculturality in Dutch and Flemish television news reports', in M. Hooghe, K. De Swert and S. Walgrave (eds), *Nieuws op Televisie: Televisiejournaals als Venster op de Wereld/ News on Television: Television News as Window on the World*, Leuven: Acco, pp. 57–77.

d'Haenens, L., van Summeren, C., Saeys, F. and Koeman, J. (2004), *Integratie of Identiteit? Mediamenu's van Turkse en Marokkaanse Jongeren/Integration or Identity? Media Menus of Turkish and Moroccan Youngsters*, Amsterdam: Boom.

d'Haenens, L., El Sghiar, H. and Golaszewski, S. (2010), 'Media en etnisch-culturele minderheden in de Lage Landen: Trends in 15 jaar onderzoek'/'Media and ethnic-cultural minorities in the Low Countries: Trends in 15 years of research', in S. Van Bauwel, E. Van Damme and H. Verstraeten (eds), *Diverse Mediawerelden: Hedendaagse Reflecties Gebaseerd op het Onderzoek van Frieda Saeys/Diverse Media Worlds: Contemporary Reflections Based on the Research by Frieda Saeys*, Ghent: Academia Press, pp. 210–32.

Devroe, I., Driessens, O. and Verstraeten, H. (2010), '"Minority report": Ethnic minorities' diasporic news consumption and news reading', in S. Van Bauwel, E. Van Damme and H. Verstraeten (eds), *Diverse Mediawerelden: Hedendaagse Reflecties Gebaseerd op het Onderzoek van Frieda Saeys/Diverse Media Worlds: Contemporary Reflections Based on the Research by Frieda Saeys*, Ghent: Academia Press, pp. 233–49.

Devriendt, J. (2008), 'Culturele diversiteit in *Thuis*: Beleid en representatie'/'Cultural diversity in *At Home*: Policy and representation', MA dissertation, Antwerp: University of Antwerp.

Dhoest, A. (2004), 'Negotiating images of the nation: The production of Flemish TV drama, 1953–1989', *Media, Culture & Society*, 26: 3, pp. 393–408.

Dhoest, A. (2007), 'The national everyday in contemporary European television fiction: The Flemish case', *Critical Studies in Television*, 2: 2, pp. 60–76.

Dhoest, A. (2009), 'Establishing a multi-ethnic imagined community? Ethnic minority audiences watching Flemish soaps', *European Journal of Communication*, 24: 3, pp. 305–23.

Dhoest, A. and Simons, N. (2009), 'One nation, one audience? Ethnic diversity on and in front of Flemish TV', *Quotidian: Dutch Journal for the Study of Everyday Life*, http://www.quotidian.nl/vol01/nr01/a04. Accessed 31 May 2011.

Geraghty, C. (1991), *Women and Soap Opera: A Study of Prime Time Soaps*, Cambridge: Polity.

Gillespie, M. (2007), 'Security, media and multicultural citizenship: A collaborative ethnography', *European Journal of Cultural Studies*, 10: 3, pp. 275–93.

Horsti, K. and Hultén, G. (2011), 'Directing diversity: Managing cultural diversity media policies in Finnish and Swedish public service broadcasting', *International Journal of Cultural Studies*, 14: 2, pp. 209–27.

Kundnani, A. (2012), 'Multiculturalism and its discontents: Left, right and liberal', *European Journal of Cultural Studies*, 15: 2, pp. 155–66.

Lentin, A. & Titley, G. (2011), *The Crises of Multiculturalism: Racism in a Neoliberal Age*, London/New York: Zed Books.

Leurdijk, A. (2006), 'In search of common ground: Strategies of multicultural television producers in Europe', *European Journal of Cultural Studies*, 9: 1, pp. 25–46.

Loobuyck, P. and Jacobs, D. (2006), 'The Flemish immigration society: Political challenges on different levels', in L. d'Haenens, M. Hooghe, D. Vanheule and H. Gezduci (eds), *'New' Citizens, New Policies? Developments in Diversity Policy in Canada and Flanders*, Ghent: Academia Press, pp. 105–23.

Malik, K. (2002), 'Against multiculturalism', *New Humanist*, 117: 2, http://newhumanist.org.uk/523/against-multiculturalism. Accessed 31 May 2011.

Malik, K. (2007), 'The failures of multiculturalism', *The Secular State and Society*, http://www.kenanmalik.com/papers/engelsberg_mc.html. Accessed 31 May 2011.

Mastro, D. and Greenberg, B. (2000), 'The portrayal of racial minorities on prime time television', *Journal of Broadcasting and Electronic Media*, 44: 4, pp. 690–703.

Morley, D. (2004), 'Broadcasting and the construction of the national family', in R. C. Allen and A. Hill (eds), *The Television Studies Reader*, London: Routledge, pp. 418–41.

Peeters, A. and d'Haenens, L. (2005), 'Bridging or bonding? Relationships between integration and media use among ethnic minorities in the Netherlands', *Communications*, 30, pp. 201–31.

Ross, K. and Playdon, P. (eds) (2001), *Black Marks: Minority Ethnic Audiences and Media*, Aldershot: Ashgate.

Ross, K. (2004), *Black and White Media: Black Images in Popular Film and Television*, Cambridge, UK: Polity.

Saeys, F. (2007), 'Statuut, organisatie en financiering van de openbare televisieomroep in Vlaanderen'/'Statute, organisation and financing of public television broadcasting in Flanders', in A. Dhoest and H. Van den Bulck (eds), *Publieke Televisie in Vlaanderen: Een Geschiedenis/Public Television in Flanders: A History*, Ghent: Academia Press, pp. 23–51.

Scannell, P. (1996), 'Britain: Public service broadcasting, from national culture to multiculturalism', in M. Raboy (ed.), *Public Broadcasting for the 21st Century*, Luton: ULP, pp. 23–41.

Sterk, G. (2006), 'Visible representation and the paradox of symbolic diversity', in L. d'Haenens, M. Hooghe, D. Vanheule and H. Gezduci (eds), *'New' Citizens, New Policies? Developments in Diversity Policy in Canada and Flanders*, Ghent: Academia Press, pp. 159–70.

Van den Bulck, H. (2001), 'Public service television and national identity as a project of modernity: The example of Flemish television', *Media, Culture and Society*, 23: 1, pp. 53–69.

Van den Bulck, H. and Broos, D. (2009), 'When "Us" meet "Them": Representations and reception of Muslim women in a Flemish documentary', in E. Castelló, A. Dhoest and H. O'Donnell (eds), *The Nation on Screen: Discourses of the National on Global Television*, Cambridge: Cambridge Scholars Publishing, pp. 157–76.

Van den Bulck, H. and Broos, D. (2011), 'Can a charter of diversity make the difference in ethnic minority reporting? A comparative content and production analysis of two Flemish television newscasts', *Communications*, 36: 2, pp. 195–216.

Van Dijk, T. A. (2000), 'New(s) racism: A discourse analytical approach', in S. Cottle (ed.), *Ethnic Minorities and the Media: Changing Cultural Boundaries*, Buckingham: Open University Press, pp. 33–49.

Verhaeghe, P.-P. (2010), *De Discursieve Kracht van het Begrip 'Allochtoon'/The Discursive Power of the Concept 'Allochthonous'*, KifKif Mediawatch, http://www.kifkif.be/page?&orl=1&ssn=&lng=1&page=Mediawatch&are=2550. Accessed 31 May 2011.

Vlaamse Radio en Televisie (VRT) (2003), *Charter Diversiteit/Diversity Charter*, http://www.vrt.be/wie-zijn-we/werkingsprincipes/diversiteit. Accessed 31 May 2011.

Vlaamse Radio en Televisie (VRT) (n.d.), *Deontologisch Zakboekje voor de Journalisten van de VRT-Nieuwsdienst/Deontological Pocket Book for Journalists of the VRT News Service*, Brussels: VRT.

VRT Studiedienst (2004), *Kleur Bekennen: Monitor Diversiteit 2004: De Zichtbaarheid van Mensen van Andere Origine op de Vlaamse Televisie/Admitting Colour: Diversity Monitor 2004: The Visibility of People from a Different Origin on Flemish Television*, Brussel: VRT.

VRT Studiedienst (2007), *Monitor Diversiteit 2007: Kwantitatieve Studie naar Zichtbaarheid van Diversiteit op het Vlaamse Scherm/Diversity Monitor 2007: Quantitative Research on the Visibility of Diversity on the Flemish Screen*, Brussels: VRT & ENA (Electronic News Archive).

VRT Studiedienst (2010), *Monitor Diversiteit 2009: Een Kwantitative Studie naar de Zichtbaarheid van Diversiteit op het Scherm/Diversity Monitor 2009: Quantitative Research on the Visibility of Diversity on the Flemish Screen*, Brussels: VRT & ENA.

VRT Studiedienst (2011), *Monitor Diversiteit 2011: Een Kwantitatieve Studie naar de Zichtbaarheid van Diversiteit op het Scherm in Vlaanderen/Diversity Monitor 2011: Quantitative Research on the Visibility of Diversity on the Flemish Screen*, Brussels: VRT & ENA.

Wal, J. ter, d'Haenens, L. and Koeman, J. (2005), '(Re)presentations of Ethnicity in EU and Dutch Domestic News: A Quantitative Analysis', *Media, Culture & Society*, 27: 6, pp. 937–50.

Weedon, C. (2004), *Identity and Culture: Narratives of Difference and Belonging*, Maidenhead: Open University Press.

WRR (Wetenschappelijke Raad voor Regeringsbeleid) (2007), *Identificatie met Nederland*, Amsterdam: AUP.

Notes

1. All quotes are literal translations by the author.
2. http://www.minderhedenforum.be. Accessed 31 May 2011.
3. http://www.minderhedenforum.be/media.htm. Accessed 31 May 2011.
4. http://www.kifkif.be/. Accessed 31 May 2011.

Chapter 6

Ireland, the 'Migration Nation': Public Service Media Responses Between Discourse and Desire

Gavan Titley (National University of Ireland, Maynooth)

Introduction

In the first years of the new millennium, public institutions in Ireland embraced 'diversity'. As several chapters in this volume explore, the contemporary discourse of 'diversity' is itself profoundly ambivalent. As Mary Hickman notes, "'talk of diversity" is predicated not on the acceptance of plurality but on the notion of a host who is being subject to diversification' (2007: 12). In other words, contemporary diversity discourses are dependent on a double movement: towards a recognition or valuing of human diversity in certain ways and under certain conditions, while at the same time emphasizing that the acceptance of 'diversity' remains contingent, and on 'it' continuing to be recognized as a good. This chapter explores the ambivalences of this embrace by the public service broadcaster, Raidió Teilifís Éireann (RTÉ), and examines that ambivalence in terms of the broader sociopolitical context.

'Diversity' was one among many discourses adopted for the governance of difference during what is loosely termed the 'Celtic Tiger' period in Ireland from the late 1990s to 2007–08. A period of fundamentally unsustainable economic growth attracted many diasporic Irish into return migration, and substantial and variegated migration from multiple sites within and without the European Union. By 2006, two years after the accession of ten new EU member states, 612,600, or 14.7 per cent of the total population, were born outside of Ireland, and included, for example, an estimated 63,000 Polish people (CSO 2006: 24).

Research on public opinion on immigration during this period is as varied as the methodologies applied and the questions asked (Mac Éinrí 2009: 40–43), however, public discourse was marked by a particular form of celebratory recognition, emphasizing the transformation of Ireland from a site of emigration to immigration, and casting the presence of migrant diversity as a dimension of positive national transformation. Concomitant to this was the discursive ordering of migrant populations along a conventional axis from 'good' to 'bad' (Titley 2008). Official state discourses reflected the same ambivalence, displaying a 'triumphalist postmodern simulacrum of diversity' (Mac Éinrí 2009: 50) woven into an over-riding 'national interest' discourse, '[which] refers to protecting Ireland's territory, economy, and labour market, welfare state, culture, identity and societal cohesion from potential threats by immigrants and their future descendants' (Boucher 2011: 126).

While many migrants experienced everyday harrassment and forms of state racism (see Lentin and McVeigh 2006), these experiences rarely featured in the mediated, 'progressive multicultural image' so central to semiotic labour in a globalized, late capitalist economy. The state's integration strategy promoted diversity as a resource, while framing integration strategy as a 'chance to get it right' – a temporal emphasis that frames Ireland as well-positioned to avoid the multiculturalist mistakes held to have been made elsewhere in Europe (Titley 2012). According to the 2008 'Migration Nation' policy, 'experiences in other countries' may guide policy-making to the extent that, 'from Ireland's point of view, we may be able to position ourselves on a more advanced cycle rather than go through earlier cycles' (OMI 2008: 35–36). In practice, however, integration policy was ultimately limited to the domain of institutional discourse for effect. Definitive, material proof of this was offered in 2008, when, in the first emergency budget of the ongoing political-economic crisis, the semi-state agencies and programmes deemed central to 'integration' policy were abolished and downscaled, and the relevant government sub-ministry was further scaled back (see Titley 2012). Arguably, then, integration and diversity policy during this period was less a substantive move towards creating the conditions for equality and 'social cohesion' than an iteration of a neo-liberal determination to cultivate 'self-sufficient and autonomous immigrants, who must work on themselves in order to be independent, and committed to contributing to the Irish economy and society, in order that they may be integrated' (Gray 2006: 130).

Beyond governmental policy, RTÉ was one of the public institutions that most noticeably invested in diversity discourses during this period. As this volume explores, most public service broadcasters in Europe have extended their historical remit of fostering commonality and recognizing pluralism to include forms of responsibility to ethnic minority audiences. Further, these institutional approaches and programme strategies have also circulated and been exchanged within the European Broadcasting Union and other fora (Horsti 2009; Leurdijk 2006). RTÉ explicitly adopted this expanded remit during this period, highlighting their emphasis on *interculturalism* as an indicator of its corporate policy reporting:

> RTÉ will be inclusive and respectful of the cultural difference and richness that exist within the population of Ireland. It will provide the diversity of output necessary to present an understanding of the cultural and ethnic backgrounds of the country's inhabitants, foster an understanding and appropriate valuing of different cultures and create a sense of cultural cohesion within our society. RTÉ recognizes that its workforce must reflect the diversity of Irish society and will promote the involvement and employment of people from different ethnic and cultural backgrounds.
>
> (RTÉ 2008: 26)

While interculturalism, like diversity, is drawn from a repertoire of somewhat elastic, positive-sounding concepts that must be assembled in context, it was the focus of a lengthy internal development process that aimed to hold together an attention to cultural diversity and a reinvigoration of the national-integrative function of public service broadcasting. Thus in its commitment to 'explain difference and promote greater understanding between the communities that make up society' (RTÉ 2006: 14), RTÉ's guiding discourse shifted from 'multiculturalism' to 'diversity', with the supplementary addition of an 'intercultural' commitment to underline the integrative function of national broadcasting. In so doing, it reflected the British Broadcasting Corporation (BBC)'s shift towards a 'social capital' understanding of diversity, where 'the policy goal has been to increase the social capital of individuals in Britain as a means to an end such as democratic renewal, social cohesion, and economic productivity' (O'Loughlin 2006: 4).

This chapter assesses RTÉ's diversity and interculturalism work, initially through an analysis of policy documents produced between 2004 and 2010, and subsequently through a discussion of the programmes and formats developed to 'promote and explore' diversity during this period, based on interviews with key producers and editors.[1]

Nothing new under the sun? Some initial dilemmas for 'multicultural programming'

As Andra Leurdijk (2006) notes in her review of multicultural broadcasting in Europe, most public service broadcasters have assumed a responsibility for extending their remit to specific forms of programmes, services or policy for minority audiences. This extension is related both to the historical remit to represent and be accessible to the whole population of their territory, and to the adaptation of the concomitant responsibility to minority audiences to include audiences defined – however ambiguously – by their ethno-national identities. These commitments demand a constant re-evaluation and adaptation of approaches to programming and the strategies of producers. The pressures of competition and technological change; a consistent focus on the legitimacy of both public service broadcasting per se and its specific services for minorities; the sociological, generational and political complexity of minority populations (and their internal diversity as audience members); and the influence of wider political discourses concerning multiculturalism and integration in the 2000s, have meant that visions and strategies of 'multicultural programming' have changed rapidly and significantly.

For all this flux, an additional source of tension for public service broadcasters is the expectation that they can and should manage to reflect the diversity and increased complexity of 'fragmented audiences' – in other words, that they can continue to mediate a unifying vision of the public and public life in a context where the shape, scope and engagement of the public is a matter of debate. As Hallin and Mancini (2004: 42–44) noted in the early years of this decade, public service broadcasting retains on average between 30 per cent and 50 per cent of audience share in western Europe, and many broadcasters retain a powerful affective status and influence in contexts where commercial competition and globalization are still relatively new processes. As a general observation then, the historical, integrative role of public service broadcasting derived from an *era of scarcity* may be increasingly difficult in an *era of abundance* (see Ellis 2000) but evidence suggests that aspects of this role are still widely expected. Certainly, public service broadcasters interviewed for this chapter – see the next section – still identify with a vision of public service that has a unifying, integrative social mission.

Within the context of the nation-state, demographic and cultural shifts in territorial space must be reflected in *media space as public space*. The question, of course, is how, and this is not only an issue of how mediated representation grapples with the complexities of social life. Public space is not neutral – it is implicitly understood as national. In this space, the legitimacy of the presence, and the degree of belonging of migrants and other minorities, is frequently questioned. It is predominantly – but not exclusively – questioned by those who are themselves free to assume an unquestioned legitimacy and belonging on the basis of nationality, citizenship or race. Therefore public service broadcasters, in attempting to mediate this changed public space, are inevitably involved in negotiating this politics of boundaries and legitimacies.

This is one of the reasons why multicultural programming assumes a significant burden of different aims, aims that are time- and context-bound, and that are inevitably pregnant with contradictions and tensions. Public service broadcasting has tended to adopt aims which are adapted from their core mission – to 'open and broaden minds' – and which cohere with wider public rhetoric and policy – to 'celebrate diversity' and to 'promote integration'. Shaped by the need to maintain mainstream audiences while representing migrant and minority presence, programming often attempts to combine a broad educative function for the established majority with a desire to communicate directly to migrant audiences.

However, while so-called 'first contact' programming may fulfil a contextual function, it quickly throws up irreconcilable tensions. How can programmes specifically aimed at the needs and interests of migrants and minorities be developed while heading off the double-edged accusation of 'ghetto programming'? How can they 'open the minds' of the established mainstream audience without 'closing the eyes' of the migrants (broadly) represented? How can programming aimed at mainstream audiences provide 'windows on their worlds' without producing limited and sometimes tokenistic, celebratory content? Can programmes aimed at *introducing* and *explaining* migrants and minorities to a 'national public' ever begin to do justice to the diversity of experiences, perspectives and opinions of people who migrate? Can multicultural programming ever escape the charge of worthiness and liberal proselytizing? Does multicultural programming unwittingly confirm ethno-national boundaries by fixating on difference? How can multicultural programming produce sufficiently different perspectives to do justice to the complexities of migration and migrant lives, while guarding against the strategic perception that it is *favouring* minorities?

The development of RTÉ policy: Beyond multiculturalism, at least

The implications of these questions provide an important reason for the general shift in European public service broadcasting towards the more elastic discourses of *diversity* discussed in this volume. RTÉ have very publicly embraced the idea that their public service remit must include not only serving new minority audiences, but also adapting the historical role of the public service broadcaster as an integrative agent to the context of contemporary society in Ireland.

The Broadcasting Authority (Amendment) Act (1976) places RTÉ under an obligation to "'be responsive to the interests and concerns of the whole community" and "ensure that programmes reflect the varied elements which make up the culture of the people of the whole island of Ireland"'. The Broadcasting Authority (Amendment) Act 2001 states that RTÉ must

> provide a comprehensive range of programmes in the Irish and English language that reflects the cultural diversity of the whole island of Ireland and include, both on radio and television … programmes that entertain, inform, educate, provide coverage of sporting, religious activities and cater for the expectations of the community generally as well as members of the community with special or minority interests and which, in every case, respect human dignity.
>
> (Department of Energy 2001: Section 28[2][a])

These two articles are regularly cited as the basis on which the diversity shaped by migration is to be integrated into pre-existing visions of the varied elements that coexist in society in Ireland. These articles are also related in the corporate literature to the principles of expectation set out in 2004's Public Service Charter (Dublin: Department of Communications, Marine and Natural Resources):

> Public service remit: RTÉ, as the national public service broadcaster, shall reflect the democratic, social and cultural values of Irish society and the need to preserve media pluralism / RTÉ shall, at all times, strive to reflect fairly and equally the regional, cultural and political diversity of Ireland and its peoples / No editorial or programming bias shall be shown in terms of gender, age, disability, race, sexual orientation, religion or membership of a minority community.

Taken together, these articles and principles constitute a consistent articulation of one of public service broadcasting's enduring characteristics and tensions: that universality of service be complemented by particularity in the representation of and service provided to minority interests, variously defined. Following the introduction of the Charter in 2004, RTÉ committed to publishing an annual reflection on its 'guiding principles' in relation to the Charter's provisions. From 2006, this annual statement of guiding principles was absorbed into an annual report on 'corporate responsibility'. Taken as a series over time, these reports show the increasing centrality of *interculturalism* and *diversity* to RTÉ's statements of principle and policy, and also to its corporate image. They also give a limited if interesting sense of how different themes, aims and indicators are positioned and adapted over time.

The first such report, *RTÉ's Guiding Principles: Implementing the Public Service Broadcasting Charter* (November 2004) does not yet make explicit reference to Ireland as a migration society, but statements of intent and action concerning the specific needs of minorities and the value of 'diversity' are prominent. In the elaboration of its role as a PSB the established goal of regional diversity is related to the goal of social cohesion: 'provide programming that recognizes regional interests and cultural diversity including language and music, and encourages understanding and tolerance' (RTÉ 2004: 10). In the section outlining the broadcaster's goals for 2004–07, goals are juxtaposed with specific actions for different output divisions. In News and Current Affairs, the goal of 'holding and attracting new audiences' is related to the need to produce 'output of interest for minority groups' by 'ensuring minority groups and their interests are reflected in the News and Current affairs programming agenda' (2004: 15). Under the goal of working to 'project Ireland's cultural heritage' the sub-goal of 'celebrating diversity' is related to a specific set of reviews concerning the relevance and responsiveness of news coverage and formats (2004: 17).

Radio's goal of 'celebrating diversity' is specified as 'broadcasting the cultural expression of new communities in Ireland' and specifically included in the goal of 'output of interest for minority groups'. When the same exercise is conducted for television, a more detailed set of actions is documented. The aim to 'produce output of interest for minority groups' is based on (1) a review of diversity programmes pursued by other broadcasters; (2) the promotion of diversity and multicultural policy to include the issue of recruitment from minority groups; and (3) an ongoing review of RTÉ Television's diversity programming output (RTÉ 2004: 19).

Interestingly, the goal of 'projecting Ireland's cultural heritage' includes a dynamic sense of projection through 'developing a strategy for reflecting diversity consistently in our output' (2004: 20).

In the 2005 review, no new goals in this theme are added, and the existing goals and their actions are updated. The production of output of interest to minority groups in News and Current Affairs is noted as an ongoing target where progress is recorded as 'News and Current Affairs programming provides ongoing coverage of issues relating to and or involving ethnic minority groups' (RTÉ 2005: 8). The specific television actions concerning 'output of interest for minority groups' involve noting the development of new programmes (such as *No Place Like Home* [RTÉ 2006–08], see next section), the presentation of a 'diversity policy review' to the Audience Council in 2005, and the ongoing consideration of an 'ethnic minority media training scheme' modelled on an initiative by the Finnish public service broadcaster, YLE (see Horsti, this volume).

The 2006 document does not replicate this same general template for stating and tracking goals, and specific commitments to 'diversity goals' are entirely absent. This general shift can be explained by the absorption of the 'statement of principles' into a broader *Strategic Corporate Plan 2006–2010* and the production of an annual corporate responsibility report. The first such report, in 2006, introduces the idea of 'public interest tests' and lists several of relevance: 'Schedules that include programming for minority groups and interests / programming that recognizes regional interests and cultural diversity / programming that encourages understanding and tolerance' (RTÉ 2006: 6). The approach of publicly declaring measurable targets is replaced by a narrative of general aspirations and completed actions (programmes, support for the Media and Multicultural Awards) and an adaptation of the programming mission to 'hope our programmes will help to explain difference and promote greater understanding between the communities that make up society' (2006: 14).

The 2007 report marks a return to more specific articulations of intent as well as aspiration. A new report section, 'Looking Forward' features an extended discussion of *RTÉ and Interculturalism* and the first explicit links drawn between broadcasting legislation, the public service remit, and the needs and interests of people who are 'dual or non-Irish in nationality'. Framed by the prevalent narrative of a rapid shift from a society of emigration to one of immigration, the section links the rapidity of this change to social and political challenges, and the power of media to play 'both a decisive and responsible role in determining attitudes and levels of understanding between communities and cultures' (RTÉ 2007: 52). Specifically, for RTÉ, this means committing to combating 'racism and racial discrimination' and to 'reflecting cultural diversity in Ireland'. Following a list of new and ongoing programming, the report signals specific programming and policy approaches, including an 'emphasis on integrating non-Irish nationals and intercultural themes and viewpoints into mainstream programming' as 'ultimately the challenge over time is not [...] to produce more niche programming but rather more fully reflect the society and people we exist to serve, in all that we broadcast and in our staff profile' (RTÉ 2007:53).

To that end a commitment to interculturalism in corporate policy is described with a commitment to publishing a comprehensive action plan on interculturalism by the end of 2008:

RTÉ will be inclusive and respectful of the cultural difference and richness that exist within the population of Ireland. It will provide the diversity of output necessary to present an understanding of the cultural and ethnic backgrounds of the country's inhabitants, foster an understanding and appropriate valuing of different cultures and create a sense of cultural cohesion within our society. RTÉ recognizes that its workforce must reflect the diversity of Irish society and will promote the involvement and employment of people from different ethnic and cultural backgrounds

(RTÉ 2007: 53)

The 2008 report recalls this commitment to publishing an action plan, and describes a process of internal research and discussion culminating in a 'cross IBD intercultural group' report being presented to the Director General in May 2008, with recommendations subsequently discussed at a 'Corporate Editorial Board meeting' in July 2008. However this overview of ideas and process cannot be understood as 'publishing a comprehensive action plan on interculturalism' as signalled in 2007. The section relates how internal discussions considered 'who and what do we mean when we talk about intercultural diversity and how RTÉ currently represents cultural and ethnic diversity across its services' (RTÉ 2008: 38). In citing (1) output (2) staff development/training and (3) recruitment as core pillars of policy among other European PSBs, the document notes the different strategies other institutions have deployed in these areas, particularly in the area of recruitment. It concludes that 'just as different country's experiences of immigration are different, there is no obvious template of best practice to follow in developing a comprehensive intercultural strategy' (2008: 38). The need for changes in attitudes, leadership at all levels and a 'willingness to embrace and value diversity' is signalled, with the qualification that

> while programme-makers were, for the most part, well disposed to having greater diversity on-air and on-screen, there was a real difficulty, given the relatively recent nature of Ireland's immigration, in finding new voices from minority ethnic and cultural groups who have the necessary skills and confidence to contribute on a broad range of issues [...] the same challenge exists in relation to recruitment.
>
> (RTÉ 2008: 38)

As a result of the report, two relevant objectives are set for 2008/09:

- Senior management in Television, Radio and Current Affairs will agree specific, realistic and measurable targets with managers, editors and programme makers for ethnic and multicultural representation in all or parts of their respective output areas by end Q4 2008;
- RTÉ is to provide intercultural awareness training for all new staff (as part of staff induction training) and identify where intercultural training can be integrated into existing IBD training programmes by Q4 2009 (RTÉ 2008: 44).

In the 2009 report, the extent to which these objectives have been met is assessed as part of the general assessment of annual objectives. With respect to the question of targets for programme makers, the report notes that 'intercultural representation was included as a Performance Development System measure for all TV commissioning editors in respect of performance in 2009' (RTÉ 2009: 4). The ways in which intercultural representation is understood, framed and evaluated within this system of indicators is not discussed, and the information is not in the public domain. With regard to the 'intercultural awareness training', the report notes that all staff received introductory training by early 2009, and that the 'recruitment freeze' in public service employment meant that no induction training was required subsequently. The 2009 report was the last 'corporate responsibility' report issued, presumably as the strategic plan for 2005–10 had run its course. However, at this point, no further mention of 'interculturalism' or 'diversity' occurs in RTÉ corporate literature or subsequent annual reports.

RTÉ thus very publicly committed to developing relevant forms of policy, and given the recurring prominence of diversity and interculturalism in its corporate literature decided to foreground this as a key dimension of its contemporary identity and brand. A reading of the different documents and statements available suggests a prolonged internal discussion of sporadic intensity, and a sustained reflection on which precise terminology and headline categories best represents RTÉ's analysis of sociocultural change, and its mediation of it. Reflections on this in interviews I conducted with senior management noted that the sequential development of these policy documents can broadly be seen as one prolonged process, shaped by the complexity of the issues and the often divergent opinions of different managers and departments.

The corporate literature presents highly ambitious aspirations that mirror the tensions in public service broadcasting's engagements with migration societies. It seeks to play a role in educating and shaping attitudes, in fostering understanding between communities, including an 'appropriate valuing' of other cultures by the established mainstream, while adequately reflecting diversity across its different services. The integrative role of PSB is expressed in the contemporary discourse of 'social cohesion'. Given these aspirations, it is notable that the last document to specifically discuss cultural diversity notes fundamental discussions concerning 'who and what do we mean when we talk about intercultural diversity', but it does not go into detail about the substance of those discussions, and their conclusions. Following this, what could be regarded as a creative form of ambivalence is resolved through silence – specific objectives, diversity branding and the overt mediation of a sense of ongoing institutional consideration are conspicuous in their absence. It is noticeable also that this occurs in parallel with the intensification of the political-economic crisis, and the explicit jettisoning and downgrading of 'diversity' and 'integration' discourse in official pronouncements and initiatives. The significance of this is taken up in the conclusion.

Broadcasting responses (1): A general invitation to 'diversity'

RTÉ's accelerated progress through institutional discourses that have evolved in other European PSBs over a far longer period of time is mirrored in the programme provision during this period. A significant dimension of this in both radio and television involved jettisoning multicultural magazine formats – or so called 'niche programmes' – for a transversal emphasis on *diversity* and the integration of relevant perspectives, issues and voices into hybrid formats and mainstream programmes. This acceleration displayed some commitment to reflect on the adequacy of programming to social realities, and to avoid tokenism and programming so driven by normative visions that they are undermined by an 'aura of persuasion' (Browne and Onyejelem 2007). However it also, much like the policy nexus, generated a dominant vocabulary for branding RTÉ productions as 'diversity' or 'intercultural', without necessarily communicating a coherent sense of what these ideas mean institutionally and how they are processed and activated.

Since the early 2000s, 'multicultural programming' has been shaped by the programme department Cláracha Gaeilge [programming in the Irish language], Multiculture and Education. Since 2005, much of this programming has been broadcast under the 'super-strand' – or programme category – of *Diversity*. RTÉ television's approach has involved broadcasting a 'flagship' multicultural programme with regularity since the early 2000s, beginning with the multicultural magazine programme *Mono* (RTÉ 2002-5). These series have been commissioned from independent production companies, and the format, focus and style of programming have changed significantly over time. This section provides a critical discussion of the main flagship programmes developed to fulfil the intercultural mission, based on interviews conducted with programme producers, and with the commissioning editor for the diversity programme strand, Mairéad Ní Nuadháin.[2]

Mono was the first series produced by this new arrangement, and followed a magazine format for all but its last series, normally including three features in its 26-minute slot. Each series comprised of 12–13 episodes. It was presented for three seasons by Shalini Sinha and Bisi Adigun, with these presenters joined by Kusi Okamura in Series 3. The commissioning editor, Mairéad Ní Nuadháin, reflects that *Mono* was a series that had a number of guiding ideas, and a central one was familiarizing a mainstream Irish audience with the factuality of multiculturalism in Ireland:

My thinking never was to make a programme for the multicultural audience. My thinking was originally [...] to make a programme for the wider audience. In those years we were really introducing the Irish audience to the idea that now you are a multicultural society. This is the way it's going to be. These are people who are living in Ireland, who have interesting stories. Their children are going to have Irish accents. They're not going to go away. And I tried to steer away from stories and programmes about refugees. I tried not to cover things that were problematic, although I'm sure we did from time to time, because I never wanted the programme itself to become a stereotype.

(Ní Nuadháin 2010)

A format that attracts a broad mainstream audience is not just an educative goal, it is also held to be broadcasting pragmatism, as Mairéad Ní Nuadháin and other programme contributors were in agreement that the role of RTÉ was not, and is not, to cater in particular cultural or linguistic terms for 'niche' migrant audiences. However a central goal of *Mono* was professional development, in front and behind the camera, and Anne O'Brien of the responsible production company Kairos Communications notes that:

> I think what I admired about it was its agenda which was very clear from the start that it was to be a training ground for people to try and get into the industry and that became more explicit in the second year. We had an internship essentially for somebody who was from an ethnic minority or who was black and Irish to train with us, and the whole agenda was that those people would then move on into mainstream programming. I think that was massively important.
>
> (O'Brien 2010)

The series was positioned not only as an initial reflection of a multicultural Ireland, but as a vehicle that could develop presenters who would subsequently move into fronting other programmes, and a production crew that could do similarly. As Anne O'Brien recalls, the desire to avoid a conventional Irish production team, in order to involve minority background producers that could contribute knowledge, perspective, stories and contacts, meant that the presenters also played a role in shaping the programme. Nevertheless, Anne O'Brien reflects that it took the programme some time during its first series to develop an approach that departed from a 'very classic Irish way of looking at new communities':

> I think we were looking at them instead of giving them the airspace to bring stories to the screen. So it was all about how black and ethnic minorities coming to Ireland was affecting the majority Irish audience rather than what it evolved into later, that is, what was going on within ethnic minority communities.
>
> (O'Brien 2010)

From Mairéad Ní Nuadháin's perspective as commissioning editor, it made sense for the programme to leave 'politicized' issues of asylum-seeking and migrant rights to News and Current Affairs, a move that nevertheless replicates the wider discursive emphasis on multicultural positivity discussed in the introduction. A format that could relate good, attractive stories, often the stories of individuals, was held to be more important at that juncture. However it was argued that 'attractive' stories did not mean simplistically positive stories. Early episodes tackled challenging material such as examining the mistreatment of migrant workers, experiences of torture and the imprisonment of 'drug mules' in Mountjoy Prison. As Anne O'Brien recalls, the remit was broad, with the sole stipulation that the pieces came from contacts and suggestions in 'ethnic minority' communities. The development of a story involved several overlapping phases:

> What happened at the research phase is somebody would say let's do a piece on someone who has converted to Islam, and we'd end up going to the Imam in the Mosque, and we'd

say listen we're doing this piece on conversion, is there anyone who has converted to Islam? He might say I have two, and I'd ask to come and meet them. At that point we'd talk to people, get their stories and get a sense of will it work on camera, would they be comfortable doing these angles on their stories, and for a five-minute piece you'd do three or four set-ups to sustain a bit of (visual) movement.

(Ní Nuadháin 2010)

In its fourth series *Mono* moved away from the magazine format to a half-hour documentary approach, a shift that reflected wider industry dissatisfaction with the dated style of magazine programming (Leurdijk 2006). Mairéad Ní Nuadháin also notes that during this period she began to question whether a different format could deliver a wider audience to the 'multicultural slot' as defined by scheduling prerogatives. Here, however, the economics of the independent media sector had a decisive impact on programme formatting, as pitching companies tended to opt for conventional multicultural food and music programmes, a conservatism arguably shaped as much by the intense competition for the commission as by the prevailing assumptions about what such programmes should aim to communicate. Mairéad Ní Nuadháin noted that this is a recurring limitation, and that stock and reactive approaches to representation have dominated most approaches, including that of RTÉ:

People thought diversity, ethnicity, equals problems, equals refugees. So it has to be about people who have […] there's a racism problem if they're black. If they are of ethnic origin – obviously we have to write in a racism line. We must have somebody who's here illegally. Obviously they are ethnic, so they can't be here legally. I used to say about television drama: 'why can't you just have a sweetshop owner or a doctor in the series. So I was really happy to see in *The Clinic*[3] that there was a very very middle-class black character […] I just thought, that's a really positive outcome, her storyline is not predicated on her ethnicity. It took years.

(ibid.)

Broadcasting responses 2: Reality formats and diverse realities

The pendulum swing illustrated above, between 'negative' portrayals determined to signal the prejudices and barriers faced by migrants, and 'positive' representations equally determined to project their *normality*, is an inevitable product of few-to-many broadcasting aiming to communicate the right messages to as large an audience as possible. The shifts in television programming that are critiqued by Sarita Malik in this volume were regarded in an interview by some producers as bypassing this polarizing dynamic, if not of transcending it altogether (see chapter 2).

The increased importance of reality formats to RTÉ mainstream programming has influenced the approach to multicultural programming, and the ways in which 'diversity' can be stitched into the unquestioned and unremarkable fabric of mediated social reality. Debates about competition-based reality formats, and what they say about production values and audience sensibilities, often obscure the more profound changes that have been wrought. As Jonathan Bignell argues (2006), it makes little sense to think of 'reality television' as a genre, but rather as a term for a wider shift in orientation towards the role and function of television. Reality formats have developed in societies characterized by increased complexity and diversity, where life-paths are increasingly flexibilized and non-linear, and where every area of life – from health, to parenting, relationships, and so forth – is subject to endless speculation about the correct approach and the 'right values'. In this milieu, observational and quasi-participatory formats offer some possibilities for curiosity, comparison and self-reflection.

Therefore, as Mairéad Ní Nuadháin points out, RTÉ programmes such as *The Health Squad* (RTÉ 2007-12) and *Baby on Board* (RTÉ 2008) can unobtrusively include migrants and ethnic minorities as people focused on personal and domestic issues, rather than as ciphers burdened by messages they have to convey. Most particularly, the future-seeking series *21ˢᵗ Century Child* (RTÉ 2007-13) took the implications of migration and settlement as a central principle in sourcing families for the programme, 'otherwise the programme wouldn't reflect Ireland in the future' (ibid). However, reality formats amplify the ambivalence of 'diversity' work, because they also allow a problematic spectrum of programming to be branded as 'diversity' simply because of the presence of something or somebody foreign. The unobtrusive inclusion of 'diversity' in reality formats can be as depoliticizing as it can be normalizing, bypassing rather than tackling questions of minority and migrant inclusion and involvement in media work, and declaring all questions of representational politics to be 'solved'. There is also the risk, as Anne O'Brien pointed out, that this form of 'mainstreaming' dissipates the expertise in multicultural programming accumulated in previous productions and projects.

No Place Like Home was broadcast between 2006 and 2008 over three series of eight, ten and nine programmes. Presented by Bob Kelly, the format involved Kelly 'bumping into the new Irish' in public spaces and asking 'why did you come to Ireland and what have you left behind?' The programme then explores the person's life in Ireland while Kelly travels to meet their friends and family. Mairéad Ní Nuadháin argues that it

> was a really good vehicle. We visited a huge range of countries, so it was a mix of travel and multiculture. Some people found fault with it because they thought it was too travel oriented and it was too focused on what you could do and what you could see in the countries the people came from. And that was true to some extent, but it actually got a good audience in its slot and that for me was positive. Also […] by showing the back lives and back stories of immigrants it told something that television hadn't previously. In *Mono* the stories were here, so you had maybe neurosurgeons

from Pakistan making galvinised gates or something in Ballyhaunis. Whereas in *No Place Like Home*, you took somebody like a Mongolian doorkeeper in Temple Bar, who just looks like every other bouncer. Bob goes back to Mongolia and finds out that his family are Olympic wrestlers, a certain amount about what Mongolia is like, and why they hate being called Chinese.

(ibid.)

The ambiguous assessments referred to can be viewed in a number of ways. The programme was criticized as a travel show in disguise, a much-vaunted commitment to multiculturalism programming merely being lacquered on a clever format designed to maximize audiences. However, this poses the question as to as what a format explicitly designed to maximize audiences can achieve as a 'multicultural' programme. Reality/observational formats thrive through generic hybridity, that is, through blending elements of programme genres previously thought of as distinct. The blending of travel show with 'window on their world' multicultural television can be read in two ways. The addition of the travel element – and the touristic viewing it may encourage – serves to, at best, distract attention from what a flagship multicultural programme should be attempting to do, and at worst it may amount to just another form of exoticization of migrants.

As against this, the format can be seen as less about travel and more about mobility and immobility, though this is a question of motivated reading rather than an explicitly developed theme of the programme. In very many of the stories featured, there is a stark, unavoidable contrast between the ease with which Bob Kelly can access the other home, and the legal, financial and employment barriers participants face in organizing annual visits, at best. At the end of each episode Kelly would bring back video messages from family and friends, and the re-mediation of this hugely prevalent form of migrant communication – even in an era of instant messaging and webcams – served as an unsettling reminder of how the (racializing) politics of mobility and immobility shape lives and relationships. To some extent also, the programme served as an anecdote to the stereotype of the biography-less migrant, and it represented something of the transnational connections and spatial relationships that are lost in programmes fixated on the localized experience of migrants in Ireland, and their impact on Ireland. In keeping with the ambivalences of diversity's capacious embrace, these analyses depend very much on the experience and contexts featured – the travel show element is always more likely to dominate on a trip to Finnish Lapland, the power relations of mobility and movement are inevitably more pronounced in the experience of sub-Saharan Africans in Ireland.

No Place Like Home was sponsored by Western Union, a form of sponsorship that, as Mairéad Ní Nuadháin notes, had an institutional impact in RTÉ on the status of multicultural programming as it indicated the wider potential importance of migrant audiences. Looking to attract an audience of people transferring remittances and savings, the sponsorship was based on the assumption that a substantial non-EU migrant population[4] was actually watching the programme:

> So then they [management] started to take notice and think 'maybe there's a reason to take numbers' [referring to targeted migrant audience research]. They're big. Suddenly we are talking about 10% of the population. Now I know that's including people from the UK as well. But there was a point where people woke up and thought the numbers are big, they are people who are paying their licence fee, they're spending money in the country.
>
> (ibid.)

Subsequent to *No Place Like Home*, two four-part series have been made under the rubric of 'diversity programming'. *Small World* was broadcast in 2011, and extended the formula of *No Place Like Home* in a changed sociopolitical context by visiting emigrant sites and experiences. Of the four programmes the first dealt with Brazilians who had left the meat-packing industry in Ireland to establish businesses with savings from this labour. The other three programmes in the series dealt with dimensions of the Irish diasporic experience.

The four-part documentary series *Meet the Neighbours* was broadcast in May and June 2009. The neighbours in question congregate in Balbriggan, Co. Dublin, the hometown of the documentary director Liam McGrath. The series was described by RTÉ in its press release:

> Balbriggan was once a sleepy fishing village. But in the space of less than five years, its population increased by over 50% and many of the newly arrived residents have come from foreign shores. No town in Ireland has seen a greater percentage population increase between the last two censuses than the ethnically diverse town of Balbriggan in North County Dublin. *Meet the Neighbours* gets to know the people and lives behind this story – creating a snapshot of a moment in time in Ireland's multicultural journey, entering the human lives of migrants who have settled in Balbriggan as well as the lives of the native Irish that they have decided to live amongst.
>
> (ibid.)

The relatively rapid diversification of Balbriggan has attracted much attention in public debates on migration in Ireland, from controversies over schooling, to anxieties about 'ghettoization' and to racist YouTube videos promising future Balbriggan civil wars.[5] In an interview, prior to its broadcast, Mairéad Ní Nuadháin alludes to this sensationalism as one dimension of the programme:

It will be a portrait of a town that has hit the headlines for sometimes the wrong reasons in Ireland. I hope it will be a nice gentle, but intimate portrait of this very, very multicultural town. It could be a very important programme in the future, the kind of programme that in twenty years time you go the archives and you say 'God, look what Balbriggan was like in 2008'

(ibid.)

Meet the Neighbours follows three to four different people per episode for a short period of time in spring 2009, filming them in different contexts, observing work, hobbies and local interaction. As a documentary series it is another formal departure for multicultural programming, however the focus on a specific place also shifts the ways in which 'migrants' are understood and represented. If a criticism of previous programmes has been the tendency to gather an enormous range of identities, status positions and experiences into the category 'migrants', and to then represent them to an Irish audience, *Meet the Neighbours* like the BBC's 2008 series *Meet the Immigrants*, is interested in representing everyday life routines and practices in place. Mairéad Ní Nuadháin argued that the shift to documentary allowed for different dimensions of storytelling to be developed. Commenting on the story eventually featured – in a slightly different form – in Episode 2, of a Balbriggan-born prawn fisherman, she says:

In this programme it's little portraits. So there's a portrait of a fisherman, and the fisherman (I remember this because I saw a rough cut) starts off as really being from Balbriggan stock and he's shelling prawns and there's a mate beside him. He starts giving out about immigrants. He's not terribly acid about it or anything. Of course the guy beside him is Latvian, and then it transpires later in the story that his own mother was Czech. He doesn't see any irony in that. He just tells it himself, and there's no commentary, there's no reporter saying, 'and wait till you hear where he came from'

(ibid.)

Thus good documentary work is capable of capturing not only the limited dimensions of how speech represents the involved fabric of people's lives, but also how assumed boundaries are less fixed in practice than is often articulated. Yet of course, that they are articulated as fixed is also important. The series' spectrum of migrant experiences is given a cohesive focus by locating them in place and observing the different ways in which they are embedded in it. From the producer's perspective, by featuring the stories of people born in Balbriggan; Irish people who have moved there; international relationships which have been formed there, it subtly throws up a cloud of questions concerning how belonging is thought about, and where belonging is thought about, in a migration society.

142

Conclusion: Assembling and dissembling diversity

There is a striking congruence between the political decision in Ireland, in 2008–09, to in effect draw a line under the overt governance of difference organized through the rubric of 'integration', and the somewhat sudden demotion of interculturalism as a strategic priority for RTÉ. The broadcaster ceased issuing corporate responsibility reports in 2009, and the annual reports subsequent to this date make no mention of 'interculturalism' or the indicators previously published. Concomitantly, the institutional emphasis on 'diversity' shifts from an explicit relationship with those who have migrated to Ireland to a more capacious category encompassing the 'cultural and regional diversity of the people of the whole island of Ireland' (RTÉ 2011: 107). Further, the programming listed as relating to this priority is a mix of religious, sports and Irish-language programming, and programmes commissioned to cover the visit of the British Queen Elizabeth II to Ireland in May 2011. The forms of specific, slot-driven programming discussed previously are absent. It would appear that, in tandem with the strategic governmental repudiation of the rubric of the 'migration nation', the national broadcaster has all but eroded the high-profile commitments of the previous ten years.

Nevertheless, there is no evidence that this abrupt diminution has any causal relation to the broader shift in governance priorities or rhetoric, though its influence cannot be fully discounted. Rather, it is arguably the case that RTÉ's acceleration through the generic possibilities and limitations experienced over a longer period of time in more established migration sites resulted in a form of generic exhaustion. The swift turn to 'diversity' integrated in and across reality television programmes represented an adequate and plausible solution, and one that is congruent with the over-arching need to compete for audience share. If meaningfully implemented, the integration of diversity as a banal component of programme composition and as a representational statement of the sociocultural real represents a considered outcome from a process of intensive, if limited, institutional engagement. However, as Sarita Malik argues in this volume, the turn to diversity in and through reality television may have a depoliticizing, 'smoothing-out' impact, emphasizing commonalities through lifestyle themes and eliding situated and structural differences. The irony of such approaches is that they run the risk of being more 'bolt-on' and superficial than the exhausted genres they are designed to supersede.

References

Bignell, J. (2006), *Big Brother: Reality Television in the Twenty-First Century*, Basingstoke: Palgrave Macmillan.

Boucher, G. (2011), 'Official discourses for managing migration', in Bryan Fanning and Ronnie Munck (eds), *Globalization, Migration and Social Transformation*, Farnham: Ashgate, pp. 125–40.

Browne, H. and Onyejelem, C. (2007), 'Textualising radio practice: Sounding out a changing Ireland', in Alan Grossman and Aine O'Brien (eds), *Projecting Migration: Transcultural Documentary Practice*, London: Wallflower Press, pp. 183–98.

Central Statistics Office (CSO) (2006), *Population and Migration Estimates*, http://www.cso.ie/releasespublications/documents/population/current/popmig.pdf, Dublin: CSO. Accessed 12 May 2012.

Ellis, J. (2000), *Seeing Things: Television in the Age of Uncertainty*, London: I.B. Tauris.

Government of Ireland (2004), *Public Service Broadcasting Charter*, Dublin: Department of Communications, Marine and Natural Resources.

Gray, B. (2006), 'Migrant integration policy: A nationalist fantasy of management and control?', *Translocations*, 1: 1, pp. 118–38.

Hallin, D. and Mancini, P. (2004), *Comparing Media Systems: Three Models of Media and Politics*, Cambridge: CUP.

Hickman, M. (2007), 'Immigration and monocultural (re)imaginings in Ireland and Britain', *Translocations*, 2: 1, pp. 12–25

Horsti, K. (2009), 'Anti-racist and multicultural discourses in European Public Service Broadcasting: Celebrating consumable differences in the Prix Iris Media prize', *Communication, Culture & Critique*, 2: 3, pp. 339–60.

Lentin, R. & R. McVeigh (2006), *After Optimism: Ireland, Racism and Globalisation*, Dublin: Metro Éireann Publications.

Leurdijk, A. (2006), 'In search of common ground: Strategies of multicultural television producers in Europe', *European Journal of Cultural Studies*, 9: 1, pp. 25–46.

Mac Éinrí, P. (2009), 'If I wanted to go there I wouldn't start from here: Re-imagining a multi-ethnic nation', in Debbie Ging, Michael Cronin and Peadar Kirby (eds), *Transforming Ireland: Challenges, Critiques, Resources*, Manchester: MUP, pp. 38–51.

Office of the Attorney General, *Broadcasting Authority (Amendment) Act 1976*, Dublin: Government of Ireland Publications.

Office of the Minister for Integration (OMI) (2006), Dublin: Government of Ireland Publications.

O'Loughlin, B. (2006), 'The operationalization of the concept "cultural diversity" in British television policy and governance', *Working Paper No. 27, CRESC Working Paper Series*, Milton Keynes: Open University.

Raidió Teilifís Éireann (RTÉ) (2004), *RTÉ's Guiding Principles: Implementing the Public Service Broadcasting Charter*, http://www.rte.ie/about/guidingprinciples.pd, Dublin: RTÉ. Accessed 16 September 2009.

Raidió Teilifís Éireann (RTÉ) (2005), *RTÉ's Guiding Principles: Implementing the Public Service Broadcasting Charter*, http://www.rte.ie/about/gprinciples05_eng4.pdf. Dublin: RTÉ. Accessed 16 September 2009.

Raidió Teilifís Éireann (RTÉ) (2006), *RTÉ's Guiding Principles: Implementing the Public Service Broadcasting Charter*, http://www.rte.ie/about/guidingprinciples2006.pdf. Dublin: RTÉ. Accessed 17 September 2009.

Raidió Teilifís Éireann (RTÉ) (2007), 'Interculturalism', *RTE and Corporate Responsibility, 2007*, http://www.rte.ie/about/pdfs/Final%20CR%20Report%20English%2028%20 August.pdf. Dublin: RTÉ. Accessed 17 September 2009.

Raidió Teilifís Éireann (RTÉ) (2008), *RTÉ and Corporate Responsibility.* Dublin: RTÉ.

Raidió Teilifís Éireann (RTÉ) (2009), *RTÉ and Corporate Responsibility.* Dublin: RTÉ.

Raidió Teilifís Éireann (RTÉ) (2006), *RTÉ Independent Productions: 2006 Commissions*, www.rte.ie/commissioning/.../2006%20Commissioning%20Round.doc. Accessed 16 February 2013.

Raidió Teilifís Éireann (RTÉ) (2011), *2011 Annual Report*, http://www.rte.ie/documents/ about/RTE%202011%20Annual%20Report%20-%20English.pdf. Dublin: RTÉ. Accessed 18 February 2013.

Titley, G. (2008), 'Media transnationalism in Ireland: An examination of Polish media practices', *Translocations*, 3: 1, pp. 29–49.

Titley, G. (2012), 'Getting integration right? Media transnationalism and domopolitics in Ireland', *Ethnic & Racial Studies*, 35: 5, pp. 817-833.

Notes

1. This analysis draws on material from the research project report *Broadcasting in the New Ireland: Mapping and Envisioning Cultural Diversity* (NUIM, 2010).

2. The interviews were conducted in March and April 2009, in RTÉ and in the relevant production companies. They were semi-structured interviews aiming to discuss the process of development of specific programmes, guiding evaluations of institutional discourses and their relation to programme-making.

3. An RTÉ character drama.

4. The availability on Eurozone inter-bank transfer (IBAN) means that Western Union services are less utilized by EU citizens in Ireland.

5. The YouTube video entitled 'Balbriggan Civil War' was removed at some point in spring 2009.

Chapter 7

A Vulnerable Diversity: Perspectives on Cultural Diversity Policies in Swedish Public Service Media

Gunilla Hultén (Stockholm University)

Introduction

Around the turn of this century, Swedish public service companies commenced the move from multicultural to more vague cultural diversity policies. The first policies were a direct result of the post-war immigration to Sweden and the multicultural goals expressed by the parliament. From a principled pluralism closely linked to minority communities and group membership, the policies evolved towards a pragmatic pluralism that emphasized mainstream content and audience choice. This shift must be seen in the light of the increasing pressure on public service media to successfully adapt to market forces while still maintaining a large enough audience to guarantee its legitimacy and survival.

In this chapter, it is argued that as a consequence of this change, cultural diversity has become a vulnerable value (Blumler 1992). Drawing on the analysis of the two major Swedish public broadcasting corporations, Swedish Television (Sveriges Television – SVT) and Swedish Radio (Sveriges Radio – SR), I contend that the present policies and regulations are not sufficient to ensure or improve cultural diversity in either their programming or their workforces.

The chapter starts by discussing some general features concerning diversity, difference and representation, followed by a brief historical background of the companies' diversity policies. I then present the legal requirements of public broadcasters concerning cultural diversity, and examine SVT's and SR's current cultural diversity policy documents. Next I introduce the views of eight managers responsible for formulating and/or implementing the companies' diversity policies and how these managers interpret and put the policies into practice.[1] The analysis of the interviews indicates discrepancies between the principles and practices of cultural diversity policies. In the concluding section of the article, I call attention to the companies' focus on bringing diversity into the newsrooms through recruiting journalists with migrant backgrounds, with an intention of securing market shares. I argue that this market logic is potentially threatening to the companies' cultural diversity, making it a vulnerable value.

Between unity and diversity

In this chapter media diversity policy refers to the representation and participation of ethnic/cultural minorities in order to enhance diversity in media content and staffing.

A driving force in this direction was provided by PSBs, since in many countries public broadcasters were explicitly required to represent the diversity of the national societies (McQuail 2001: 73). The promotion and protection of diversity has also been a justifying argument of PSB. Diversity is thus viewed as difference, which has inherent positive effects, such as pluralism of ideas and a variety of opinions and outlets.

Traditionally cohesion has been within the core remit of public television and radio, as a service to the entire population. In the Reithian sense, public service broadcasting and its values entailed plurality and diversity, thus involving the provision for minorities, a concern for national identity and community, and the addressing of audiences as citizens, not as consumers (cf. Scannell 1990). Thus, PSB have been seen as having a nationally unifying and integrating effect, and of providing common values. This nationally homogenizing tendency, built on territorial logic, is disputed by the diverse composition of the 'public' in terms of divisions into different ethnic or cultural groups.

In Sweden, these ideals harmonized with the core principles of *Folkhemmet* (The People's Home). The concept is closely linked to the Swedish Social Democratic Party and the building of the Swedish welfare state. Sweden should become a good home, as it were, marked by equality and consensus. In the post-World War II decades the import of foreign labour to support Swedish industry was considered necessary to secure the welfare state project. Swedish journalism has been closely associated with the construction and diffusion of the welfare state, and with promoting a welfare nationalism (Hultén 2006). The Swedish public service companies were given an important role in an inclusive national conversation, bringing audiences together (cf. Löfgren 1997: 36).

In the mid-1960s immigration to Sweden declined as a result of the implementation of entry regulations. The public debate and media rhetoric also shifted, from viewing immigration as an indispensable resource, towards regarding it as an economic burden to the welfare state (Hultén 2006: 221). There has been much variation in immigration to Sweden in recent decades. During the period of 2004 to 2010 there was a significant increase of immigrants due to the conflicts and unrest in Iraq, Somalia, Afghanistan and Ethiopia.

In the face of processes of globalization, with large migratory movements, and commercialization, public service institutions have been criticized for failing to be a service for everyone. Des Freedman observes a shift in the discourse of media policies from understanding diversity as a public good towards seeing diversity as efficiency in the marketplace. He sees the risks with narrowing down aspirations towards initiatives designed to maximize consumer choice and market penetration. Therefore diversity cannot just be equated with competition, and he argues that policy makers need to take on a broader definition of diversity. In his mind, diversity ought to be about acting on contemporary economic, social and political divisions, and not simply about celebrating difference (Freedman 2008: 77–78). According to Jay G. Blumler, increased commercialism is potentially threatening to a diversity of content, allowing for only that amount and those forms of diversity that are likely to attract enough audience interest to protect the companies' market shares. Less powerful and commercially less attractive segments of the population risk not finding materials in the schedules which are reflective of their interests and with which they can identify (Blumler 1992: 32–39).

Simon Cottle claims that efforts concerning cultural representations have increasingly become an issue of the politics of difference and diversity. This change also indicates a shift in institutional arrangements and production regimes. Among the shaping forces that he identifies are the intensified commercial imperatives and the changing politics of multiculturalism (Cottle 1997: 6–8, see also Cottle 2000). Sonja Kretzschmar notes a twofold media development. On the one hand, she observes that competitive media markets enhance mainstream content, which largely reflects ethnic majority opinions. On the other, she sees the rising problems of the disintegration of ethnic minorities in western European countries (Kretzschmar 2007: 230–31).

Obviously the concept of difference can have a variety of meanings. In a negative sense, it is about the exclusion and marginalization of those who are perceived as Other. On the other hand, difference can be construed favourably as a source of diversity and heterogeneity. Difference is then seen as enriching and as a basis for opportunities (cf. Lentin and Titley 2011). However, the notion of difference does not capture the mechanisms that produce and reproduce inequality between different groups in society. As Michel Wieviorka reminds us, difference also evokes inferiority, subordination, exclusion and domination (2001: 59, 161). In addition, differences contain a potential threat to society, implying the dissolution and division of society. He contends that contemporary debates on cultural difference proceed from the observation that it is an internal problem in our societies, emphasizing the friction between different cultural groups (2001: 89). In doing so, he raises the questions of power relations, and touches upon the politics of representation. For Wieviorka, the challenge of contemporary societies is rather to ensure intercultural communication, and to realize that all cultures are susceptible to alteration or dissolution.

In the policy documents of the Swedish PSM, difference is regarded as something desirable. It is primarily described as an absence or deficiency in the present programming and workforce, which can be and ought to be corrected by its presence.

From multiculturalism to mainstreaming

In the 1960s the concept of multiculturalism came into wider use, and multicultural policies were introduced in many countries. Michel Wieviorka identifies Sweden together with Canada and Australia as one of three countries that has provided concrete and significant expressions of multiculturalism (2001: 112). One example is the Swedish immigration and integration policy from 1975. It rested on three core objectives: legal equality between minority groups and the rest of the population, freedom of choice regarding ethnic and cultural identities, and cooperation. These multicultural principles gave immigrants the right to preserve their languages and cultural identities. The essence was that integration should take place without the need for cultural assimilation, thus taking on a pluralistic cultural approach.

The first Swedish radio and TV programmes directed at immigrants were not initiated by the public service companies, but were the results of immigrants' opinion-groups and a decisive ruling in the former Radio Commission in 1975. The decision stated that programming did not conform to the requirements of the broadcasting licence. Later that same year SVT started its first multicultural programme, *Invandrardags/Immigration-time*. Another outcome of the ruling was a new clause in the legal requirements, making the companies accountable to ethnic minorities (Andersson 2000: 5–7). The new stance was closely linked to the government's new integration policy, which called attention to advocacy and change in public attitude (Hultén 2006: 190). PSM also compete within a highly diversified market, including a multitude of media outlets. New technologies have also involved a change in the nature of journalistic work. These changes have compelled PSM to re-think their mission, and to reconceptualize their diversity policies.

The Swedish media system is a 'duopoly', where public service broadcasters coexist alongside commercially funded companies, with the public service broadcasters still remaining comparatively strong (Hallin and Mancini 2004: 145). Nevertheless Swedish public service companies are on the retreat, as they face difficulties in maintaining their audiences and have implemented major reorganizations in recent years, including staff cuts and reductions in budgets. In the past years declining shares of viewers have challenged Swedish public service television, whereas the commercial TV channels have strengthened their positions. In 2012 the public service television market share was 37 per cent in Sweden (Nordicom 2012). The two public service television channels, SVT1 and SVT2 taken together, still have the highest number of television viewers, followed by the commercial channel TV4 (The Swedish Broadcasting Authority 2013: 25). Since commercial radio broadcasting channels first began operating in the early 1990s, public service radio's share of daily listeners has steadily declined from 70 per cent to 48 per cent of the population in 2008 (Carlsson and Harrie (eds) 2010). The changing conditions have also had an impact on both companies' diversity policies, promoting the shift from multicultural programmes to a mainstreamed general diversity within all programming.

Concurrent with this discursive shift, intensified commercial interests have changed the functioning of the public service companies, and they have reorganized their address of immigrants and minorities (Horsti and Hultén 2011). Both SVT and SR have cancelled their specific multicultural programmes, including the radio programme *Brytpunkten/ Breaking Point* and the television programmes *Mosaik/Mosaic*, *Språka/Let's Talk* and *Aktuellt för invandrare/News for Immigrants*.[2] Mainstreaming is one key concept in the companies' current policies, which state that diversity should permeate the content, programming and staffing. Another key notion is difference. The subtitle of SR's diversity policy is 'Differences in interaction' and in the opening clause of SVT's diversity policy the company states: 'SVT welcomes and respects differences regarding gender, age, ethnicity, religion or faith, sexual orientation and disability' (Sveriges Television 2008).

In brief, SVT's and SR's shifts in diversity policies can be characterized by a move from ethnically-marked forms of cultural difference and the support for ethnic minorities, towards broader approaches of cultural diversity.

Regulations

SVT and SR are financed by compulsory license fees. The underlying principles of the Swedish broadcasting licence are formulated in the Radio and Television Act. The Act stipulates certain fundamental rules regarding the assertion of democratic values and the principle of all people's equal value. Moreover, SVT's and SR's broadcasting licences require the companies to provide a diverse array of programming that reflects the various cultures present in Sweden.

In addition, the companies must comply with the Swedish Discrimination Act, aimed at promoting equal rights and opportunities regardless of gender, transgender identity or expression, ethnicity, religion or other beliefs, disability, sexual orientation or age. By law, employers are required to actively promote equal rights and opportunities and to fight discrimination. These measures are to be goal-oriented and accounted for annually (SFS 2008: 567).

Moreover, SVT and SR are required to submit an annual report to the Swedish Broadcasting Authority,[3] stating that the content of the programmes conforms to the regulations of the Radio and Television Act. In addition, the authority monitors whether programmes already broadcast are in compliance with the Act as well as with the terms of the licences the Government has granted. SVT's and SR's public service annual reports include an account of the programming in the national minority languages Finnish, Sami, Meänkieli and Romany. SR's latest report also account for the programming in Albanian, Arabic, Assyrian, Kurdish, Persian, Serbian,[4] Somali and English. However, ethnic and/or cultural diversity in the programming is not monitored on a regular basis, and is not presented in the annual reports. Nor do the companies' diversity policies contain strategies concerning the monitoring of diversity efforts.

The cultural diversity goals of the companies are therefore controlled by at least four decision making levels: the Radio and Television Act, the broadcasting licence, the companies' cultural diversity policies and local diversity plans made up by divisions and/or editorial offices.

Cultural diversity policies in SVT and SR

Sweden has been an immigrant country since the late 1930s, and has a long history of political debate concerning media's role and responsibility in a multi-ethnic society. Given the changing demographics of Sweden, ethnic and cultural diversity is taken into account in the PSM's formulation of media strategies to attain new markets and audiences. In Sweden, 15 per cent of the current population is foreign-born, whereas the percentage for persons with a migrant background is 20 (Statistics Sweden 2012a).[5] The five largest migrant groups by country of origin are Iraq, Finland, Yugoslavia, Iran and Poland (Statistics Sweden 2012b). Among journalists, foreign-born professionals are under-represented. Recent figures from Statistics Sweden suggest a slight increase of foreign-born journalists from 5.4 per cent in 2006 to 6.6 in 2011. However only 2.5 percent were born in a non-European country (Statistics Sweden 2011). The past years' media diversity initiatives have seemingly had marginal effects (cf. Hultén 2009).

Journalists in Sweden express very strong support for the idea that the composition of journalists should reflect the composition of the population. Nearly nine out of ten journalists think it is important that representation of immigrant groups should correspond to that of the population as a whole (Djerf-Pierre 2007: 18–19). This can be viewed as a type of descriptive representation, with the idea that journalists should be descriptive of, or mirror, the people at large. In this context, it refers to the assumption that migrant groups may be represented by *descriptive representatives*, that is, individuals whose backgrounds reflect some of the experiences and outward features of belonging to the group. The functions of these representatives would be to add trustworthiness and to bring innovative thinking to the organizations. This standpoint is manifest in SVT's and SR's official documents, and is to a large extent shared by the interviewees. However, the mirror view provides few guidelines for selecting which characteristics merit representation. It says nothing about which groups should be represented or on what grounds.

Swedish Television
The diversity issues in SVT gained momentum when the company in 2002 denied a woman wearing a headscarf a position as a presenter. The DO [Ombudsman against ethnic discrimination] concluded that SVT's decision was against the law. As a result, SVT reconsidered its position. The shift of policy was not generated within the company but was the result of general and political changes in the society, one manager claimed. The debate and the publicity that followed were crucial to SVT's increased interest in diversity issues, reasoned respondent #3 (R3).

> It showed that SVT had lagged behind and forced us into a useful process. [...] These types of questions are not always highly prioritized, but the headscarf debate placed diversity concerns into focus in a new way. The discussions SVT had with the DO opened the way to a new diversity policy.

(R3)

Another consequence of DO's ruling was the establishment of the SVT Multicultural Centre, with the task of examining to what extent the company's programming complied with SVT's obligations. The centre was inspired by British Broadcasting Corporation

(BBC)'s Multicultural Programmes Department, set up in 1991. SVT developed a diversity policy, which was implemented by the end of 2002. One of the main features was that diversity should permeate the content, programming and staffing of SVT. An immediate consequence of the new alignment was the cancellation of *Mosaik*, which first aired in 1987. The programme was targeted at minority audiences and the objective was to 'reflect on and examine multicultural and multilingual Sweden' (Andersson 2000). A key notion in the new policy was mainstreaming, signifying that ethnic and cultural diversity should be taken into account in SVT's programmes, and that they should target a broad audience.

In SVT's 2002 annual report to the Swedish Radio and Television Authority, the word *diversity* is used to designate a variety of programme categories, voices and sources. The part of the report that deals with ethnic and cultural diversity is instead labelled 'multicultural Sweden' and includes sections concerning 'the multicultural society' and 'multicultural dimensions' of the programming as well as 'multicultural programmes' and 'multicultural perspectives' (Sveriges Television 2002: 33).

A new diversity policy was adopted in 2004, and was revised two years later. In the policy of 2006 the word 'multicultural' has been replaced by 'diversity'. The most common words in the policy are *ethnic, cultural, diversity* and *backgrounds*. The word *multicultural* is only mentioned in one context, which relates to SVT's commitment 'to regard multicultural qualifications' in recruiting and staffing (Sveriges Television 2006: 6). In April 2008 SVT adopted a new diversity policy that replaced the previous one. The word *multicultural* is now not mentioned at all. The new document is less than a page in length and states that SVT serves all and that:

> SVT shall assert the principle of equality of all people by promoting gender equality and increased diversity. SVT shall also combat discrimination in all forms. This should be reflected in both content and staffing
>
> (Sveriges Television 2008)

The policy also rules that generalizations should be avoided in SVT's programming. Moreover it asserts that different experiences and skills are to be considered as assets to SVT. The responsibility of implementing the policy is assigned to all managers at all levels. In the document *Om alla. För alla* (*About Everyone. For Everyone*) published in 2011, SVT firmly stresses the 'serve all principle' of public service broadcasting and emphasizes the company's democratic mission and the responsibility to reflect all of society.

> SVT allows programming about everyone, for everyone. And we really mean everybody, not only audiences that are commercially viable. By broadly reflecting the entire country, SVT can build bridges between people with different backgrounds. SVT has a special mission regarding some groups, such as children and the young, linguistic and national minorities and persons with disabilities.
>
> (Sveriges Television 2011: 33)

The document also states that 'SVT believes in the equal value of all viewers, but Sweden is becoming an increasingly divided country' (2011: 33). With programming that is 'permeated by the fact that Sweden consists of people of different ethnic and cultural backgrounds and with different beliefs and experiences' the company signals its integrative ambition to evoke a national conversation (2001: 26).

Swedish Radio

SR's first diversity policy, launched in 2002, had a different point of departure than that of SVT. According to respondent #5 the new orientation was a part of a general policy shift at that time. In 1999 the Swedish parliament passed a new anti-discrimination law. The Act on Measures Against Discrimination in Working Life on Grounds of Ethnic Origin, Religion or Other Belief entered into force. The multicultural policy that concentrated on ethnicity gave way to a diversity policy that covered the discriminatory categories mentioned in the law. This was in line with the wider concept of diversity that circulated among European policy makers, commented respondent #5 (R5). 'There was pressure from the EU in different contexts and documents in this direction. The shift didn't arise from within the company, more than anything we felt demands from outside' (R5).

This can be interpreted as adhering to the harmonizing principle of a European media policy dominated by an economic logic (cf. McQuail 2001: 76). A revised policy, appearing in 2006, emphasizes the democratic mission of the company and declares that Sweden is a multicultural society. Therefore, overall programming aims at appealing to all. 'SR has a mission to provide a range of programming that reflects the diversity of society. SR's central position demands, among other things, that the company set an example with regard to gender equality and ethnic diversity in programming' (Sveriges Radio 2006: 2).

The diversity policy has specific objectives for managers and supervisors. They are requested to analyse diversity efforts regarding both staffing and programming. They also have to annually formulate concrete and measurable goals, to consider diversity issues in recruitment, and to ensure that employees are aware of SR's diversity policy (Sveriges Radio, 2006: 7). The policy states that diversity should be a natural part of all of the company's programming and stresses that those differences are regarded as resources. In a handbook targeting all employees, SR details the policy, and gives instructions as to how to put the guidelines into practice. It states:

> We shall describe, examine and bring to life the multicultural Sweden in our regular programming in a natural way, which does not exclude programmes on ethnicity and cultural diversity.
>
> Diversity means that we choose topics, music and perspectives in an inclusive manner and fight the division between 'us and them', moreover that participants, experts and sources have different ethnic and cultural backgrounds.
>
> (Granér Magnerot 2012: 45)

In a recent strategic document outlining vital future issues, Swedish Radio stresses the company's role as an integrating factor in society: 'SR contributes [...] more than other media companies to create a common basis for the whole of Swedish society. The need to reach the entire population is of particular importance to the Swedish Radio' (Sveriges Radio 2011: 19).

Cultural diversity has a minor role in the document, and is actually only brought up once in connection with finding skilled employees. SR underlines that its mission 'presupposes diversity and breadth in both the social and ethnic backgrounds of the staff' (2011: 35). Recruitment is a major issue in the responses of the managers, an issue that will be discussed below.

Diversity at stake

In this and the following section I will discuss some of the key themes appearing in the interviews with eight managers responsible for formulating and/or putting the companies' diversity policies into practice. The interviews concern the attitudes towards and the implementation of the companies' cultural diversity policies. Before going into the managers' responses, I will give a give a brief account of how their staff perceive diversity.

A survey study was conducted in October 2008 in order to explore attitudes toward diversity among all employees at the three Swedish public service companies, SR, SVT and Utbildningsradion[6] (*Zebraprojektet vid SR, SVT och UR* 2009). The study was based on answers from some 2,400 employees and revealed that about 80 per cent of the respondents were of the opinion that more diversity was required in the workplace (2009: 7). The concept of diversity was foremost linked to gender and ethnicity. The survey showed that the Swedish public service companies are very homogenous workplaces, with only 6 per cent of the employees born in a non-Nordic country and 3 per cent born in a non-European country. Most of the respondents were in favour of efforts to enhance diversity but foresaw major hindrances in achieving those goals.

One-third felt that their working teams did not live up to the goals expressed in the companies' diversity policies. When those respondents were asked to state what most holds back diversity they identified the following factors (2009: 9):

- Severe workload and working against the clock
- Homogenous workteams
- Older patterns of recruitment
- Stereotypical thinking
- Fear of conflicts

The main measures that the employees proposed to promote diversity were management training and more active and wider forms of recruitment.

The diversity policy documents of Swedish Television and Swedish Radio demonstrate the companies' celebration of diversity and pluralism. Both SVT and SR are highly hierarchical organizations, which means that diversity policy support comes from above. Even if personal engagement in diversity issues is of importance, you need the backing of the top management, some of the interviewed managers commented. 'You can't lead your own diversity guerilla', as one respondent (R6) put it.

> I think most managers believe that diversity is important, so it is more a question of their mandate being clearly formulated. […] Instructions are required, as well as clarity regarding their assignments and it must be known by the company that diversity is a prioritized issue. In addition, there must be tools to follow up the results.
>
> (R2)

Several interviewees point to the dilemma of putting the policies into practice in a commercialized media climate. The market values of diversity are not articulated in SVT's and SR's policy documents, but are openly discussed within the companies and are brought up by the respondents. One manager's experience was that there was less room and money for pursuing various cultural goals. The respondent was critical of what SR had accomplished so far in terms of diversity. 'This issue [diversity] has been discussed a lot and for a long period of time. At one level there has been all talk and maybe not so much action' (R8).

Other interviewees argued that in a situation where the public service companies are challenged and put under pressure by commercial competitors, diversity strategies could prove to be of vital importance to PSM. 'We need to be role models in this field. It's imperative that we reach a variety of listeners and viewers and that we are able to equalize access to information, and in that way maintain a democratic function' (R1).

Market benefits were even considered by some to be the driving force to enhance diversity, and that the way to do it is by mainstreaming diversity in all programming.

> We are entering a media landscape of intense competition where more and more people realize the business benefits of diversity. There are audiences that SVT can't disregard. In the monopoly situation it was different perhaps. We can't afford to not make our programming accessible to as many as possible.
>
> (R3)

In some responses the serve-all and commercial arguments merged. Respondent #2 believed that what is good for business is good for the public.

> Of course there is a business value to diversity. The more people whose backgrounds are included in our programmes the more they are likely to watch them. So more diversity on the screen is also good from a commercial point of view. If large groups don't feel included, they make other choices since the range of channels and services is so vast.
>
> (R2)

But one respondent opposed the view that commercial values overshadow the serve-all principle of SVT.

> To me that is a very odd way of arguing. It is self-evident that a programme that doesn't have any viewers has no raison d'être. [...] If we don't hit the target, we won't have any viewers. If the news programmes looked exactly the same as they did 15 years ago, when SVT was more dominant within the market, I don't think we would have had as many viewers as we have today.
>
> (R4)

Several remarks concerned the difficulties in reaching certain groups. Immigrant groups listen to Swedish Radio to a very little extent, one interviewee (R8) said and continued: 'It is a problem that we don't reach these [migrant] groups with what we presently offer.' A minority of the managers believed that they could organize their diversity work better. In response to why this had not already been done, they mentioned that there are other issues that are 'more important to prioritize', such as dealing with reorganizations or budget matters. To others this attitude was not acceptable, and they considered goal-oriented efforts and monitoring to be indispensable tools in order to increase diversity in programming and staffing. One respondent addressed the lack of penalties if managers fail to address the issue of cultural diversity.

> Managers need to be aware of the importance of diversity and they must put pressure on the staff, otherwise diversity is easily forgotten. [...] If you don't fulfil the diversity goals it should have consequence: no increase in wages, for instance.
>
> (R1)

The interviewed managers expressed an awareness that their companies do not live up to the principles and goals expressed in official statements and policies. They indicated the difficulties in increasing diversity in a climate of budgetary restraints and growing market competition.

Representation and identification

Diversity efforts in SVT and SR have mainly focused on recruitment of journalists with migrant backgrounds. From 2005 to 2007 SVT took part in the FAIR project that focused on competence in the recruiting process.[7] The company declared that it was SVT's responsibility to be at the forefront in changing the workplace climate so as not to lose essential competence (Sveriges Television 2007: 66). The importance to the public service companies of opening themselves up to employees with varying backgrounds has been stressed in a variety of documents. But for the past few years both SVT and SR have instead reduced their staff.

The cultural diversity policies at Swedish Television and Swedish Radio declare that managers and supervisors are expected to consider diversity issues in recruitment and ensure that employees are aware of the content of the diversity policies. Several respondents point to the difficulties of increasing or even maintaining the diversity of the editorial staff in times of employment freezes and downsizing. The uniformity of the newsroom and the tight deadlines are regarded as hindrances to achieve the goal expressed in the news policy (cf. Hultén 2009). The interviewees singled out the white middle-class culture as a reason that innovative ideas were held back. An SR manager was responsible for a project aimed at recruiting persons with different cultural and ethnic backgrounds to the department and offer them training. 'We wanted to reach groups that we otherwise have difficulties in reaching,' the manager explained (R7). The newsroom was described as 'extremely homogenous' and the respondent continued: 'All have similar backgrounds, are the same age and come from the white middle class. That is what society looks like so we needed to do something very drastic.'

The interviewees considered the homogenous compositions of the newsrooms as a major hurdle. One SVT manager was of the opinion that the uniformity created a strong monoculture that was resistant to change and brought inertia to the system. 'Therefore it is difficult to enter a large news organization if you have a different cultural background,' respondent #4 concluded. Respondent #8 described the dilemma in this way:

It is problematic that most of the reporters [at this station] have the same values and backgrounds. If you have the journalistic notion that you should provide a multifaceted, complex picture of reality, it is not satisfying that only one perspective of this reality is described.

(R8)

Audience identification was a crucial argument for managers to take on journalists with diverse cultural backgrounds. 'In our programmes too few are heard that the listeners are able to identify with,' one respondent (R8) explained. SVT managers attached significance to the visibility of diversity and to the idea that people appearing in the programmes should visually signal cultural diversity. In a climate of staff reductions and budget cuts, some respondents felt that the recruitments became even more important. One manager (R8) drew attention to the risk-taking involved in the recruiting process and explained: 'I have to assess if this will cost more than it is worth for everyone involved.'

This is a very slimmed down organization and the rate of production is high. If I'm going to take on someone who is not immediately able to step into the production rate this creates greater demands on the rest of the staff.

(R8)

Both the scarcity and the importance of minority representations produce what many have called *the burden of representation*. One interviewee clarified (R4): 'When someone [with a different background] is hired, that person is easily regarded as a representative of the entire immigrant community, which is not ok.' And respondent #7 added: 'When you take on a person with a different background in the newsroom, editors may feel that now this person can cover integration issues. We don't want to have it that way.' But having a different background is a quality that is sought after. Managers were looking for competences that were lacking in the newsrooms and for a network of contacts that the other employees did not have. One respondent (R4) commented that the employees of the station rarely were visible in neighbourhoods with large immigrant populations and that those perspectives were easily lost.

The arguments for a descriptive representation are salient in the responses. The presence of *diverse individuals* would then function as a symbolic marker and would increase the legitimacy of the Swedish public service corporations. It can be argued that the interests of migrant groups in principle can be looked after as well by representatives that are not members of the group in question. One manager touched upon this and on the need to change attitudes among those already employed. 'We have our democratic mission of reflecting all dimensions of society. My impression is that most of our employees strive for that. So that's not the problem. It's more about our own values and experiences' (R3).

A study presenting interviews with journalists who have migrant backgrounds in the Stockholm region revealed that they often expressed disappointment with their company's efforts to improve diversity in hiring and in content. The journalists drew attention to the need to change editorial organization patterns, reporting practices and newsroom cultures as well as the need to redefine journalistic missions regarding ethnic diversity (Hultén 2009).

The responsibilities of public service news media regarding diversity affect the established routines and the occupational ideology of journalism. Traditional newsroom practices and news patterns are persistent. Only two of the interviewed managers mentioned difficulties in building diversity in the news processes, and pointed out the difficulties in controlling the journalists because professional standards of questioning authorities guide their work, rather than the management requirements. Respondent #5 was not convinced that recruiting staff with minority backgrounds would change the content. 'Do you really get something different? Will there be different perspectives or other news stories, or will they be the same? The structures of journalism are very firm. If you have totally different ideas, you will be punished' (R5).

The conclusion was that diversity entails unequal power relations and that minority groups will remain marginalized until they enter mainstream institutional structures. In addition, the respondent stressed that diversity generates more conflict in a workplace, and described Swedish companies as extremely afraid of conflicts. 'I do not know if we really are prepared for diversity.' (R5).

Conclusion

This chapter illustrates the gap between principles and practices in SVT's and SR's diversity policies and the tension between unity and diversity. Diversity in media content and in staffing is perceived as a good thing, however complex to operationalize and achieve. Cultural diversity policies can contribute to newsrooms that are more open to pluralism, but cannot eliminate or resolve the complexity of the challenges of the media industry. The dynamics of diversity are connected with – or even propelled by – market mechanisms. In a transforming media climate where PSM are under increased market pressure, cultural diversity is identified as a vulnerable value at stake in the Swedish public service companies Sveriges Television and Sveriges Radio.

The recruitment strategies in SVT and SR have focused on finding and hiring persons with minority backgrounds based on Sweden's demography. This approach of descriptive representation remains strong. In a document outlining SR's strategy for the coming years it is stated that:

> Newsrooms are excluded from further cuts, and the local channels have been given additional resources enabling them to recruit staff from other ethnic backgrounds, to better cover areas that Swedish Radio traditionally has not reached. The editorial mission, and efforts to reach out to everyone in the Swedish society, requires diversity and breadth in both the social and ethnic backgrounds of the people.
>
> (Sveriges Radio 2011: 45)

The issue of representation is equally central among the interviewed managers. The main motivation cited for recruiting journalists of migrant backgrounds was that they would bring different and new newsbeats and perspectives to journalism. However it remains unclear to what extent this strategy has been successful.

Efforts to reach specific target groups, such as migrant groups, have an underlying business purpose. Market considerations were strong in getting managers to seek journalists with migrant backgrounds who can provide identification with a potential audience. This type of recruitment is not unproblematic. Journalists with foreign backgrounds experience and oppose the burden of representation in the newsrooms (see Hultén 2009). The analyses of the policy documents and the responses raise questions as to what *diverse* really is and what *difference* is meant to accomplish. The effectiveness of the implementation of cultural diversity policies is often hard to assess and difficult to measure (Love 2001: 93–94). As Sarita Malik concludes, most diversity policies are well-meaning and difficult to implement but also easy to dodge (Malik 2002: 184). Further research needs to analyse more clearly how this *new* and *different* is taken up by SVT's and SR's editorial offices and made present in mainstreamed media content.

One conclusion that may be drawn is that diversity as formulated and interpreted by the Swedish PSM has its limits. Only to a restricted extent do policy documents and interviews touch upon the companies' hierarchic organizations, newsroom structure, organizational structure and power relations, all of which have impact on diversity in the workplace. It is not sufficient to consider the presence/absence of people with migrant backgrounds in content and in the workforce. Nor is it viable to rely on the market logic in order to ensure ethnic/cultural diversity in programming and workforce.

Taking diversity seriously would call for more nuanced strategies of representation and a broader view on diversity. This would include increasing the range of views, values, interests and opinions expressed. The envisioned changes of bringing a diversity of voices into PSM will not be facilitated by primarily focusing on who represents them. Attempts to appeal to new audiences may however be less attractive to the present core and mainstream audiences. That is the core groups that Swedish public service companies need to rely on in order to survive on the market and legitimate the public in PSM.

References

Andersson, M. (2000), *25 färgrika TV-år: De mångkulturella programmen från SVT 1975 – 2000/25 Colourful Years in TV: SVT's Multicultural Programming, 1975–2000*, Stockholm: SVT.

Asp, K. (2007), *Mångfald och kvalitet: Public service-TV 1998–2006 – en utvärdering/ Diversity and Quality: Public Service TV 1998–2006 – An Evaluation*, Haninge: Granskningsnämnden för radio och TV.

Blumler, J. G. (1992) 'Vulnerable values at stake', in J. G. Blumler (ed.), *Television and the Public Interest: Vulnerable Values in West European Broadcasting*, London: Sage, pp. 22–42.

Carlsson, U. and Harrie, E. (eds) (2010), *Nordiska public service-medier i den digitala mediekulturen: Pengar, politiken och publiken/Nordic Public Service Media in the Digital Media Culture: The Money, the Politics and the Audience*, Gothenburg: Nordicom.

Cottle, S. (1997), *Television and Ethnic Minorities: Producers' Perspectives: A Study of BBC In-house, Independent and Cable TV Producers*, Aldershot: Avebury.

Cottle, S. (1998), 'Making ethnic minority programmes inside the BBC: Professional pragmatics and cultural containment', *Media, Culture & Society*, 20: 2, pp. 295–317.

Cottle, S. (ed.) (2000), *Ethnic Minorities and the Media: Changing Cultural Boundaries*, Buckingham: Open University Press.

Djerf-Pierre, M. (2007), 'Journalisternas sociala bakgrund'/'The social background of journalists', in K. Asp (ed.), *Den svenska journalistkåren/Swedish Journalists*, Gothenburg: JMG, pp. 17–31.

Freedman, D. (2008), *The Politics of Media Policy*, Cambridge: Polity.

Granér Magnerot, A. (ed.) (2012), *Public service-handbok/Public Service Handbook*, Stockholm: Sveriges Radio.

Hallin, D. and Mancini, P. (2004), *Comparing Media Systems: Three Models of Media and Politics*, Cambridge: CUP.

Horsti, K. and Hultén, G. (2011), 'Directing diversity: Managing cultural diversity media policies in Finnish and Swedish public service broadcasting', *International Journal of Cultural Studies*, 14: 2, pp. 209–27.

Hultén, G. (2006), *Främmande sidor: Främlingskap och nationell gemenskap i fyra svenska dagstidningar efter 1945/On the Strange Side: Estrangement and National Community in Four Swedish Daily Newspapers after 1945*, Stockholm: Stockholm University.

Hultén, G. (2009), 'Diversity disorders: Ethnicity and newsroom cultures', *Conflict and Communication Online*, 8: 2, http://www.cco.regener-online.de/. Accessed 11 June 2013.

Kretzschmar, S. (2007), 'Diverse journalists in a diverse Europe? Impulses for a discussion on media and integration', in K. Sarikakis (ed.), *Media and Cultural Policy in the European Union*, Amsterdam: Rodopi, pp. 203–226.

Lentin, A. and Titley, G. (2011), *The Crises of Multiculturalism: Racism in a Neoliberal Age*, London: Zed.

Love, A. J. (2001), 'Assessing the implementation of cultural diversity policies', in T. Bennett (ed.), *Differing Diversities: Transversal Study on the Theme of Cultural Policy and Cultural Diversity*, Strasbourg: Council of Europe Publishing, pp. 93–106.

Löfgren, O. (1997), 'Att ta plats: Rummets och rörelsens pedagogik'/'Taking up space: A pedagogy of room and movement', in G. Alsmark (ed.), *Skjorta eller själ? Kulturella identiteter i tid och rum/Shirt or Soul? Cultural Identities in Space and Time*, Lund: Studentlitteratur, pp. 21–37.

Malik, S. (2002), *Representing Black Britain: A History of Black and Asian Images on British Television*, London: Sage.

McCracken, G. D. (1988), *The Long Interview*, Newbury Park, CA: Sage.

McQuail, D. (2001), 'The consequences of European media policies and organisational structures for cultural diversity', in T. Bennett (ed.), *Differing Diversities: Transversal Study on the Theme of Cultural Policy and Cultural Diversity*, Strasbourg: Council of Europe Publishing, pp. 73–92.

Nordicom (2013), *Statistik om medier i sverige/Statistics on Swedish Media*, http://www.nordicom.gu.se/?portal=mt&main=showSveStats.php&menu=menu_sve&me=7&media=Television&type=media. Accessed 13 October 2013.

Scannell, P. (1990), 'Public service broadcasting: The history of a concept', in A. Goodwin and G. Whannell (eds), *Understanding Television*, London: Routledge, pp. 11–28.

SFS 2008:567, *Diskrimineringslag/Discrimination Act*. Stockholm: Integrations-och jämställdhetsdepartementet, http://www.ud.se/sb/d/108/a/115903. Accessed 13 October 2013.

Statistics Sweden (2011), Arbetsmarknad/Labour market, http://www.scb.se/Pages/SSD/SSD_TreeView.aspx?id=340478. Accessed 13 October 2013.

Statistics Sweden (2012a), Befolkningsstatistik/Population statistics, http://www.scb.se/Pages/ProductTables_____25795.aspx. Accessed 13 October 2013.

Statistics Sweden (2012b), Befolkningsstatistik/Population statistics, http://www.scb.se/Pages/SSD/SSD_TreeView.aspx?id=340478. Accessed 13 October 2013.

The Swedish Broadcasting Authority (2013), *Media Development 2011*, http://www.radioochtv.se/Publikationer-Blanketter/Publikationer/. Accessed 13 October 2013.

Sveriges Radio (2006), *Policy: Mångfald på Sveriges Radio/Policy: Diversity in the Swedish Radio*, http://sverigesradio.se/sida/artikel.aspx?programid=3113&artikel=2058657. Accessed 13 October 2013.

Sveriges Radio (2011), *Sveriges Radio mot 2019: Avsiktsförklaring vid Kontrollstationen 2011/Swedish Radio towards 2019: Declaration of Intent at the Control Station 2011*, http://sverigesradio.se/sida/artikel.aspx?programid=3088&artikel=4854114. Accessed 13 October 2013.

Sveriges Television (2002), *Sveriges Televisions public service-redovisning 2002/The Swedish Television's Public Service Report 2002*, Stockholm: SVT.

Sveriges Television (2006), *Policy för etnisk och kulturell mångfald i SVT 2006/Policy for Ethnic and Cultural Diversity within SVT 2006*, Stockholm: Sveriges Television.

Sveriges Television (2007), *Sveriges Televisions public service-redovisning 2007/The Swedish Television's Public Service Report 2007*, Stockholm: SVT.

Sveriges Television (2008), *Mångfaldspolicy för SVT/Diversity Policy for SVT*, Stockholm: SVT.

Sveriges Television (2009), *Sveriges Televisions public service-redovisning 2009/The Swedish Television's Public Service Report 2009*, Stockholm: SVT. http://www.svt.se/omsvt/fakta/public-service/. Accessed 13 October 2013.

Sveriges Television (2011), *Om alla. För alla/About Everyone. For Everyone*, Stockholm: SVT.

Wieviorka, M. (2001), *La Différence/The Difference*, Paris: Les Éditions Balland, http://classiques.uqac.ca/contemporains/wieviorka_michel/la_difference/la_difference.html. Accessed 13 October 2013.

Zebraprojektet vid SR, SVT och UR . Rapport av förprojektering/The Zebra Project at SR, SVT and UR. Report of a Project Plan (2009). Unpublished document.

Notes

1. The interviews were conducted in the respondents' workplace between April 2008 and October 2009 and between November 2010 and March 2011. The method used was the semi-structured individual interview. The interviews were between 40 and 60 minutes long, and were recorded and transcribed in their entirety. In writing up the results, the analysing process aimed at discerning and organizing the emerging patterns and themes in the respondents' answers (McCracken 1988). The examination has been inspired by Simon Cottle's concept 'professional pragmatics' (1998), here used as the managers' professional and practical responses to policy-

making and implementation in an institutional context. At the time of the interviews the respondents were Managing Diversity Officials, Managing Editors and/or Executive Producers. The investigation focuses on how professional aims in their programme and/or policy-making activities are articulated. The interviews focused on the following overarching themes: attitudes, interpretations, strategies and implementation regarding policies for cultural diversity.

2. *Mosaik* was broadcast from 1987 to 2003, *Språka* from 1976 to 1998 and *Aktuellt för invandrare* from 1976 to 1995 (Anderson 2000). *Brytpunkten* was broadcast from 1998 to 2007.

3. The Swedish Broadcasting Authority was formed on 1 August 2010 after the Radio-och TV-verket (The Swedish Radio and TV Authority) and Granskningsnämnden för radio och TV (The Swedish Broadcasting Commission) were wound up.

4. Including Croatian and Bosnian.

5. The definition of migrant background used by Statistics Sweden implies a person born abroad, or whose parents were both born abroad.

6. The Swedish Educational Broadcasting.

7. FAIR, Future Adapted Inclusive Recruitment, was developed by the EU Equal partnership.

Chapter 8

The Politics of a Multicultural Mission: Finland's YLE in a Changing Society

Karina Horsti (University of Jyväskylä)

Introduction

Ramadan fell in August in 2010, which was not that easy for those Muslims who happen to live in the Nordic countries. Daylight began at 6:00 a.m. and lasted until 9:00 p.m. This was a newsworthy aspect of the religious festival, and in Finland Ramadan was covered on the front page of the nationwide newspaper *Helsingin Sanomat* (28 August 2010) and in the main newscast of the public service television news channel *Yleisradio* (YLE) TV1 (11 August 2010). Both media outlets ran the story from the perspective of Muslims living in the metropolitan Helsinki region. It is only recently that Finnish news began to cover Ramadan as a domestic event.[1] Before, if Ramadan was covered, it appeared in the foreign news section, or if it was treated as a domestic issue, the story was scheduled in a multicultural 'niche' programme such as *Basaari/Bazaar* (YLE, 1996–2008) (e.g. 11 October 2004).

The shift in the treatment of Ramadan reflects the *YLE Erityis – ja vähemmistöryhmien palvelustrategia/YLE Policy on Services for Minorities and Special Groups* (YLE 2005b), which guided the company towards the mainstreaming of cultural diversity across all programming during 2006–2010. The aim of this policy was both to reach minorities – ethnic, national and disabled minorities – and to tell stories about culturally diverse Finland for mainstream audiences. In 2008, the multicultural *Basaari* programme ended, and the editorial office that trained and supported media practitioners of minority backgrounds was closed. The decision manifests as a turning point in the implication of the minority policy (YLE 2005b). The company shifted from a multiculturally oriented media policy to a cultural diversity policy that highlights mainstreaming diversity across all programming and the production of cross-cultural entertainment programmes. Ethnic minority journalists no longer have the support of the *Basaari* editorial department but are on the market 'as any other journalist', as Ismo Silvo, a manager at YLE, puts it in an interview that I had with him just before *Basaari* ended (Silvo 2008).

The minority policy (YLE 2005b) lasted only five years as a transition from the period of *Basaari* to the current situation where YLE does not have a specific policy for ethnic minorities but applies the more general principles set by YLE law and general strategy documents. The analysis of programming after *Basaari*, between 2009 and 2013, shows that YLE highlights cross-cultural formats that construct media personalities, make comedy out of group identities and invite audience participation in multiple media platforms. The only exception is the Russian-speaking minority which, contrary to the general policy of mainstreaming diversity, receives stronger services in the minority language, Russian. YLE justifies extending the news service in Russian not only on the grounds of providing a minority service but also as a means to balance the news flow from neighbouring Russia with 'credible news from a Finnish perspective' (YLE News 2013).

This chapter analyses policy documents, websites and other textual materials and interviews with YLE policy makers and programme makers to examine why, when and how policy that recognizes immigrant and ethnic minorities has developed and changed in Finland. Furthermore, I analyse how the policy shifts connect to the demands set by both commercialization and democratic principles that influence PSM policies today. Particularly, the analysis is contextualized in the current politicization and polarization of immigration and integration topics. The policy changed from multiculturalism to cultural diversity at a time when nationalist populism began to take root in Finland and a general Europe-wide 'crisis of multiculturalism' discourse began to shape policies elsewhere in the region. Through policy-making, YLE aimed to carefully balance its public position between the nationalist sentiments and its responsibility to serve, as its slogan says, 'the whole people', including ethnic minorities. Yet in a country that has relatively recently shifted from a country of emigration to that of immigration, the imagined 'wholeness' of the people is undergoing redefinition.

Diversity in Finland

Finland has a tradition of diversity policy in the form of bilingualism, and YLE has developed sensitivity to linguistic diversity issues since its foundation in 1926. The second official language group, the Swedish-speaking minority has traditionally gained relatively strong resources and positions within the public service broadcasting company YLE. The Swedish-language media in Finland forms an institutionally complete media system (Moring and Husband 2007) and, therefore, it cannot be seen as minority media in the same sense as media catering to ethnic minorities, including the so-called national minorities of the Roma and Sami, which have been subject to discrimination and marginalization in several ways throughout history (for more about multilingualism in Finland, see Latomäki and Nuolijärvi 2005).

Only since the early 1990s, the number of migrants to Finland has grown, but it still is one of the smallest in the European Union. Only about 3 per cent of the population has a foreign nationality, and 4.4 per cent has a 'migrant background'.[2] However, in some areas, namely in the metropolitan region, the numbers are higher than elsewhere in Finland. In the capital, Helsinki, 9.2 per cent of the population and 12.2 per cent of children up to 15 years old have a mother tongue other than the official national languages of Finnish, Swedish or Sami (City of Helsinki, City of Espoo and City of Vantaa 2010: 9–11).[3]

In Finland, the anti-immigration sentiments have become more organized only recently. The populist (True) Finns Party[4] has had a series of successes from the municipal elections of 2008 and the European parliamentary elections of 2009 to the parliamentary elections of 2011, when the party increased its number of seats from the previous 5 (2007) to 39 (2011). It became the third-largest party and the main opposition party. The Finns Party has roots in the more traditional populist protests against modernization and the European Union rather than in right-wing populism. However, the anti-immigration group inside the party is visible and active and has gained a foothold in its organization and political agenda, particularly after the parliamentary elections of 2011. In addition, the other larger parties – the Social Democrats, the Coalition Party and the Centre Party – are divided when it comes to immigration issues.

Since the elections of 2008, the Internet has turned out to be a popular and influential space where anti-immigration arguments are debated and developed. In 2008, an online debate forum, *Homma-forum*,[5] launched the concept of *maahanmuuttokriittinen* (literally, immigration criticism) to argue that sentiments against immigration were not racism, but a realistic social critique. Some of the main issues championed by these populist movements are 'direct civic democracy', as they call it, and critique of the current immigration politics in Finland.[6] This framing of 'immigration criticism' turned out to be successful, and the position of 'realism' gained support, also amongst many in the mainstream parties and media. The discursive space in Finland shifted from a politically correct silence to politicization of the immigration topics after 2008 (e.g. Keskinen, Rastas and Tuori 2009; Horsti and Nikunen 2013).

Public service media in Finland

In the Nordic countries, some level of state intervention in the media market has been understood to be important for democracy (Hallin and Mancini 2004: 145), thus public service broadcasters are still important. For instance, in Finland, YLE television channels had a 42.2 per cent audience share in 2012 (Finnpanel 2012), and they have a reputation for quality and accuracy. However, increased competition and commercialism in the media landscape influenced the content, production and audience relations of PSM in Finland where economic discourse penetrated society in the 1980s and was strengthened in the economic recession of the early 1990s (Herkman 2005: 52–57). YLE develops its services across different media platforms and, as a response to digitalization, in 2013 the funding model shifted from a television licence fee to a public service media tax.

The organizational structure and YLE policy, which is bound by the Act on YLE, construct the environment where programming is produced. Parliament appoints the administrative council, and the company is state owned. YLE needs to be analysed as part of the European media system and as part of the national media system, where it has a unique institutional position as a publicly funded and supported media company (Jääsaari 2007: 24). Media policies are crucial for managing the institution and explaining the need for it to the society. Through policy-making, PSM organizations balance their practice and programming and define their role, particularly when market pressure tends to overrule public interest (see Raboy 2003: 42).

Thus, at the beginning of the new millennium, YLE was influenced from several directions to voice out their strategy regarding minorities. First, immigration began to rise, and second, commercial imperatives strengthened while democratic principles needed to be sustained. Third, mushrooming of multicultural media policies across European public service media (see the other chapters in this volume) pressured the Finnish YLE to 'internally put together thoughts and establish the line' (Silvo 2008). The outcome was the *YLE Policy on Services for Minorities and Special Groups*. In the next section, I analyse empirically how the policies pertaining ethnic minorities are articulated in the YLE policy documents and in the interviews with producers and managers in 2005–08, a time period when the first minority policy document was created and adopted. In the concluding chapter, I discuss the later policy developments in this field.

Critical policy analysis

Critical policy analysis (e.g. Stevens 2003; McGuigan 2002; Bacchi 2009) treats policy as a culturally, socially and politically constructed problematization of an issue. The idea of 'policy' is critically scrutinized, and thus this approach differs fundamentally from general policy research, which has the main aim of making more efficient policy. Reports, strategy papers, policy papers and websites are understood as written institutionalized accounts. 'An ethnography of texts' (Ahmed et al. 2006) is compiled for the purposes of analysing a variety of texts and interviews with managers and producers. These interviews at YLE add to, interpret and sometimes critique the more official policy papers. I have collected policy briefs and papers, documents, training materials and websites of YLE that deal with ethnic minorities, immigration, multiculturalism or cultural diversity. (For a detailed list of research materials, see the reference list at the end.)

The interviews at YLE in the summer of 2008 took place right after the decision to end the multicultural 'niche' programme *Basaari* was announced. I interviewed five people who have contributed to or implemented minority policies at YLE (see the list of interviews in references). The interviews were transcribed and analysed using the methods of critical discourse analysis. One central figure in the multicultural programming, Seppo Seppälä, had already retired; and the former chief of cultural programming, who had a history of developing *Basaari*, Elina Paloheimo, and departmental manager Mauri Vakkilainen retired soon after the interviews. Project manager for Mundo (2004–2007) Marita Rainbird, who had been a key figure for *Basaari*, had a temporary contract, which was not renewed. Actually, only the director of strategy and planning, Ismo Silvo, continues to work for YLE. Thus, it comes as no surprise that while I was doing the interviews, the atmosphere amongst many at YLE was affected by puzzlement.

The ending of YLE's *Basaari* programme connects with a generational shift in the organization as many of those who were first to sensitize their organization to gender and diversity issues in the 1980s and 1990s retired from their positions. Ms Paloheimo had proposed establishing a multicultural office for the YLE management, claiming that it would restore the organization's competence and would make use of the networks the *Basaari* office had created amongst minority communities. The management did not support this, and currently there is no person appointed to take responsibility for cultural diversity within the institution. The issue of cultural diversity is 'business as usual' as Mauri Vakkilainen (2008) puts it in the interview.

Multiculturalism in YLE's media policy

The YLE Act and EBU regulations (see Chapter 3 in this volume) guide the responsibilities YLE has for minorities in Finland. In the research interviews, the law is raised as an important motivation for creating the *YLE Policy on Services for Minorities and Special Groups*. (See also similar arguments in the case of Sweden in Christensen [2001: 92].) The YLE Act (YLE 2012) demands programming, in order of importance, in the Finnish and Swedish languages as well as in Sami, Romani and sign language and, 'where applicable, in those of other language groups'. Thus, the act avoids commitments to programming in the languages of new migrants, yet it makes such commitments possible, an opportunity that YLE took in 2013 when it extended Russian news programming to television. In addition, it also requires the development of civic skills across the population and the promotion of 'tolerance and multiculturalism' (YLE 2012). These ideals are in the line with the democratic corporatist tradition, which values high professional standards of conduct, commitment to a common public interest and autonomy from other social powers (Hallin and Mancini 2004: 145).

The case of *Basaari*

In the interviews, Elina Paloheimo, who was the manager of cultural programmes of YLE TV1 in the 1990s, recalls that YLE adapted ideas from other European PSM organizations:

> When the number of immigrants began to rise, an idea was raised. Should we somehow understand this and should the public receive more knowledge? […] I think I had seen funny and good programmes in the festivals and thought that we should be able to do something like that.
>
> (Paloheimo 2008)

Paloheimo and some other individual producers at YLE picked up the idea for an immigrant-specific programme slot from European examples such as *Mosaik/Mosaic* (SVT, 1987–2003) in Sweden. The *Basaari* programme began in 1996, and it was a product of multiculturalist-policy thinking that had taken root in European public service broadcasting collaborations (see Chapter 3). The programme had a two-dimensional goal. First, it aimed to offer services to minorities, and second, to disseminate stories of other cultures and the multicultural reality to the mainstream population.

YLE ended the *Basaari* programme and closed the editorial department at the end of 2008 after twelve years of programming. Audiences and television critics did not seem to care about the ending of the programme as there was no public debate about the issue. Maasilta, Simola and af Heurlin's (2008) survey amongst audiences of 'migrant background' demonstrates that the programme was not very important to them. Many television viewers of immigrant origins prefer a commercial channel to the public service channel when they watch Finnish television (Maasilta, Simola and af Heurlin 2008: 36, 45). However, *Basaari* should not be treated only as a programme slot as it was, from the beginning, also an educational project and an editorial community that supported journalists and media students who were of minority backgrounds. An example of the educational function was a training programme, the Mundo Project, which was largely funded by the European Commission's European Social Fund's EQUAL programme in 2004–07. It offered a stepping stone for 24 students of minority backgrounds who completed the programme.

Ending *Basaari*, which was located in the Factual Programme Department in 2008, was in line with the policy directions taken by the EBU and by several leading European public service broadcasters such as the NPS, SVT and the British Broadcasting Corporation (BBC) (see chapters 2, 6 and 8 in this volume). The decision is also in line with the YLE minority policy that was in effect between 2006 and 2010 (YLE 2005b). The preliminary report to the policy paper requires YLE to increase 'a general visibility of minority groups'; offer more services in 'experiential, fiction and entertainment programmes'; and 'in YLE's brand/imago, strengthen the message that YLE serves special and minority groups and fosters dialogue' (YLE 2005a). The only exceptions to the new policy of mainstreaming diversity across all programming are the programmes in Sami, Romani, English, Russian and sign language. Russian speakers are the only immigrant group for which YLE provides online, radio and television programming in their own language (other than the English language). Russian speakers make the largest minority language group (after the second national language, Swedish) in Finland. However, this is not the sole reason for the deviation from the general policy of mainstreaming cultural diversity. Programming in Russian is also argued to be necessary because YLE assumes that Finnish Russians' close connections with Russia and the other Russian speakers in Finland would hinder integration and increase biased information, a belief that is widely shared in Finnish society. Programming in a minority language is argued on the basis of integration. In 2008, manager Ismo Silvo argued,

YLE wants to provide YLE journalism in Russian because, could we say, the character of Russian speakers is to live amongst themselves. Their media behaviour grounds on Russian-language media in Russia. We see that it would be a good thing if the Finnish-language media would have a connection to the Russian-speaking minority living in Finland.

(Silvo 2008)

This concern for the Russian minority's integration is not only present in YLE, but it is a wider understanding amongst Finnish media managers. The nationwide newspaper *Helsingin Sanomat* maintained that a Russian-language newspaper produced in Finland deserves to be subsidized because supporting the 'integration of Russian speakers into Finland would be worthwhile' (Blåfield 2008). In 2013, the newspaper praised the launch of YLE television news in Russian, arguing that '[n]ews made with Western journalistic principles are a splendid way to strengthen the integration of a growing linguistic minority into the Finnish society. Providing quality news also in television will help us avoid misunderstanding and purposeful communication' (Anon. 2013). The issue referred to in the editorial is not only the integration of Russian immigrants in Finland but also the concerns over the ways in which the Russian media have covered child welfare practices and child custody disputes that involve Finnish authorities and Russian parents. The media conflict between the two countries on child welfare was particularly acute in 2012 and 2013, the time when YLE expanded its news production in Russian.

Missionary intervention and the market approach

The interest in minority policies at YLE developed in the 1990s from ideas of equality and human rights that those inspired by other European experiences promoted. Gender equality had been an issue in the 1980s, and ethnic minority equality grew out of this heritage. Gender equality has remained on the policy agenda, and it is measured in different ways every year. As the company was sensitized to one type of equality and ethics – gender – ethnic minority equality was a continuum to that debate in the late 1990s. In addition, the national minorities of the Sami and the Roma and the disabled raised their demands for identity recognition. Furthermore, bilingualism sensitized the company to issues of minority languages and cultures. However, whereas gender equality, bilingualism and services for the disabled have become institutionally recognized and are monitored as part of the company strategy, commitment to multiculturalism is vaguer, and to some extent, it rests on the individuals. Elina Paloheimo, now-retired Chief of Cultural Programming at YLE, has concerns over the success of the mainstreaming policy: 'Things tend to change as long as there are at least a few people who stubbornly keep these issues on the table. Of course, I am scared now when I leave. I have been one of those thorns in the flesh' (Paloheimo 2008).

Multiculturalism entangles with mission discourse as the following examples demonstrate. Department Chief Mauri Vakkilainen stresses personal interest in minority equality when he mentions a former director, Ann Sandelin, who influenced multicultural policy-making at the managerial level:

> She was the director of Swedish-speaking programming, and thus, in a way, she had social experience of being in the minority [...] her cultural background, minority perspective was a natural part of her thinking. There were her type of people in the management [...] those who naturally understood [multiculturalism] and who had a strategic eye for this.
>
> (Vakkilainen 2008)

Likewise, Marita Rainbird, who directed an EU-funded multicultural recruitment programme, Mundo, stresses individual involvement. There is a sense of an emotional and more profound meaning of equality and dedication that seems to drive her work:

> Multiculturalism [...] has pended on the personal interest of one or two people. [...] I think the key to success is that the company can find people who have the soul of a human rights fighter, that you believe in the cause and work like crazy endlessly for that. If there is no one who believes in these issues [...].
>
> (Rainbird 2008)

In this quote, I recognize that Rainbird is not only relying on the enthusiasm and mission of herself and people like her but also argues that this devotion energizes and inspires others in the organization. This is why she is so concerned about the future scenario (which has actually been realized) that there is no particular individual, that there is 'no one' left to fight for the cause. This focus on exceptionally brave individuals positions multiculturalism as a quality of an individual journalist, programme maker, producer or manager. Multiculturalism in this line of thought is understood as a mood or an attitude, and a wrong kind of attitude can be retrained, or people with the right attitude can be hired to work for the organization. There are several accounts in the media sector (e.g. Cottle 1998; Malik 2002; Hultén 2009) and in other sectors (Ahmed et al. 2006) of 'racial positioning' and the 'burden of representation', particularly when professionals of ethnic minority backgrounds are positioned as diversity champions embodying diversity for the organization. Ahmed et al. (2006) consider an even distribution of diversity and responsibility across an organization very crucial for success and equality amongst professionals. However, they stress that it is not enough to say everyone is responsible as it typically ends up that no one is responsible. Committed individuals need strong support from the leadership and support from the internal structures and systems of the institution. This was not the case at YLE at the end of the *Basaari* period. A quote from Marita Rainbird about her visit to the YLE management to introduce a European training kit called *A Diversity Toolkit* (FRA 2007) illustrates this well: 'We went to see the management with Elina Paloheimo [producer of *Basaari* at the time] and presented the toolkit. I could see that everything we said went into one ear and came out from the other. It was shocking' (Rainbird 2008).

When she experienced this in 2008, the mission-oriented understanding of multiculturalism had already become a burden in the minds of the YLE management. In the interview, Ismo Silvo argues that the effect of niche programmes is limited exactly because of their mission ethos: 'Since this type of factual program [*Basaari*] serves only the believers – those who are tolerant already, understand and support the cause - it has no effect. The believers strengthen, but the sinners became more sinful' (Silvo 2008).

As we can see, understanding multiculturalism as a mission appears both amongst the managers at YLE and the editors close to *Basaari*. However, the worth of the mission is valued differently: as a resource amongst the *Basaari* editors and as a politicized burden amongst the managers. Both sides understand multiculturalism as one social paradigm of thinking, and for the management, the multicultural mission discourse has become politicized along with the more general politicization of immigration and integration topics in Finnish society. This politicization is not only a Finnish issue, but it also comes up amongst other European cultural diversity promoters. For instance, a diversity editor for the BBC, Elonka Soros, mentioned in a European workshop that the BBC would not publish the European training tool *A Diversity Toolkit* on its website because cultural diversity is a politically delicate issue.[7] Furthermore, immigration and integration issues are not necessarily understood as important fields of competence. *A Diversity Toolkit* was also used at YLE as training material. However, implementing the training was not without suspicion amongst the news editors, as Elina Paloheimo (2008) explains, 'It is clear that, particularly, news reporters are, well, quite a self-important and arrogant crowd. They are not easily advised.'

The strategy that led to the cancellation of *Basaari* on YLE distanced itself from a mission-oriented discourse that relied on enthusiastic individuals. Instead, it approached the issue more with a market-oriented policy, which is articulated differently at YLE compared to countries that have larger migrant communities – for instance, Sweden (Horsti and Hultén 2011). In terms of the audiences, YLE needs to fulfil its legal requirements and construct a progressive public image of equal and inclusive public service 'for all'. However, it should not irritate those audiences that feel threatened by the recent social and demographic changes. This complex situation is articulated in the interview with Ismo Silvo (2008). First, he explains the concerns: 'YLE cannot be that much ahead of Finnish society because it will hit back […] the majority, the intolerant majority – that is, the intolerant majority hits back.' Later in the interview, he reminds of the responsibilities to serve minorities: 'The strategy is that we will increase multicultural programming as Finland becomes more multicultural. Like I said, a bit on the forefront. That is the responsibility.'

A visible difference on-screen was a crucial target of the minority policy (YLE 2005b). The company wanted audiences to see that YLE is fulfilling its legal and ethical requirements. The *YLE Policy on Services for Minorities and Special Groups* (YLE 2005b) highlighted that in its public image, YLE needed to 'strengthen the message that YLE serves also special and minority groups and promotes dialogue between them and the general public' (YLE 2005b). The policy document continues, 'This increases the popularity of the public service amongst the eyes of the audiences'. The *Preliminary Report* (YLE 2005a) talks about recruitment and visibility of 'diverse personnel' on-screen. Yet there is a discrepancy between policy documents. The recruitment of media experts of diverse backgrounds is not mentioned in the heavier yearly human resources reports until, suddenly, the issue appeared once in the report of 2011:

> Multicultural structure of the personnel is an added value for the YLE that promotes good client relations. In order to reach all Finns, we need men and women of diverse ages and from diverse ethnic and cultural backgrounds as programme and service makers. The goal is that in 2014, YLE personnel will be more diverse than it is today, reflect the surrounding Finnish society more than it does now. For instance, this means more recruitment of those who have an immigrant or disabled background.
>
> (YLE 2011b)

In the policy papers and in the interviews, there is no discussion about quotas or monitoring of cultural diversity. Recruitment and visibility of minorities is a sensitive issue for YLE as it does not wish to displease any major section of Finnish society. Opposition to these affirmative action types of policies is one of the targets of the anti-immigrant section of the (True) Finns Party.[8] Niche funding, recruitment on the basis of 'affirmative action' and 'immigrant slots' are policies the nationalist-populists would strongly oppose. Whereas the management at YLE seemed to be between these two fires, those close to *Basaari* were more confident that the audiences were open to diversity in content, recruitment and representation. However, as Ms Rainbird explains, they felt that the structural support in the organization was not adequate enough: 'I am not in doubt that the audience would not be ready [for more diverse programming], but are they here [at YLE] ready for it? There are some people who have strong prejudices' (Rainbird 2008).

The importance of minorities as audiences and media professionals still remains a future scenario in Finland. The idea of reaching relevant audiences and collaborators is mentioned only in the *Human Resources Report* of 2011 (YLE 2011b), yet the audience reports do not mention cultural diversity. The audience reports are based on quantitative monitoring such as panel surveys; methods that cannot capture ethnicity and cultural diversity. The managerial level at YLE assumes that once the number of immigrants grows and the new generation reaches adulthood, the current lack of media professionals from minority backgrounds gets 'naturally' solved. Ismo Silvo explains,

> It is important to recruit people with an ethnic background, but it is easier said than done. This person needs to fulfil all the high professional criteria. Perhaps today we have such a time window that these types of people exist in Finland, perhaps even

the second-generation immigrants or the first generation who arrived in Finland as children. Some have taken a university degree and speak Finnish better than me. We have seen these amongst those seeking for employment. We aim at getting that [the number of professionals with ethnic backgrounds] to a certain level.

(Silvo 2008)

Conclusion

YLE has been sensitive to cultural and linguistic diversity since its establishment in the 1920s in the form of bilingualism. In the 1980s, gender issues and the national Indigenous Sami minority's and the disabled interests groups' stronger identity politics paved the way for the claims of the new immigrant minorities in the 1990s. YLE is required by law to provide programming for the national minorities and for the Swedish speakers, but policies regarding other minority groups are less explicit. YLE recognized the new immigrant minorities, first through a multiculturalist policy, by setting up a niche programme, *Basaari,* and a specific editorial office. The transition phase from multiculturalism to a more general policy of mainstreaming cultural diversity across all programming emerged in the form of a specific policy for minorities (YLE 2005) during 2006–10. After these two explicit interventions, YLE now articulates its minority policy only at a very general level. Since 2005, discourse that considers multiculturalism as a mission has lost its attractiveness in Finnish PSM policy. This is a policy orientation that follows shifts in neighbouring Sweden and beyond in northern Europe. One development that has shaped policy in this direction is the increased commercialization and competition in the media environment.

Interventions such as assistance for journalists with a minority background and niche programming for and about minorities are difficult to articulate in market-oriented terms in a country that still has a relatively young history of international migration. Furthermore, the rapid rise of nationalist populism and a general Europe-wide 'crisis of multiculturalism' mentality have shaped the ways in which policies are articulated and implemented in PSM. The recent general policy documents like the *Annual Report* (YLE 2011a) and the *YLE of the people – YLE strategy* (YLE 2012) reflect a national discourse. The terms Finnish and Finnishness are repeated in connection to culture, audience and citizenship. Cultural diversity is not mentioned in these texts at all (except for the one paragraph in the *Human Resources Report* [YLE 2011b]). The national framing also prevails in the YLE justification for expanded news service in Russian, a position that is echoed in privately owned national media like the *Helsingin Sanomat.* The dominance of Russian-language media use amongst the Russian minority has generated concerns in Finnish society, both in terms of (non)integration and (mis)framing.

Nevertheless, in the interviews for this study, the YLE policy makers foresee audiences from minority backgrounds as a future concern. In addition, in 2011, the

YLE *Human Resources Report* for the first time publicly announced a goal to increase recruitment of media experts from minority backgrounds. In addition, the multiplatform media landscape opens up new types of opportunities for ethnic minorities. The new commercialized and digitalized media environment has generated programming that involves audience participation, media personalities and spreadable content. The most recent examples of YLE programming show that ethnic minorities have made it to the mainstream, particularly via social media. A Sami sketch comedy programme called *Njuoska bittut/Märät säpikkäät* (*The Wet Leg Warmers*) (Tarinatalo/YLE TV2, 2012–13) featuring two young Sami women, Suvi West and Anne Kirste Aikio, attracted attention in social media before the actual television programme began airing. Similarly, a radio talk show called *Ali ja Husu* (*Ali and Husu*) (YLE Puhe, 2013) hosted by Ali Jahangiri and Mohamed Abdirahim Hussein, both from refugee backgrounds, involves audience participation through social media.

These examples show how the new media and participatory formats open up spaces for minorities and marginalized voices. Yet the focus on media personalities individualizes minority politics, a process that reflects the current broader discursive shift away from group-oriented multiculturalism. In addition, it gives the impression that anyone could participate on equal terms, omitting the inequalities that exist in Finnish society and media representations. Social media and participatory culture have also given space for polarization and anti-immigrant voices (Horsti and Nikunen 2013).

The *YLE of the people – YLE strategy* (YLE 2012) offers a promise for a more structural change that in principle could open up to more inclusive policy and practice regarding multiculturalism. This, however, is only an opportunity yet to be realized. The strategy orientation at YLE is to 'fulfil promises to targeted audiences' and to produce programming and projects with 'partners', 'companies' and 'social actors' (YLE 2012). These could mean collaboration with ethnic minorities and understanding culturally diverse audiences as 'targeted audiences'. However, cultural diversity, multiculturalism or citizens of ethnic minority backgrounds are not specifically mentioned in these policy documents. What this omission means for YLE is yet to be seen.

References

Ahmed, S. et al. (2006), *Race, Diversity and Leadership in the Learning and Skills Sector* [Final report], Lancaster: Lancaster University.

Anon (2013), 'Novosti YLE on hyvä uutinen'/'Novosti YLE (YLE News in Russian) is good news'. Editorial, *Helsingin Sanomat*, 7 May 2013.

Bacchi, C. (2005), *Analysing Policy: What's the Problem Represented To Be?*, French Forest: Pearson.

Blåfield, A. (2008), 'Suomalaisin silmin'/'With Finnish eyes'. Editorial, *Helsingin Sanomat*, 8 March 2008.

Christensen, C. (2001), 'Minorities, multiculturalism and theories of public service', in U. Kivikuru (ed.), *Contesting the Frontiers: Media and dimensions of identity*, Gothenburg: Nordicom, pp. 81–102.

Cottle, S. (1998), 'Making ethnic minority programmes inside the BBC: Professional pragmatics and cultural containment', *Media, Culture & Society*, 20: 2, pp. 295–317.

Finnpanel (2012), 'TV-mittaritutkimuksen tuloksia'/'TV-rating results', http://www.finnpanel.fi. Accessed 13 May 2013.

European Agency for Fundamental Rights) (FRA) (2007), *A Diversity Toolkit for Factual Programmes in Public Service Television*, Barcelona: FRA.

Hallin, D. and Mancini, P. (2004), *Comparing Media Systems: Three models of media and politics*, Cambridge: CUP.

City of Helsinki, City of Espoo and City of Vantaa (2010), *Vieraskielisen väestön ennuste Helsingin seudulla 2010–2030/Estimate of foreign language population in Helsinki region*, Helsinki: Helsingin kaupungin tietokeskus.

Herkman, J. (2005), *Kaupallisen television ja iltapäivälehtien avoliitto: Median markkinoituminen ja televisioituminen/Marriage of commercial television and tabloid press*, Tampere: Vastapaino.

Horsti, K. and Nikunen, K. (2013), 'The ethics of hospitality in changing journalism: The response to the rise of the anti-immigrant movement in Finnish media publicity', *European Journal of Cultural Studies* 16: 4, pp. 489–504.

Horsti, K. and Hultén, G. (2011), 'Directing diversity: Managing cultural diversity media policies in Finnish and Swedish public service broadcasting', *International Journal of Cultural Studies*, 14: 2, pp. 209–27.

Hultén, G. (2009), 'Diversity disorders: Ethnicity and newsroom cultures', *Conflict and Communication Online* 8(2).

Hultén, G. and Horsti, K. (2010), 'In case of diversity: Dilemmas of sharing good practices across borders in European broadcasting', in E. Eide and K. Nikunen (eds), *Media in Motion: Cultural Complexity and Migration in the Nordic Region*, Oxford: Ashgate, pp. 19–35.

Jääsaari, J. (2007), *Consistency and Change in Finnish Broadcasting Policy*, Turku: Åbo Akademi University Press.

Keskinen, S., Rastas, A. and Tuori, S. (2009), 'Suomalainen maahanmuuttokeskustelu tienhaarassa'/'Finnish immigration debate at crossroads', in S. Keskinen, A. Rastas and S. Tuori (eds), *En ole rasisti mutta … Maahanmuutosta, monikulttuurisuudesta ja kritiikistä/I am not a racist but … On immigration, multiculturalism, and criticism*, Tampere: Vastapaino, pp. 7–21.

Latomäki, S. and Nuolijärvi, P. (2005), 'The language situation in Finland', in R. B. Kaplan and R. B. Baldauf Jr (eds), *Language Planning & Society: Europe Vol 1: Hungary, Finland and Sweden*, Clevedon: Multilingual Matters.

Maasilta, M., Simola, A. and af Heurlin, H. (2008), *Maahanmuuttaja mediankäyttäjänä/An immigrant as a media user*, Tampere: Tampereen yliopisto.

Malik, S. (2002), *Representing Black Britain: A History of Black and Asian Images on British Television*, London: Sage.

Moring, T. and Husband, C. (2007), 'The contribution of Swedish language media in Finland to linguistic vitality', *International Journal of the Sociology of Language*, 2007: 187-188, pp. 75–101.

McGuigan, J. (2002), 'Cultural policy studies', in J. Lewis and T. Miller (eds), *Critical Cultural Policy Studies*, Oxford: Blackwell, pp. 23–42.

Paloheimo, E. (2008), interview by K. Horsti, Helsinki, 3 June.

Raboy, M. (2003), 'Rethinking broadcasting policy in a global media environment', in G. Lowe and T. Hujanen (eds), *Broadcasting & Convergence: New Articulations of the Public Service Remit*, Gothenburg: Nordicom, pp. 41–56.

Rainbird, M. (2008), interview by K. Horsti, Helsinki, 25 June.

Silvo, I. (2008), interview by K. Horsti, Helsinki, 25 June.

Statistics Finland (2010), *Väestö syntymämaan, kansalaisuuden ja äidinkielen mukaan 2010/Population according to country of birth, nationalism and mother tongue*, Helsinki: Statistics Finland. http://www.stat.fi/til/vaerak/2010/vaerak_2010_2011-03-18_kuv_002_fi.html. Accessed 3 June 2011.

Stevens, L. P. (2003), 'Reading first: A critical policy analysis', *Reading Teacher*, 56: 7, pp. 662–69.

Vakkilainen, M. (2008), interview by K. Horsti, Helsinki, 3 June.

YLE (2012) *Act on Yleisradio Oy* (1380/1992; amendments up to 474/2012 included), http://www.finlex.fi/en/laki/kaannokset/1993/en19931380.pdf. Accessed 7 October 2013.

YLE (2005a), *YLE Erityis – ja vähemmistöryhmien palvelustrategian valmistelu: HR-työryhmän raportti/YLE preliminary report for the strategy for special and minority groups service*, 31 October, Helsinki: YLE.

YLE (2005b), *YLE Erityis – ja vähemmistöryhmien palvelustrategia/YLE Policy on Services for Minorities and Special Groups*, http://www.yle.fi/fbc/palvelustrategia.pdf. Accessed 28 August 2009.

YLE (2011a), *Vuosikertomukset/Annual Reports*, http://yle.fi/yleisradio/vuosikertomukset. Accessed 11 January 2013.

YLE (2011b), *Henkilöstökertomus/Human Resources Report*, http://yle.fi/yleisradio/vuosikertomukset/henkilostokertomus-2011/toimintakulttuurin-tasa-arvoisuus. Accessed 11 January 2013.

YLE (2012), *Koko kansan YLE – YLEn strategia/YLE of the people – YLE strategy*, , http://yle.fi/yleisradio/yle-lyhyesti/koko-kansan-yle-ylen-strategia. Accessed 11 January 2013.

YLE News (2013), 'Mitä mieltä olet venäjänkielisistä tv-uutisista?'/'What do you think of the TV-news in Russian?', *YLE News*, http://yle.fi/uutiset/mita_mielta_olet_venajankielisista_tv-uutisista/6638137. Accessed 13 May 2013.

Notes

1. Since 1990, the nationwide *Helsingin Sanomat* has reported on Ramadan as a domestic news event only occasionally, in 2001, 2007 and 2010. Ramadan has been a regular topic of the foreign news section of the newspaper. News items dealing with Ramadan were searched for on dates between 1 January 1990 and 7 September 2010. A similar archive is not available for YLE.
2. Official statistics in Finland do not use race/ethnicity categories. Foreign nationality, country of birth and mother tongue are classified in the statistics. 'Migrant background' refers here to those who have a foreign nationality, have been born in another country, have a mother tongue other than Finnish, Swedish or Sami and those who have been born in Finland but have another mother tongue (Statistics Finland 2010).
3. The statistics use the concept of *vieraskieliset* (foreign language), which refers also to 'strange' or 'alien' in the Finnish language.
4. The party Perussuomalaiset changed its English name from True Finns to Finns in 2011.
5. http://cms.hommaforum.org/. Accessed 13 August 2010.
6. They argue that immigration politics is run by elites and that the majority of Finns would like tougher immigration and integration policies. This they prove with surveys and polls. According to their agenda, immigration and integration politics should be decided by the people in direct voting, and new technology should be developed for this type of politics.
7. Elonka Soros, Diversity Editor, BBC, *Diversity Show*, 'Diversity Toolkit: Working group discussion', 6 November 2008, Hilversum. Notes of the workshop by Karina Horsti. The Diversity Toolkit for Factual Programmes in Public Service Television is an initiative of the European Broadcasting Union and the Fundamental Rights Agency that can be downloaded at http://fra.europa.eu/fraWebsite/media/materials_trainings/diversity_toolkit_en.htm. Accessed 28 June 2011.
8. For instance, a member of parliament, Mr Jussi Halla-aho strongly opposes any preferable treatment of ethnic minorities in his blog and in the address of the True Finns, a parliamentary group that uses multiculturalist discourse to argue against affirmative action: http://www.halla-aho.com/scripta/katsaus_julkilausuman_kirvoittamiin_kommentteihin.html. Accessed 28 June 2011.

Chapter 9

The Multicultural Mission in Public Service Broadcasting:
The Case of Norway

Gunn Bjørnsen (Volda University College)

In an afternoon broadcast of the Norwegian Broadcasting Corporation (NRK) during the fall of 2008, we heard an interview with two Norwegian Pakistani men who were recruiting ethnic Norwegians to their local cricket club. A feature on the upcoming Hajj, the Muslim Pilgrimage to Mecca, was also broadcasted. Topics like these are rarely covered in Norwegian prime-time broadcasts. Both reporters had bicultural backgrounds and at the time they were participating in the newly established FleRe[1] project, a recruitment initiative started by NRK in order to increase the number of journalists with multicultural backgrounds on its staff. In January 2010, news anchor Fawad Ashraf, whose parents are Pakistani, moved to Islamabad to report news from the region on behalf of NRK. Ashraf's long-term assignment was path-breaking in the sense that NRK acknowledged that a multicultural background was a useful journalistic competence in international reporting.

These examples illustrate a public broadcaster in motion regarding how it relates to multicultural[2] Norway. NRK is in the process of defining itself in an increasingly diverse and heterogeneous society. Public broadcasters have an explicit social responsibility with regard to how they present and *re*present ethnic minorities in their broadcasts. NRK thus has a particularly central role in the 'reality production' of the public multicultural discourse. When the public changes, public service must change with it. Today's major demographic and cultural transitions represent one of the most fundamental challenges facing journalism today. Formally and factually, what do these changes mean for NRK as the most important public broadcaster? This article aims to explore how NRK shapes its role in the multicultural and rapidly changing Norway.[3]

The terrorist events of 22 July 2011 in which 77 persons were massacred, serve as a tragic background for the present Norwegian discourse and debates on immigration and integration and the role of journalism in these processes. Although the material discussed in this chapter is mainly before 22/7, in this introduction it makes sense to include the Norwegian national trauma as a contextual factor. Multiculturalism was explicitly under attack. The extreme right-wing attitudes of the perpetrator, as they were expressed in the so-called 'manifest', triggered the population to communicate togetherness across cultural differences. The political party that is furthest to the right ('the Progress Party') was silent in the weeks after the attack. Many of the victims had multicultural backgrounds, and the expression, 'the new Norwegian we' was often used. For the first time, we also witnessed a priest and an imam conducting a funeral together, according to the wish of one of the victim's parents (originally from Iraq). This was meant to symbolize the integration and reconciliation between Muslims and Christians, and got broad media coverage. In the aftermath of the terrorist events, discussions about the role of journalists in covering multicultural society before, during and after the massacre have been put on the agenda. Perspectives have included both whether the press has been too reluctant to include extreme right-wing attitudes in the immigration and integration debate and, on the other hand, whether the press to a large degree still contributes to simplification and stereotyping in describing multicultural society to itself.

The issues of the extent to which the media should play an active part in the integration of ethnic minorities have generally increased in scope throughout the last decade. These issues have arisen from and been facilitated by debates concerning multiculturalism. We observe an increasing awareness of and attention to the purpose journalism really should serve in a multicultural society. The role of the press is obviously particularly important when we take into consideration the substantial role it is assumed to have in forming the public's ideas of 'the others'. Still relatively few ethnic Norwegians socialize with minorities on a personal level (cf. Gullestad 2002; Bråthen et al. 2007).

NRK plays a unique role in this setting. The oldest and only licence-funded public service broadcaster bears a special responsibility for how the media deals with immigration and integration issues and has a vital role in the construction of national identity. One of NRK's prominent goals is to 'strengthen Norwegian language, identity and culture' (3-3 of NRK's bylaws). What 'Norwegian' identity and culture really means, however, is not obvious, taking into account the so-called 'new Norway'.

This chapter concerns NRK's role as public service broadcaster in multicultural Norway, with the goal of fulfilling a 'journalistic mission'. I will describe some key features of the multicultural policy and illuminate its development throughout the last decade by presenting selected 'multicultural events' in NRK's history. NRK's self-presentation relating to the coverage of multicultural Norway, as expressed in the institution's annual reports from 2000 to 2010, will also be discussed. An underlying issue is the tension between 'the multicultural' as a special trait/field/theme and as a potential *dimension* of mainstream broadcasts. What is Norwegianness, and how is 'Norwegian language, identity and culture' understood in the NRK context?

The chapter is based on studies of documents, both public and in-house, as well as interviews and meetings in NRK. A central background is an ethnographic fieldwork spanning over four months in a newsroom in NRK.

Migration, policy and journalism

Although Norway always has been an immigration society (Kjelstadli 2008), the country has a relatively short history of welcoming inhabitants from (previously[4]) so-called non-western countries. The main immigration from these countries began in the early 1970s with worker immigrants from Pakistan. Labour immigration ended in the 1980s and most immigrants during the last 20 years have been family members and refugees. In the late 1990s, the European Union and European Economic Area legislation allowed people from former Eastern Europe to immigrate to Norway for employment. Today Poles represent the largest immigrant group in Norway. The largest group of immigrant descent is Pakistani (i.e. born in Norway of two foreign-born parents). The other large immigrant groups are Somali, Iraqis and Vietnamese. Today 13 per cent of Norway's population has an immigrant background (including 'western' countries) (Statistics Norway 2012).

The challenges facing journalism in a multicultural society have continually been included as a topic in government documents in recent years. During the spring of 2010, the Directorate for Integration and Diversity (IMDI) released its annual report with (the bold) title, *Immigrants in Norwegian media: Media-created fear of Islam and invisible daily life*. An entire chapter of the report of the Norwegian Directorate for Immigration (UDI) on racism and discrimination in Norway (2001–02) was dedicated to 'Ethnic discrimination in the media'. In a report by the Norwegian government (2003–04), *Diversity through inclusion and participation: Responsibility and freedom*, it was stated that 'if someone's way of life, faith and experiences are repeatedly scrutinized in the media, it will affect the general image of immigrants' (Ministry of Labour 2003: 66).

In recent years, the Norwegian immigration debate has increased in both intensity and volume. Disputes over the Muhammad caricatures and hijab debates (in multiple, repetitive rounds), forced marriage and female circumcision are examples. Public debates on integration have been heavily attended. Comments on the Internet have reached new heights, in both number and content. A relatively new phenomenon in recent years is that also the voices of opposing participants with multicultural backgrounds are increasingly heard in the public sphere. In the aftermath of 9/11, the caricature disputes and the terrorist events of 22 July, the challenges facing the role of the press in a transnational and highly globalized world have become increasingly prominent and linked to fundamental issues concerning freedom of speech in a transnational context.

NRK has a long and broad history of conducting programming to represent the Norwegian population. NRK Sami Radio, a channel targeting the Sami segment of the population, has become a miniature-NRK, with multiple local offices and daily broadcasts covering most aspects of society on TV and radio as well as online. NRK's policy concerning the Neo-Norwegian (*Nynorsk*) language also illustrates their idea of public representation and diversity. There are two official written languages in Norway, Norwegian and Sami. Norwegian has, however, two different versions: Neo-Norwegian (or, as the Language Council of Norway prefers, 'Norwegian Nynorsk') and Norwegian (*Bokmål*). The so-called Neo-Norwegian is based on the original dialects in the countryside and was established during the mid-nineteenth century to provide an alternative to Danish, which was the written language at the time.[5] Around 10 per cent of the population use Neo-Norwegian as their preferred written language (Grepstad 2005). The use of Neo-Norwegian is an important identity marker and accentuates issues of minority/majority relations in several ways. The focus of this chapter is, however, on the 'new' ethnic minorities. Nevertheless, it is useful to understand NRK and multiculturalism from a broader perspective of diversity with regard to experience gained from coverage and representation of the Sami people, the Neo-Norwegian language and the hearing impaired.

'The mission of journalism', or rather the idea of it (cf. Roppen and Allern 2010), is an integrated part of the self-understanding of Norwegian journalists, and can be said to have a legitimizing function in their influence in society (Allern 1997, Hovden 2008). The journalistic mission can be understood as a democratic ideal (political), as part of the professional ideology, as a 'false ideology', and possibly as sugarcoating for commercial purposes (Allern 2001: 22). A central principle is the self-governance of the press. The guidelines concerning the multicultural programme requirements for public service broadcasters and the rules of the regulatory authority for media (Medietilsynet) may thus seem paradoxical because such regulations can be seen as restrictions on the idea of an independent and self-governed press.

Problematic programme requirements

It is obvious that licence-funded public broadcasters are in a special position with regard to general expectations of how to conduct their business. They are subject to political guidelines to ensure that basic democratic values are fulfilled, such as mirroring the demographic of the country and reaching every segment of the population.

In Norway, both the Swedish public service broadcaster SVT and the British Broadcasting Corporation (BBC) have been role models for the coverage of ethnic minorities. The BBC has had a policy on diversity and equality for almost thirty years and SVT[6] for almost ten (since 2004). An 'equal opportunities employment policy' was implemented by the BBC as early as 1983, and in 1999 over eight per cent of their workforce stemmed from a background of ethnic minorities (Born 2004: 201–02). It should, however, also be noted that critical voices have been raised concerning how the BBC deals with and portrays multicultural society (Horsti and Malik in this volume).

In the case of Sweden, SVT's multicultural guidelines have gone from a clear multicultural profile (reflecting multiculturalism as a policy) to become increasingly vague under the label of 'cultural diversity' (Horsti and Hultén 2011a). The development of public broadcaster policies in different countries reflects national values that contribute to a better understanding of the role of the media in the representation of (ethnic) difference in varying societies. Differences in how different countries handle issues of migration in the media must obviously also be understood in the context of their various migration patterns.

The Norwegian Media Authority formulated guidelines, which apply to media institutions with the status of public broadcasters (i.e. government funded or concession dependent). The following summary shows the official requirements for the different Norwegian public broadcasters:

- Radio Norge ('Radio Norway'): *The concessionaire must have a weekly broadcast that explores multicultural themes, recruits workers with foreign-cultural backgrounds and includes multicultural perspectives in their programming in general, particularly in their news and current affairs programming.*
- P4: P4 must broadcast … *80 editions and 70 hours of programmes for and about multicultural Norway.*
- TV 2: *TV 2 must have programmes or segments specifically produced for ethnic minorities.*
- NRK: … *NRK's nationally broadcasted programming must, both in radio and TV, at the least maintain programming for national and linguistic minorities.*

(Medietilsynet/The Norwegian Media Authority 2009)

These directives indicate various levels of details and ambitions for each individual broadcaster, which must be understood historically. NRK's programme requirements have deep and long roots, which is evident in other managerial documents as well. TV 2's requirements have few details with regard to programming, whereas the very precise requirements for Radio Norge and P4 must be understood in the light of the competition among channels for the main radio concession in 2004.

The requirements again show how problematic categorizing minorities can be. What and who 'the multicultural' are is not at all evident. The word used the most often in the programme-requirements is 'multicultural'. In addition the terms 'ethnic minorities', 'national and linguistic minorities' and 'foreign-cultural' are used. These terms have similar connotations and challenges (cf. note 2). The term 'foreign-cultural' is also a non-accepted and outworn expression within Nordic migration research; 'foreign' implies distance. NRK uses the expression 'national and linguistic minorities'. The term 'linguistic minorities' refers to 'the new multicultural people', while 'national' minorities include Finnish descendants, Jewish people, Rom and Romani people.

Furthermore, challenges exist concerning how the programming should be modelled, that is, whether it should be *for* and/or *about* the multicultural Norway. There is a significant difference between being the target audience and the *subject* of a programme.

The multicultural programme requirements can be viewed as emphasizing the main goals of Norwegian public service broadcasting in general. The ambition is to reach both large and small or narrow audiences, contribute to strengthening Norwegian identity *and* serve a democratic function that ensures that all voices are heard. NRK's obligations must also, and especially, be understood in light of the NRK charter, which was put into practice in 2008 and emphasizes the government's expectations of NRK as a public broadcaster (Bjørnsen 2009).

Because it is licence funded and state owned, NRK has a particular responsibility to meet all different kinds of programming obligations. NRK's multicultural programme requirements are generically formulated as follows: 'NRK's collective national programme assortment must, both in radio and TV, at the very least contain programmes for national and linguistic minorities' (NRK bylaws 2004 [programme requirements]: para. 3–5, sect. g). The NRK bylaws also state that in their core business, NRK must 'offer content that appeals to broad layers of the population and protect the interests of minorities and special groups'. Programmes and broadcasts must 'collectively offer wide socially relevant coverage and thus reflect the diversity of culture, life views and living conditions that exist in different parts of Norway' (NRK bylaws 2004: 2). Other managerial documents also deal with multicultural issues. The most relevant is, as mentioned, the NRK charter of 2008 (incorporated in the bylaws in 2009). It states that 'NRK shall spread knowledge of, and reflect the diversity of the Norwegian society. NRK shall create arenas for debate and information about Norway as a multicultural community. [And] […] NRK shall offer programmes for minorities' (NRK plakaten/the NRK charter 2008: sect. 3[b], 3[c]).

With regard to these sections of the charter, we observe a development from the earlier wording 'NRK shall offer programmes for national and linguistic minorities on both radio and TV' (i.e. the original bylaws) to also include the formulation 'spread knowledge of and reflect the diversity of the Norwegian society' and 'create arenas for debate and information about Norway as a multicultural community' (NRK 2008). These directives are, however, general and say nothing about either the *scope* or the *type* of programming.

NRK's first committee for diversity was established in December of 2009 and with it, NRK's first diversity strategy. This committee 'works with increasing representation of multicultural people – both as staff workers and as contributors and sources in programs' (FleRe 2010). The strategy also includes a gender perspective.

From ethnic humour to affirmative action

How has NRK historically actually managed and shaped its multicultural mission? In this section, I explore some selected events in NRK's relatively recent history of immigration with particular attention to programming and the recruitment of workers with multicultural backgrounds.

From a historical perspective, ethnic diversity at NRK has mainly been represented by immigrant radio programming with news broadcasts in the language of the largest immigration groups as well as Sami programmes. In a broader understanding of diversity, as previously mentioned, we must also note that sign language and the widespread subtitling of programmes have long traditions at NRK. In addition, the requirement that 25 per cent of the broadcasts be conducted in Neo-Norwegian is interesting in a broader perspective of diversity. The processes linked to the social organization of significant differences have common features independent of *which* differences are made relevant (as elaborated in Eriksen and Breivik 2006).

Immigrant radio in Norway was established in 1976. The first radio broadcasts for immigrants consisted of news in Urdu. In the 1980s, the programming expanded to include broadcasts in Turkish and Vietnamese. In 1997, the immigrant editorial staff was fused into *Østlandssendingen*, the NRK district newsroom for Oslo and surroundings, because of reorganization and low listening numbers, among other reasons. News broadcasts for immigrants reemerged under the name *Migranytt* (*Migranews*) in 1998, and included broadcasts in Somali and Bosnian, Croatian and Serbian, although Turkish was dropped. This change was not a complete success (cf. headline in Enger 2006: 281; 'Migranews: No big success'), and the programmes were halted in 2001.

In 1997, the multicultural magazine *Migrapolis* went on-air for the first time, and in 2005, the programme debuted as a weekly magazine on radio as well. The goal of *Migrapolis* was to cover multicultural Norway across the entire population and to 'create dialogue among cultures' (NRK's annual report 2007). After a major editorial overhaul in 2004, and in particular, a change of channel from NRK2 to the main broadcast NRK1, the viewership doubled. *Migrapolis* had become a mainstream programme. It is interesting to note that Norway is the only Nordic country still running this kind of multicultural programme, which is considered 'anachronistic' in our neighbouring countries. In Sweden, *Mosaik* (*Mosaic*) (SVT, 1987–2003) ended in 2003, and the Finnish *Basaari* (*Bazaar*) (YLE, 1996–2008) ended in 2008 (Horsti and Hultén 2011b).

In a different genre, *Radio Yalla* (literally meaning 'Radio let's go') went on-air for the first time in 1999. This programme featured in the show *Ukeslutt* (*End of the week*) between 1999 and 2001 and with segments on the Saturday main news (*Radio Yalla TV*) beginning in 2000. *Radio Yalla* consisted of humorous skits about immigrants encountering the Norwegian reality, which were presented in a witty, partly satirical style and a strong accent. The programme is especially interesting as an example of a relatively early ethnic humour programme about multiculturalism by NRK. *Radio Yalla* can also be understood as an expression of making immigration seem non-threatening during a period when most ethnic Norwegians did not know people with minority backgrounds. The programme went on-air when very few key voices with migrant backgrounds were heard in the public sphere.

Migrapolis and *Radio Yalla* are examples of two very different expressions of how NRK has related to the multi-ethnic society during the last decade. A systematic progression of programmes and pieces with a multicultural dimension and themes since the waves of immigrants from Pakistan started in the 1970s might be expected to illustrate patterns that in varying degrees mirror the developments in society during the same time. Much has happened since 1971 when the question, 'Do you think that Pakistani foreign workers have any right to come to *our* country?' was asked in the programme *Mennesker søker ny fremtid* (*People Seeking a New Future*) (aired 20 November 1971). In the 1980s, the programme series *Mot et mangfoldig samfunn* (*Towards a diverse society*) dealt with immigration issues to a large extent framed through comparisons with the Norwegian emigration to USA during the 19th century. A Saturday guest on the news of 31 January 1987 was simply introduced, and objectified, as 'a Pakistani'. In the 1990s, questions concerning Norwegian dietary habits arose: 'is the potato on its way out and the kebab in?'*Sommeråpent* (*Summer Open*, 10 July 1996). And in the programme *Ordspor* (*Word Tracks)* the leader of the organization 'African Youth', Amani Olubanjo Buntu, pointed out that

> Parts of the Norwegian media are stuck in earlier times. It's still funny to take pictures of an African person skiing. […] What do you think about the snow? What's your position on fishcakes? It's like Africans got here *yesterday*! There are indeed some questions and descriptions which really should have been history by now.

This statement was made in 1999.[7] In the new millennium, reporter Noman Mubashir explores his Pakistani roots in the series *En Noman i Pakistan* (*A Noman in Pakistan,* 2006). And in the *Eurovision Song Contest* final in Oslo in 2010, only one of the three hosts was 'monocultural'. Since 2008, the recruitment initiative 'FleRe' has also left its mark on broadcasts in multiple programmes and formats.

New Norwegians in NRK

Because of the recognition that there is a correlation between journalists' ethnic backgrounds and journalistic content (Jensen 2000; Pham 2002; Bjørnsen 2003; Mikkelsen 2009), recruitment is considered central. NRK as 'the white house' has been discussed both internally and in public for many years. NRK journalists Atta Ansari and Rajan Chelliah have promoted increased recruitment of journalists with multicultural backgrounds for NRK as well as other media corporations for many years, primarily through a minority project organized by the Oslo branch of the Norwegian Union of Journalists. Colleague Noman Mubashir was also engaged in the lack of recruitment, as for example expressed in the chronicle 'Ali kurerer gruff' /'Ali cures rust' (*Aftenposten*, 31 December 2007). A milestone in Norwegian broadcasting was achieved when the same Mubashir appeared as the first news anchor with Norwegian Pakistani roots on *Østlandssendingen* in 1998. Mah-Rukh Ali became the first multicultural anchor on nationally broadcasted television when she appeared on the evening news in 2006.

The recruitment project, FleRe, has made a difference in the presence of multicultural staff. Former *Migrapolis* chief, Marianne Mikkelsen, was one driving force that led to the establishment of the project in 2008. Each semester, five journalists are recruited as interns. They receive paid training and practice in NRK over a period of six months. In the fall of 2010, the project was extended to a one-year period instead of six months. Group number eight started in August 2012, and most interns continue to work in different branches of NRK after completing their internship. An interesting fact is that the FleRe-project was inspired by and built on the same model as the Neo-Norwegian Media Center, which was pioneered in 2004. Their project recruits ten Neo-Norwegian-speaking interns a year for training and practice over a period of six months.[8]

Simultaneously and probably in interaction with the establishment of FleRe, multicultural issues have been increasingly raised in other areas over the last couple of years. In 2008, NRK established a directory of multicultural sources. The idea was to stimulate and increase the use of different kinds of sources with multicultural backgrounds. The Christian monopoly was suspended the same year, not without debate, and was launched on NRK's websites under the title 'All religions have a place in NRK' (NRK 2008). The first Eid-prayer (Muslim holiday after the Ramadan month) was broadcasted on NRK in September 2008. In 2009, NRK conducted a study among listeners and viewers on their attitudes towards reporters with accents. The study showed that only one out of three persons thought reporters must be able to speak Norwegian without an accent. In NRK, accents have moved towards recognition as on par with dialects.[9]

Something for everyone? Always?[10]

One way of mapping developmental traits and changes in NRK's attitudes and actions in multicultural Norway is to study the annual reports. These reports can be understood as documents representing NRK's self-presentation and narration as well as the institution's view of to what degree and how it fulfils the programme requirements. The following discussion is based on annual reports from the last decade, 2000 to 2010.

The most eye opening, clear and not unexpected differences between NRK's annual reports from 2000 to 2010 is (the physical) *scope* of content with a multicultural dimension and the *complexity* of the articulations. In 2000 'only' the Sami are mentioned (briefly), and other national or ethnic minorities are not mentioned at all. This report also announces the implementation of a new interpreter service for the hearing impaired. In the annual report for 2001, a single paragraph is devoted to 'other ethnic groups' in addition to a description of the programmes *Migrapolis* and *Migranytt*. 'The Sami population' are given one whole page (in 2001, Sami in Norway and Sweden got their own joint news broadcasts on TV), while the programming for the hearing impaired is weighed as for 'other ethnic groups'. These sections on diversity amounted to two pages in the annual report for 2001 (of which one page consisted of illustrations). In comparison, multicultural matters (i.e. 'other ethnic groups') alone (excluding Sami and the hearing impaired) were described over more than three pages in the annual report for 2008 (illustrations cover about half a page) and five pages in the 2009 report (one and a half of the pages are illustrations).

In 2001, the description consisted of a brief characterization of programmes regarding time of airing and content. There was one sentence about the content of *Migrapolis*: 'This is a journalistic and critical society-oriented programme that explores both positive and negative sides of Norway becoming a more complex and international society' (NRK annual report 2001: 47). Single sentences were allotted to language (in *Migranytt*; Bosnian, Croatian, Serbian, Somali, Urdu and Vietnamese) and the number of viewers. At the end of the decade, the number of topics mentioned had increased, and the descriptions were more complex. Under the main headlines 'Integrate the multicultural' (in 2008) and 'Mirrors the entire population' (2009) a study on the use of NRK by 'immigrants' was included. The goal was stated to be reaching 60 per cent of the immigrant population. The importance of recruiting multicultural staff was emphasized, a multicultural source archive had been established, and examples of multicultural content in mainstream broadcasts were described as important and meaningful. In addition, in 2008, *Migrapolis* is supposed to 'crack codes' and to make 'the public think in new ways' (NRK annual report 2008: 70).

The annual reports comprise multiple multicultural milestones. The ethnic heritage of media producers was first described in an annual report in 2002: 'NRK Østlandssendingen, which produces *Migrapolis*, is proud to have the most ethnically diverse editorial staff' (NRK annual report 2002: 52). This was also the first annual report to bring attention to the so-called *Black list* (established in 1999). The list is a critical summary of descriptions of 'the others' and meant as an eye opener and linguistic guideline of how people with multicultural backgrounds are described. In the annual report for 2004 an intention of 'not creating an "us" and "them" mentality and [...] therefore programmes such as *Migrapolis*, should aim to reach all segments of the viewership equally' was expressed under the headline 'The multicultural as target groups' (NRK annual report 2004: 27). Accordingly, the timeslot and channel for *Migrapolis* changed from NRK2 to prime-time on NRK1. The goal that at least 20 per cent of NRK programming should reflect cultural diversity was also stated in the 2004 report. In the annual report for 2005 under the mainstream chapter on 'News', multicultural background is described as a useful additional competence for news journalists. Illustrating this point is the coverage of an earthquake in Pakistan conducted by Norwegian Pakistani reporter Mah-Rukh Ali. *Radio Migrapolis* was established in that year, with Norwegian Ugandan Asta Busingye Lydersen as the first host. In addition, the music editors of P2 were reported to have sought out 'immigrant areas in Norway and their music for several years', in part by having guest-hosts from East Africa (NRK annual report 2005: 18). In the report for 2006, multicultural perspectives are also described under the chapter 'Life philosophy' through a description of the series *12 commandments* in which host Veslemøy Hvidsteen (from the *Migrapolis* staff) and social anthropologist Thomas Hylland Eriksen explored different rules of living from the perspective of diversity.

In the annual report for 2007, the chapter 'Minorities' noted the celebration of the tenth anniversary of *Migrapolis*. The airing of Bollywood movies was described as a major multicultural activity. Nevertheless, we find the statement 'the minorities are also represented in NRKs programmes through their *peculiar* music' (NRK annual report 2007: 46, emphasis added).

In the 2010 report, an interesting development has taken place. The topics of minorities and multiculturalism no longer are in a separate chapter. The objective evidently was to integrate the multicultural dimension into the 'mainstream' chapters. An example is the main illustration for the chapter, 'Drama'. In the online version of the report, this category is illustrated with the face of a woman in a niqab with only the eyes visible. The

Migrapolis programmes in 2010 are described thus: 'These programmes are not mainly about immigrants, but about challenges and coexistence in a multicultural Norwegian ordinary day' (NRK annual report 2010: 32).

This summary of NRK's annual reports over the last decade is bound to be simplified and does not provide a complete overview of NRK's self-presentation regarding multiculturalism. However, the developments that have taken place are indicated in some key points of the reports as discussed here. The reports demonstrate that NRK, not unexpectedly, has developed from a relatively one-dimensional point of view in both *understanding* and *rhetoric* concerning their role in a culturally diverse and 'new' Norway to a more multifaceted and complex approach.

Conclusion

I have described some central developmental features concerning how NRK defines its journalistic mission in multicultural Norway. This multicultural mission is explicitly expressed in the NRK bylaws. These differ in both form and content from the programme requirements of other public service broadcasters and reflect the government's expectations of NRK as a frontrunner in multicultural issues. This must naturally be understood in light of the legitimization of NRK as a licence-funded, state-owned public service broadcaster.

The multicultural programme requirements, content and recruitment policy of NRK indicate that it is still *moving* towards multicultural broadcasting. The state channel seems to have been hindered by its slow pace, being more reactive than proactive in including multicultural perspectives in both organization and production. The hesitancy in meeting multicultural challenges has probably both institutional and individual explanations. Simply put, NRK is an old, huge organization with a bureaucracy that can be expected to resist new perspectives. At the individual level, it is fair to assume that the dedication to pursue ethnic diversity will vary greatly among, for instance, the central middle managers in their busy everyday editorial lives. A possible commercial explanation is that the 'multicultural drive' increased as NRK started to see the 'new Norwegians' as a potential *audience.*

The slowness may be unexpected in the light of NRK's long traditions of multiple ways of dealing with diversity and other representation issues (e.g. cities and districts, different dialects, Sami and the hearing impaired). At the same time, the multicultural mission(s) of 2013 seems increasingly clear and articulated at different levels of the institution with regard to the formal guidelines, the strengthening of affirmative action in recruitment and the inclusion of more and diverse multicultural perspectives in the actual programme offerings.[11]

To understand NRK's contribution to the presentation and inclusion of 'the others', it is necessary to consider the total volume and content of its actual broadcasts. There is for instance a seemingly higher degree of 'multicultural consciousness' in NRK's Oslo and suburban offices and in staff working with programmes for children and youth (Bjørnsen 2012). This manifests through choices of topics, use of sources, hosts and reporters, and frame perspectives. These differences and variations must be assumed to exist both within and between branches and production teams as well. It is to be expected that multiple options of discourses exist side by side and that programme content includes different elements and expressions of stereotyping, dialogue, criticism and ambivalence (Eide 2002; 2007).

We have also observed a possible duality regarding NRK as a key player in defining the 'classic Norwegian' *and* at the same time including new perspectives on ways of being Norwegian. There seems to be a built-in tension related to whether multicultural dimensions, in content, recruitment and perceptions about the audience, should be seen as a special field or be merged with new understandings of the 'mainstream'. The choices concerning the ways to reach both 'broad and narrow' segments of the population are also potentially conflicted with regard to cultural diversity. More precise expressions of heterogeneity within the broad term 'multicultural' are demanded. At the same time it is also worth exploring the degree to which the *mirror metaphor* is strong in NRK and how it is expressed in the daily broadcasts. Formulations in the NRK charter and in the title of the multicultural part of the annual report for 2010, 'Mirroring the whole population' (NRK annual report 2009), reflects this understanding of reality. It makes sense to examine the production processes in NRK in light of the idea of media content as social constructions (cf. Tuchman 1978; Berger and Luckmann 1984 [1966]). NRK does not mirror reality; it *creates* reality.

In 2009, NRK received the government's diversity award for its establishment of the recruitment project FleRe. The jury stated that 'the awarding of the Diversity Award in 2009 to the FleRe-project in NRK is simultaneously a request to the institution to work broadly and on many levels towards increased integration and diversity'. At the award ceremony,[12] the head of NRK, Hans-Tore Bjerkaas, agreed that NRK has a great responsibility and still has a long way to go when it comes to achieving diversity. In his thank-you speech, he underlined that NRK receives many awards, but that the institution values this award particularly highly: 'This prize hits *exactly* in the core of our journalistic mission. We *must* mirror reality the way it really is.' Uttering these words, he also confirmed that both the mirror metaphor and the idea of a journalistic mission still play vital roles in NRK's self-understanding.

References

Allern, Sigurd (1997), *Når kildene byr opp til dans: Søkelys på PR-byråene og journalistikken/ When the sources ask for a dance: Focus on the PR-agencies and journalism*, Oslo: Pax.
Allern, Sigurd (2001), *Nyhetsverdier/News values*, Kristiansand: IJ-forlaget.

Bjørnsen, Gunn (2003), 'Flerkulturell bakgrunn som journalistisk kompetanse?'/'Multicultural background as journalistic competence?', in G. Bjørnsen and T. Smistrup, *Journalistik i flere farver/Journalism in several colours* [Report], Nordisk Journalistcenter, www.njc. dk/farver. Copenhagen: NJC. Accessed 5 June 2010.

Bjørnsen, Gunn (2009), 'Nye nordmenn på lufta: En studie av hvordan allmennkringkasterne oppfyller sine flerkulturelle programforpliktelser'/'New Norwegians on air: A study of how the public broadcasters fulfil their multicultural programme obligations', *Allmennkringkastingsrapporten for 2008/The public service broadcasting report for 2008*, Oslo: Medietilsynet.

Bjørnsen, Gunn (2010), 'Det flerkulturelle samfunnsoppdraget: Ideelle intensjoner og redaksjonelle realiteter i NRK'/'The multicultural mission: Ideal intentions and editorial realities in NRK', in J. Roppen and S. Allern (eds), *Journalistikkens samfunnsoppdrag/ The mission of journalism*, Kristiansand: IJ-forlaget.

Bjørnsen, Gunn (2011), 'Investigators or integrators? Broadcast journalists covering multicultural Norway', in E. Eide and K. Nikunen (eds), *Media in Motion: Cultural Complexity and Migration in the Nordic Region*, Farnham, UK: Ashgate Publishing Ltd.

Bjørnsen, Gunn (2012), 'Medierte migranter: NRK og nye nordmenn'/'Mediated migrants: NRK and new Norwegians', in M. Eide, L. Larsen and H. Sjøvaag (eds), *Nytt på nett og brett: journalistikk i forandring/News on the internet and on the board: journalism in transition*, Oslo: Universitetsforlaget.

Berger, Peter and Luckmann, Thomas (1966), *The Social Construction of Reality: A Treatise in the Sociology of Knowledge*, Garden City, N.Y.: Doubleday.

Born, Georgina (2004), *Uncertain Vision: Birt, Dyke and the Reinvention of the BBC*, London: Secker & Warburg.

Bråthen, Magne, Djuve, Anne Britt, Dølvik, Tor, Hagen, Kåre, Hernes, Gudmund and Nielsen, Roy A. (2007), *Levekår på vandring. Velferd og marginalisering i Oslo/Living conditions on the move. Welfare and marginalization in Oslo*, [report], FAFO-rapport 2007, no 5, Oslo: FAFO.

Eide, Elisabeth (2002), *'Down There' and 'Up Here': 'Europe's Others' in Norwegian Feature Stories*, Dr.Arts thesis, Oslo: University of Oslo.

Directorate for Integration and Diversity (IMDI) (2010), *Innvandrere i norske medier: medieskapt islamfrykt og usynlig hverdagsliv/Immigrants in Norwegian media: Media-created fear of Islam and invisible daily life* [Annual report 2009]. Oslo: IMDI.

Eide, Elisabeth (2007), 'Gjenger, offerhelter og nye stemmer'/'Gangs, "victimheroes" and new voices', in E. Eide and A. H. Simonsen (eds), *Mistenkelige utlendinger: Minoriteter i norsk presse gjennom hundre år/Suspicious Foreigners: Minorities in the Norwegian Press Through Hundred Years*, Kristiansand: Høyskoleforlaget.

Enger, Jørn (2006), *Hele landet på lufta: Historien om NRKs distriktskontorer/The Entire Country on Air: The History of NRKs District Departments*, Oslo: NRK.

Eriksen, Thomas Hylland (2006), 'Diversity vs difference: Neo-liberalism in the minority-debate', in R. Rottenburg, B. Scnepel and S. Shimada (eds), *The Making and Unmaking of Difference*, Bielefeld: Transaction, pp. 13–36.

Eriksen, Thomas Hylland and Breivik, Jan-Kåre (eds) (2006), *Normalitet/Normality*, Oslo: Universitetsforlaget.

Grepstad, Ottar (2005), *Nynorsk faktabok/Neo-Norwegian Fact Book*, Ørsta: Aasen-tunet.

Gullestad, Marianne (2002), *Det norske sett med nye øyne: Kritisk analyse av norsk innvandringsdebatt/The Norwegian Seen With New Eyes: A Critical Analysis of Norwegian Immigration Debate*, Oslo: Universitetsforlaget.

Hovden, Jan Fredrik (2008), *Profane and Sacred: A Study of the Norwegian Journalistic Field*, Dr.Polit. thesis, Bergen: University of Bergen.

Horsti, Karina (2009), 'From multiculturalism to cultural diversity: European public service broadcasting and challenge of migration', *IMISCOE [International migration, integration and social cohesion], Cross-Cluster Theory Conference: Interethnic Relations – Multidisciplinary Approaches*, Lisbon, Portugal, 13 – 15 May.

Horsti, Karina and Hultén, Gunilla (2011a), 'Diverse directions: Multicultural media policy in Finnish and Swedish public service broadcasting', *International Journal of Cultural Studies*, 14: 2, pp. 209–27.

Horsti, Karina and Hultén, Gunilla (2011b), 'In case of diversity: Dilemmas in sharing good practices across European broadcasting', in E. Eide and K. Nikunen (eds), *Media in Motion: Cultural Complexity and Migration in the Nordic Region*, Aldershot: Ashgate Publishing Ltd.

Høydahl, Even (2008), 'Vestlig og ikke-vestlig – ord som ble for store og gikk ut på dato'/'Western and non-western – concepts that became too big and outdated', *Samfunnsspeilet/Mirror of society*, Oslo: Statistics Norway, http://www.ssb.no/samfunnsspeilet/utg/200804/15/index.html. Accessed 15 February 2012.

Jensen, Iben (2000), *Hvornår er man lige kvalificeret? Etniske minoriteters profesionelle adgang til etablerede danske medier/When Is One Equally Qualified? Ethnic Minorities' Professional Access To Established Danish Media*, Copenhagen: Nævnet for Etnisk Ligestilling.

Kjelstadli, Knut (2008), *Sammensatte samfunn: Innvandring og inkludering/Compound Societies: Immigration and Inclusion*, Oslo: Pax.

Lentin, Alana and Titley, Gavan (2011), *The Crises of Multiculturalism: Racism in a Neoliberal Age*, London/New York: Zed Books.

Malik, Sarita (2014), 'Diversity, broadcasting and the politics of representation', this volume, Bristol/Chicago: Intellect, pp. 21–42.

Medietilsynet (2009), *Allmennkringkastingsrapporten for 2008/The Public Service Broadcasting Report for 2008* [report]. Oslo: Medietilsynet.

Mikkelsen, Marianne (2009), *Verdsatt og feilvurdert: Flerkulturelle journalister i norske redaksjoner/Valued and Misjudged: Multicultural Journalists in Norwegian Newsrooms*, Master's thesis, Oslo: University of Oslo.

Ministry of Culture (2007), 'NRK-plakaten'/'The NRK charter', *White Paper no 6 2007–2008*, Oslo: Ministry of Culture.

Ministry of Labour, (2003), 'Mangfold gjennom inkludering og deltagelse: Ansvar og frihet'/'Diversity through inclusion and participation: Responsibility and freedom', *White Paper no 49 2003–2004*.

UDI/Norwegian Directorate of Immigration (2003), *Rapport om rasisme og diskriminering i Norge 2001-2002/Report on Racism and Discrimination in Norway 2001-2002* [report], Oslo: UDI.

Pham, Hong (2002), *Farget penn blant mange hvite/Coloured Pen Among Many White*, BA thesis, Oslo: Oslo University College.

Phillips, Anne (2007), *Multiculturalism Without Culture*, Oxfordshire Princeton University Press.

Roppen, Johann and Allern, Sigurd (2010), *Journalistikkens samfunnsoppdrag/The Mission of Journalism*, Kristiansand: IJ-forlaget.

Statistics Norway (2012), http://ssb.no/. Accessed May 10 2012.

Tuchman, Gaye (1978), *Making News: A Study in the Construction of Reality*, London: The Free Press.

NRK (2001), *NRK Annual Report 2000* [report], Oslo: NRK.

NRK (2002), *NRK in 2001* [report], Oslo: NRK.

NRK (2003), *NRK in 2002* [report], Oslo: NRK.

NRK (2004), *NRK in 2003* [report], Oslo: NRK.

NRK (2005), *NRK Annual Report 2004* [report], Oslo: NRK.

NRK (2006), *NRK Public Broadcaster Report 2005* [report], Oslo: NRK.

NRK (2007), *NRK in 2006* [report], Oslo: NRK.

NRK (2008), *Alle religioner skal få plass I NRK/All Religions Have a Place in NRK*, www.nrk.no, 18 April 2008. Accessed 12 March 2009.

NRK (2008), *Annual report 2007, Godt innhold gjør noe med deg/Good Content Does Something To You* [report], Oslo: NRK.

NRK (2009), *Annual report 2008, Godt innhold, tilgjengelig for alle/Good Content, Available to all* [report]. Oslo: NRK.

NRK (2010), *NRK annual report 2009, Høy kvalitet. Norsk virkelighet./High Quality. Norwegian Reality.* [report], Oslo: NRK.

NRK (2011), *NRK Annual Report 2010, Gjør dagen bedre/Making the Day Better,* [report], Oslo: NRK.

NRK (2002) *Noe for alle. Alltid. Overordnet strategi for NRK 2002-2006/Something for Everybody. Always. The NRK Superior Strategy 2002-2006*, Oslo: NRK.

NRKs bylaws.

NRKs charter.

NRK, Status reports for the FleRe project, 2008–2012.

NRKs online archive. www.nrk.no/skole. Accessed 20 April 2010.

NRKs language rules, 2007.

Notes

1. It literally means 'MoRe', referring to (more) multicultural recruitment.
2. 'Multicultural' and 'multiculturalism' are evidently multifaceted concepts that also are said to be in a state of crisis (Phillips 2007; Lentin and Titley 2011). Cultural differences can 'refer to a lot of different kinds of phenomenon, from the cosmetic and aesthetic to the moral and social-structural' (Eriksen 2006: 13). In this chapter, the concept is used merely in a descriptive manner (for lack of other words), to label people and issues that are understood to refer to experienced and constructed cultural differences (cf. Bjørnsen 2011).
3. An early version of this chapter has been published in Norwegian in the book *Journalistikkens samfunnsoppdrag/The mission of journalism* (Bjørnsen 2010).
4. 'Non-western' was ruled out as a category in Statistics Norway, acknowledging that the division of the world into two categories was clearly outdated (Høydahl 2008). For reasons of simplicity, I still (with ambivalence) use this concept to mean persons born abroad or having both parents born abroad in countries in Asia, Latin America, Africa and former Eastern Europe.
5. Norway was in a (asymmetrical) union with Denmark until 1814
6. Sweden has two public service companies, Sveriges/Sweden's Television (SVT) and Utbildningsradion/The education radio (UR), in addition to the public service radio company Sveriges Radio/Sweden's Radio (SR).
7. These examples are found by searching the NRK online broadcast archive: http://www.nrk.no/skole/. Accessed March-May 2010.
8. See Bjørnsen (2012) for a more elaborate discussion of the FleRe project and a thorough analysis of *Migrapolis*.
9. This was already expressed in 2007 when the following phrase was included in the NRK language rules: 'NRK shall mirror the diversity in the Norwegian language, also when it comes to the use of dialects and pronunciation colored by other languages.'
10. This heading borrows the title of NRK's strategic document, 2002–2006: 'Something for everyone. Always.'
11. The autumn TV 'menu' of 2012 is significant here; it offered the most multicultural content yet. This might be interpreted as a more or less conscious reaction to the 22/7 terrorist attack.
12. I had the pleasure of attending this event.

Chapter 10

Estonian Broadcasting and the Russian Language: Trends and Media Policy

Andreas Jõesaar and Salme Rannu (Tartu University)

Introduction

This chapter sets out to explore the ways in which Estonian public broadcasting tackles one specific media service sphere: how television programmes for language minorities are created in a small country, a country that had long been under Soviet rule, and which has only recently begun to introduce the tradition of free democratic journalism and public service media. The article highlights four major tensions, namely between Estonia and Russia as nation-states, Estonian and Russian media outlets, Estonian and Russian speakers within Estonia and the European Union and Estonia concerning the role of public service broadcasting.

To establish the background for our topic, we will briefly examine the time preceding World War II, and will also investigate the geopolitical turnaround that occurred during the war, leading to drastic changes in the ethnic structure of Estonia's population. The Soviet era, which lasted for 45 years, brought about the development of two language communities: Estonian and Russian. Estonia regained its independence in 1991, and the necessity to integrate national minorities living in Estonia with the new democratic society created a number of challenges and problems, which it was hoped would be solved by straightforward political and economic means during the initial years of independence. However, after 20 years, the issues still remain without an adequate solution. Estonia is officially a single-language country, with regions where a relatively large community of foreign-language speakers lives closely together. These individuals should have more active participation in Estonia's politics, civil society, economy and cultural life. We take an interest in the solutions that the national media policies and the public broadcasting organization, operating as the state's partner in democratic processes, have sought when trying to arrange and improve the information flow directed to the Russian-speaking population.

In addition, we investigate the media policies, economy and journalism-related aspects that have prevented success. After analysing the viewing rates of TV channels available to the Russian-speaking population in Estonia, we conclude that their contact with Estonian television is meagre. This could be due to the scarcity of Russian television programmes created in Estonia, or because of the programme contents themselves. Through the following analysis we hope to explain to some extent why Estonia still has no modern Russian-language television programme that could interest Russian viewers; and we will try to explore the developmental perspectives of such programmes against the backdrop of established media policies and the economic situation.

When Estonia regained its independence in 1991, the national authorities deemed it neither important nor possible to deal with the development of national Russian television because first, it was presumed that the media spaces of Estonian and Russian communities, which developed during Soviet times, would merge into one Estonian-language-based media space; second, both financial and work force resources were insufficient to establish programming in both languages during the first years of independence; and third, believing that the market would meet the media needs of all groups of society, the media industry was subordinated under market economy self-regulation. However, the 20-year development since independence has shown that there are insufficient market economy prerequisites for the development of a full-time television channel of general scope in Russian (Jõesaar 2011).

When discussing the current state of television, we have to admit that so far the Russian-speaking minority has not attained a domestic Estonia-wide Russian TV channel with their status and material resources. The market has not been capable of arousing investors' interest in a commercial channel, because the foreign competition from the Russian Federation is too strong. The local cable channels are weak in their content and their spread. Discussions concerning the launch of a public broadcaster's TV channel in Russian have yielded no results. This market failure has resulted in an offering of limited choice and a lack of fairly objective information (Jakobson 2004: 232).

Population changes from Soviet times to nowadays

Before World War II, Estonia was a relatively homogenous nation-state; 88.1 per cent of Estonia's inhabitants were Estonians. Larger minorities were Russians and Germans. Estonian was the national language; all the main spheres of the state (political leadership and management, education, science and culture) were executed in Estonian. The war led to drastic changes: from the 1940s onwards, after being incorporated into the Soviet Union, Estonia lost nearly one-fifth of its population due to mass repression, war activities and political exile. The 'nations policy' of the Soviet Union established that strategically important spheres (including communications) should be staffed by trustworthy people, the majority of whom originated from the Soviet Union. Mass immigration from the Soviet Union's member republics, especially from the Russian Federation, made Estonia's population multinational in a few decades.[1] The newcomers were mainly Russians, Ukrainians and Belarusians, who spoke Russian. In the Soviet Union, the Russian language had the status of being the language of communication between and within different nations, meaning that in practice Russian was used as the official language, even though the Constitution of the Soviet Union had not established one. Political and economic administration had been centralized to Moscow, and in those circles knowledge of Russian was obligatory.

Parallel to the education system, cultural life and the media conducted in the native language ran a Russian-language system. The majority of the Russians who had moved to Estonia never learned the local language or became part of the Estonian community;

rather, they formed their own Russian-speaking community, which, by the end of the 1980s, formed 35.2 per cent of Estonia's population. In 1989, at the height of the Singing Revolution,[2] the Supreme Council of the Estonian Soviet Socialist Republic (ESSR) passed the first Language Act, by which Estonian was stipulated as the official language of the ESSR (Supreme Council 1989). The public has considered the Language Act as an important means for the survival of the Estonian language and a tool to leverage Russian-language dominance (Tomusk 2009). The Constitution of the Republic of Estonia, adopted on the referendum held in 1992, declared Estonian as the one and only official language.

The regaining of independence by Estonia caused large-scale transformations in politics and economics, which were separated from the Soviet Union's system and founded on market economy principles. The majority of the large trans-union industries lost their market and fell apart. The Soviet army was pulled out of Estonia in 1994. Noteworthy numbers of the Russian-speaking population lost their occupations and began to move elsewhere. There has been a significant decrease and a nationality ratio change in Estonia's population during the last two decades. In 1990, the total population was 1.57 million, which included 61.5 per cent Estonians. In 2010, the total population had decreased to 1.34 million, among whom 68.8 per cent were Estonians. Although the number of Estonians has decreased by 4.5 per cent, the number of non-Estonians has dropped by 19.1 per cent, due to negative migration (Figure 1).

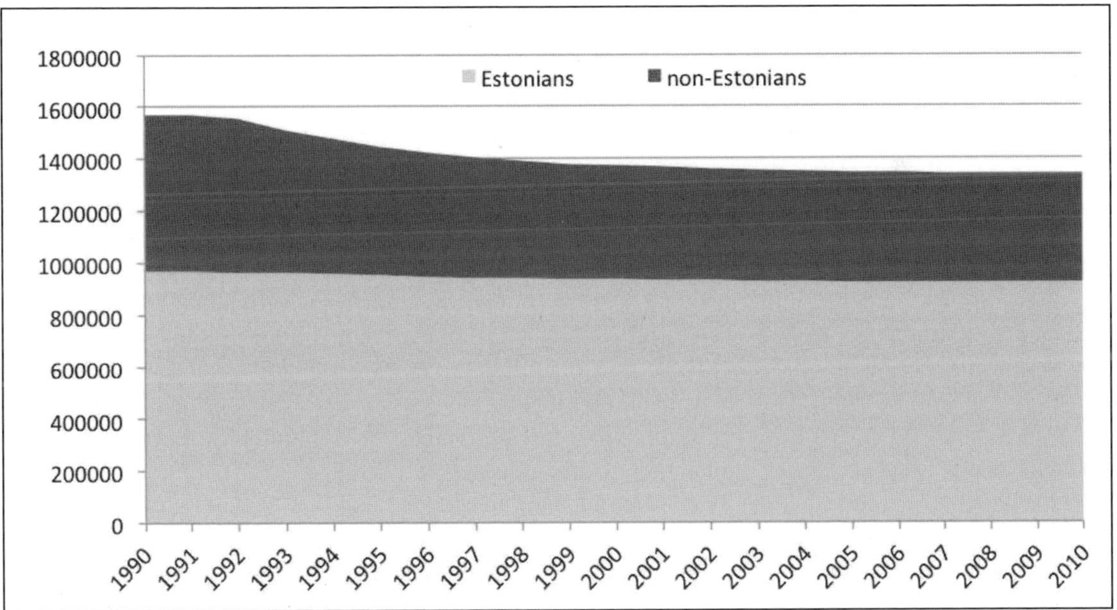

Figure 1. Estonian population trend. *Source:* Statistikaamet 2012.

Among the non-Estonians living in Estonia, half were born in Estonia and one-third in other former Soviet states.[3] From the language perspective, at least 93 per cent of non-Estonians are Russian speakers, and in Estonia these people are referred to as Russians. Nowadays, Russian is the mother tongue of 29.6 per cent of the Estonian population (Estonian Statistics 2012). The number of monolingual people among them has constantly decreased; however, 16 per cent of Russian-speaking people claim they do not understand Estonian at all (Lauristin et al. 2011).

Television broadcasting in Russian

Until the beginning of the 1990s, the main TV channels that broadcasted on Estonian territory were Estonian Television (ETV) and three channels from Russia: Ostankino TV, Russia TV (both re-transmitted from Moscow) and Leningrad TV. The re-transmission of all Russian television channels was terminated in 1993–94. The frequencies and networks they had occupied were licensed to newly-born Estonian private broadcasters. The primary objective of the first Broadcasting Act (Riigikogu 1994) passed in parliament in 1994 was to establish a dual media system; the co-existence of PSB; and a commercial sector. The former State Radio and Television Committee was reorganized into two independent public service institutions: Estonian Radio and Estonian Television. Licences for private broadcasters were issued through public tenders.

For the Russian-speaking audience, the changes taking place at the beginning of the 1990s were dramatic; the number of programme hours offered through terrestrial broadcasting in Russian dropped substantially. No domestic national TV channel targeted at Russian speakers was established. By the end of the 1990s, as a result of the state media policy, the Estonian commercial broadcasting sector belonged to Schibsted (Norway) and the Modern Times Group (Sweden). They obtained the most valuable terrestrial TV broadcasting nationwide licences. Local Russian-language TV channels were granted three limited transmission area licences. Due to the poor economic and editorial resources, the programming offered by these three Russian channels never met high-quality standards, and the channels' share of viewing and reach were much lower compared to foreign Russian (language) channels. The market demand for programmes in Russian was met by cable operators. They expanded their networks rapidly and started to re-transmit Russian channels available on satellites.

It is noteworthy that there are a number of foreign thematic TV channels in Russian, available in cable packages. In total, these 'other' channels reached 87 per cent of Russian speakers weekly and took up 39 per cent of their viewing time in 2010 (see Figure 2). However, Estonians spent only 17 per cent of their viewing time watching 'other' channels. Furthermore, their weekly reach was far lower, 64 per cent, partly because far fewer channels are available in Estonian. Compared with the Russian-speaking audience, the Estonian television audience had never been so fragmentized until digitalization at

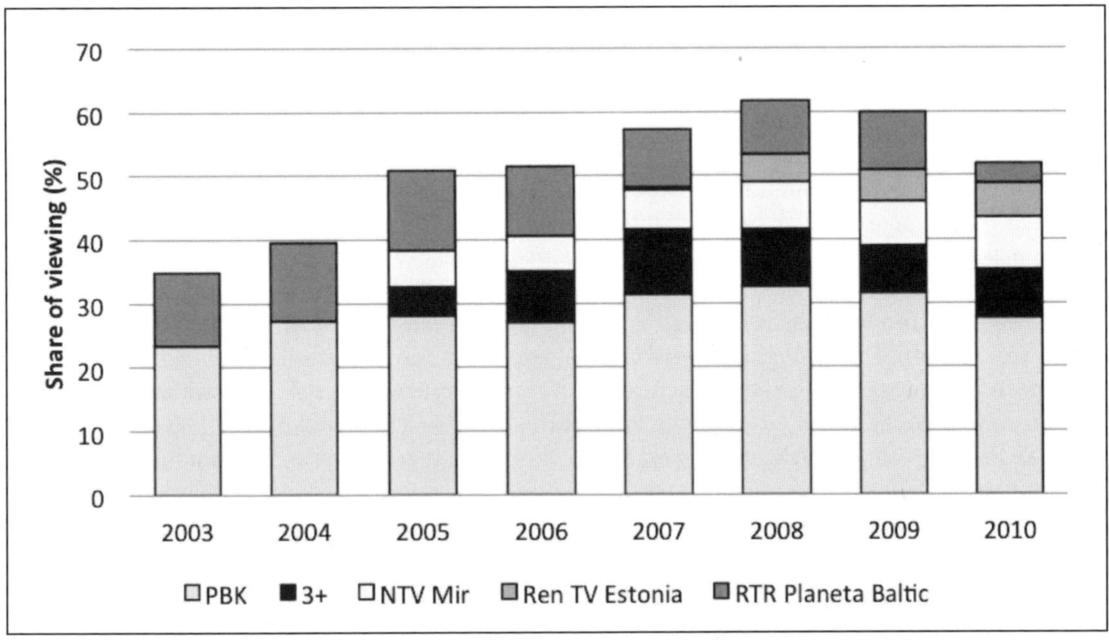

Figure 2. Russian-speakers' share of viewing of the main Russian-language TV channels. *Source:* TNS EMOR 2008.[4]

the end of the 2000s, but neither channel had been predominating. Domestic Estonian-language television still occupies nearly 80 per cent of the viewing time of Estonian speakers.

The most popular TV station among Russian speakers is Pervõi Baltijski Kanal (First Baltic Channel; PBK), which is owned and operated by a Latvian independent legal entity working under two jurisdictions; they have a broadcasting licence issued by LNRT Latvia and by Ofcom UK. The PBK programme is available in all Baltic countries on all technical platforms: satellite, cable, IPTV and DTT pay-TV packages. It primarily re-transmits the Russian commercial TV channel Obshtshtvennoje Rossijskoje Televidenije ORT (controlled by the Russian government), but also includes a daily newscast produced locally in each country in the format of ORT's main news programme (*Vremja,* broadcast since 1968), and is scheduled immediately after the latter on prime-time.

PBK's *Novosti Estonii* (*Estonian News,* broadcast since 2004) is often blamed for being Moscow-minded and supporting the Estonian Centre Party, which closely cooperates with the Russian Federation's political circles in power. This opinion was asserted very clearly during the events of Bronze Night[5] in April 2007, when PBK's Russian news programme *Vremja* and *Novosti Estonii* both aired official incriminating statements from the Russian

Government (Estonian Ministry of Foreign Affairs 2007). After Bronze Night, an intense discussion regarding the role of the media in protecting national security was initiated. The most extreme utterances demanded for prohibition of the re-transmissions of Russian satellite programmes. Of course, these positions were too unrealistic to be accomplished.

Vihalemm (2008) showed that 69 per cent of Russian speakers highly trust PBK's Russian state news programme *Vremja*. A total of 65 per cent considered PBK's *Novosti Estonii* as the most reliable source of information, and ETV's *Aktuaalne Kaamera (Actual Camera)* was trusted by 56 per cent of Russian-speakers. Vihalemm warned that this gave the Russian state media an opportunity to easily manipulate this portion of Estonia's population. To avoid any manipulation, PSB should be a trustworthy and reliable source of information. However, the viewers tend to trust more the information channels with which they have greater contact. The reach of *Novosti Estonii* was 20.1 per cent among the Russian-speaking audience, while the reach of ETV's Russian news was 3.4 per cent (TNS EMOR 2008), although the news programme is aired on two channels; ETV2 and 3+.

PSB's tradition of Russian-language programming

The next four sections of the article will focus on PSB. Estonia has generally adopted a liberal approach to media regulation. On a large scale, such a mindset is driven by economic grounds and a free market ideology (Jõesaar 2011). With regard to private broadcasters,[6] the law does not include any specific guidelines or obligations around meeting the demands and serving the interests of minorities. The remit of PSB, as stated in the Estonian National Public Broadcasting Act, is far more detailed. In the context of this article, the following clauses should be mentioned:

- Supporting the development of the Estonian language and culture;
- Enhancing the guarantees of the permanence of the Estonian state and nation, and drawing attention to the circumstances that may endanger the permanence of the Estonian state and nation;
- Assisting in the increase of the social cohesion of Estonian society;
- Transmitting programmes that, within the limits of the possibilities of National Broadcasting, meet the information needs of all sections of the population, including minorities (Riigikogu 2007).

The law does not specify the question of ethnic minorities. The Act states that PSB operates two TV channels (ETV and ETV2) and four radio stations. Of these four, the Russian-language station, Raadio 4, is a good example of high-quality programming, which is rewarded with listeners' loyalty and trust. Since its launch in 1993, Raadio 4 has had a strong position compared to Russian-speaking commercial radio stations; however, maintaining the leadership has been a challenge in recent years.

Soviet-era ETV produced news and primarily cultural and educational programmes in Russian during the 1960s and the 1970s. In the mid-1970s, the offer of pan-Union Russian programmes intensified. In the context of the USSR, local Russian-language programmes were never treated as those targeted to a minority, because the speakers of the non-native language among the population of a republic of the Union were never considered as minorities. Programmes in Russian, broadcast by the TV stations of the republics, expressed one of the Russification methods used by the USSR: the production of these programmes was not driven by the modern idea of complying with the information needs of a minority. In Estonia, where only one local TV station existed, a third of its schedule was filled with the Central Television programmes of the Soviet Union.

The content scope of local programmes in Russian developed only partially. From 1980 to 1991, ETV aired only approximately an hour of domestic programmes in Russian (including news) daily (Shein 2005). Few television journalists spoke Russian as their mother tongue, and the content they produced was limited, mainly cultural, music and educational programmes; analytical journalism was almost non-existent. The topic of ethnic minorities was subsequently raised by Estonian journalists, after the founding of the Union of Estonia's Nationalities in 1988. From 1990, with the exception of news, the Russian ETV programmes were aired on Saturday daytime and the content scope extended from information to entertainment. The volume of programmes was less than 200 hours per year. Due to the lack of viewers, attempts were made to find a better timeslot, and in the middle of the 1990s, a programme strip in Russian was created to air before the news in Russian on work days.

In the early 1990s, Russian-language TV journalism existed only on ETV. Independent producers had not yet appeared, and when they did, around the end of the decade, the majority were individual producers and fully dependent on their financiers. Commercial stations did not pay to show programmes in Russian; instead, barter deals were offered: the producers could sell advertisement time inside their programmes. The budget of PSB television was also highly dependent on advertisements, so, as the volume of other production grew, the programmes in Russian were pushed into the background, as something unattractive to advertising agencies. Although some good publicists emerged among the Russian-speaking television journalists, they probably felt the air of suspicion of disloyalty, and therefore tried to choose as neutral topics as possible; which, in return, did not help to increase the interest of viewers. The integration programme, launched in the second half of the 1990s and funded by the European Union, produced a shift in the content focus, which moved to integration-related topics (Lauristin 2004).

Notwithstanding the incompleteness of the statistics covering the end of the 1990s, we can estimate that the volume of Russian-language programming rose above 200 hours in 1998–99 (see Figure 3), when over ten different series were aired on ETV (Trapido 2000: 112; Shein 2005). Unfortunately, this was the time of the economic downturn, and the attempt by the management to increase its own production output, in circumstances whereby the state grant had been cut back by 10 per cent, caused a serious budgetary crisis. At the beginning of the 2000s, the crisis led to a recession in all activities, including the production of Russian programming on ETV. By April 2000, the budget for Russian programmes had decreased five times since 1998, and enabled the production of just one half-hour programme per week (PRTM 2000).

After the crisis, of the original Russian programmes, it was primarily the production of the news that continued to be financed from ETV's budget. The remainder of the in-house production received funding from the Integration Foundation or from other public funds. Part of the schedule was acquired from Russia, and re-runs of some Estonian programmes with Russian subtitles were also scheduled for Russian timeslots.

A budgetary crisis in ETV in 2000–02 resulted in cut-backs in several programming sectors and produced changes in management logistics. The production of Russian programmes was initiated on the orders of ETV's programme management, mainly in the form of co-production between independent producers and ETV employees; several former employees of ETV now work as independent producers, acquiring the necessary additional financing from public funds. However, a specific centre of competence, which should work on developing a cohesive concept of television programmes aimed towards non-Estonians and executing related ideas, does not currently exist in Estonia. This fact has also been pointed out in the debates discussing the launch of a television channel in Russian (Ajutrust Konsultatsioonid 2007).

Today's challenges for PSB

Estonian Television's position among the Russian-speaking audience is complicated. There is no full-scale national TV programme in Russian. In 2011, ETV's channels occupied only 1.8 per cent of the viewing time of non-Estonians. The launch of the PSB Russian-language channel, ETV2, has been debated for almost two decades. It has been mentioned in parliamentary debates and has been part of a number of PSB's development plans. A short list of arguments supporting and opposing ETV2 in Russian is as follows:

FOR

- The channel will support the enhancement, development and servicing of social, political and cultural citizenship;
- It will offer adequate and reliable information to all citizens and inhabitants;
- It will extenuate tensions between two ethnic groups;
- It will serve as a balancing force to Moscow, lowering national security risks.

AGAINST

- To attract a Russian audience (extra) high-quality programmes are needed;
- It is too expensive; sufficient additional financial resources are unavailable;

- Whatever the programme, it is unrealistic to expect that it will attract the attention of the Russian audience, because of high competition from abroad;
- There is no need for such a channel – in the long run, all citizens will understand Estonian and will therefore be capable of watching Estonian programmes;
- If state-financed propaganda is required, these programmes should be ordered from, and aired on, PBK.

In 2008, another economic downturn enforced ETV to make budgetary cut-backs and the volume of Russian-language programmes dropped to a level last experienced in the middle of the previous decade (see Figure 3). Only one series was produced for the Russian audience, which, too, received funding from external sources. Despite the lack of funding, ETV2 started broadcasting in summer 2008 and continues to be on-air. However, the original concept of this new channel, broadcasting in Russian at least on prime-time, was revised. Today, the main scope of the channel is cultural and educational programmes and this task is primarily fulfilled by using ETV's archives. As no extra financial resources are allocated from the state budget, the new in-house production is minimal, primarily consisting of original children's programmes, which also have an important role in ETV2. Notwithstanding, the launch of ETV2 opened up new possibilities and, from 2009 onwards, the volume of Russian-language programming has significantly increased (see Figure 3).

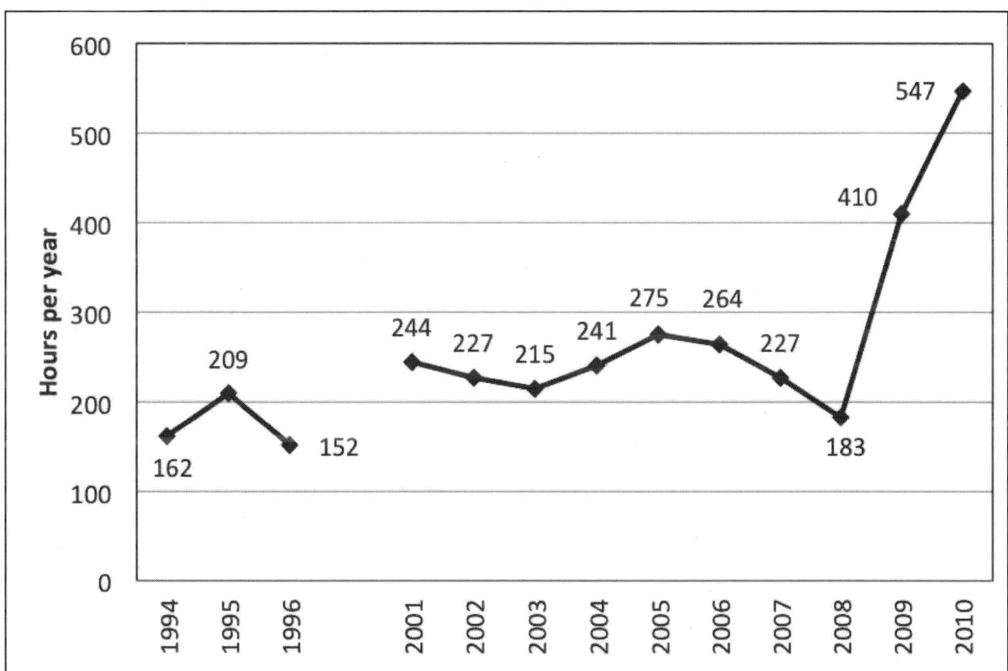

Figure 3. ETV's yearly total programme hours targeted at the Russian-speaking audience in 1994–96; 2001–10.
Source: authors' calculation.

A remarkable increase in output of Russian-language news occurred after the news was transferred to ETV2, where a longer timeslot was available. Unfortunately, the shift to ETV2 meant that the Russian news lost some of its viewers. In 2009–10, the Russian-language offering at ETV2 increased significantly, although the major part of in-house productions (with the exception of the news) was financed from external sources. Furthermore, re-runs from the ETV archives and Estonian-language current affairs programmes with Russian subtitles increased the output. The result is that a prime-time slot, including news and some information and discussion programmes scheduled for Russian speakers, today exists on ETV2. It remains to be observed whether these late changes are sufficiently efficient to attract the Russian-speaking audience and to integrate them into the Estonian information field.

Planning the future of ETV2

The mission of ETV2 remains somewhat unclear; while it is described as cultural and educational, there are also expectations that it should provide more informational and cultural programming in Russian. One could argue that this confusion is also characteristic of the state's media policy concerning the Russian-speaking section of society. Guaranteed funding for ETV2 in Russian could be a definitive answer; however, this has not been accepted by the political powers.

In Estonia, PSB is financed from the state budget, and advertising sales have been prohibited since 2001. Funding is annually designated by the State Budget Act, which means that the exact funding for the next calendar year is approved by the parliament at the end of the previous calendar year. This type of financing system makes long-term planning uncertain. In order to offer a longer development perspective, the Amendment of the Broadcasting Act introduced the system of development plans in 2001.

A review of development plans (DP) allows us to follow the attention and the planned actions concerning the Russian-speaking audience. The first document (ERR 2002) foresaw the launch of ETV2 on cable and digital networks in 2004. The channel was described as mainly cultural and educational, with prime-time programmes in Russian; and with at least 3,000 aired hours per year. The director of ETV at that time reasoned that merely to air a small number of Russian-language programmes via an Estonian channel was a waste of resources. A better solution to attract a Russian audience and to make an impact would be to launch a full-time TV channel that broadcasts in Russian (Raag 2004). As no extra state funding was granted, this plan did not come to fruition.

DP 2006–08 (ERR 2005) were more focused on programming in Russian. In part, this was to be re-runs of Estonian original productions with Russian subtitles or a voice-over on prime-time; a closer collaboration between Estonian and Russian news departments was proposed. The mission of ETV2 was formulated to support the integration of Estonian and Russian communities. In addition, 'cultural' and 'educational' are the keywords used to describe the overall strategy of the channel. It was intended that ETV2 would be launched in 2007, but this deadline passed. Even the dramatic events of Bronze Night, which heated up the question of the possibility of launching the long-debated second Estonian Television channel, did not generate specific political measures. In crisis meetings, some politicians demanded that ETV immediately launch ETV2 in Russian. The idea of targeting an ETV2 schedule towards Russians was heavily debated among politicians and covered by the media. There was even a proposal to launch a pan-Baltic Russian channel financed by all the Baltic States. However, this and all the other plans did not come to fruition, and, despite the debates, the only decision made (and supported by extra state funding) was to launch the public broadcaster's Russian-language news portal *novosti.err.ee*.

According to objectives described in DP 2010–13 (ERR 2009), ETV2 should also have a strong dedicated time zone for Russian programmes and should reach at least 75,000 Russian viewers. Neither of these tasks has thus far been accomplished.

The DP for 2011–14 (ERR 2010) aims to have a defined prime-time slot with at least 250 hours of Russian premieres (mainly news, current affairs and public debates) in the 2013/14 season. All Estonian-language programmes on ETV2 should cater for the possibility of adding Russian subtitles. The DP 2012–15 (ERR 2011), justifies the existence of ETV2 with the need for differentiation of programmes. According to the most recent development plan – DP 2013–16 (ERR 2012) – Russian-language programme development will be revised in 2013.

Integration through media

The issues of Russian-language television journalism become apparent when they are observed within the context of Russian-language journalism in Estonia on the whole. Valeria Jakobson characterized the years 1991–94, when the number of newspapers in Russian decreased by almost 50 per cent and so press runs also dropped, as a crisis of the Russian-language printed press (Jakobson 2004: 214–15). The crisis was due to the inability of publications to adapt to the new market economy and find investors; their incapability to act as a free press, independent of the constraints of the communist party's influence; their ineptitude to grasp the quickly changing political and economic situation; and also sometimes to their insufficient language skills, which hindered them from merging with the information flow, which, by that time, had adopted the Estonian language.

Conversely, the authorities were inclined to have a negative attitude towards non-Estonians as a cultural group and, therefore, also towards their media. It was believed that the majority of non-Estonians would immigrate to Russia; those who stayed would accept Estonian culture and employ the Estonian-language media. The local Russian-language journalism was sometimes accused of lacking loyalty towards the Estonian state; any form of criticism of specific issues of legislation, politicians or the overall situation was observed as an anti-Estonian disposition. This resulted in self-censorship of

Russian-language journalism; criticism of complex topics, which the Estonian-language media was actively covering, such as privatization, corruption, relationships between Estonian parties, reforms in medical and social spheres, etc., were avoided. As a result, the dissemination of information provided by the press, and the quality of that information, decreased, which in turn pushed the audience towards alienation from both Estonia's governmental institutions and the Russian-language media in Estonia.

Denis Trapido and Olga Peresild said that

Both the Russian and the Estonian language press are mutually attempting to negatively envisage the opponent: Estonian language journalism underestimates the willingness of non-Estonians to adapt to Estonian society and the political situation. Conversely, Russian language journalism underestimates the willingness of the Estonians to develop relationships connected to integration and those between nations.

(2000: 3–4)

An analysis of the Russian printed press has revealed that opinions on integration, tolerance and collaboration are sceptical and even critical. Estonians, specifically politicians and officials, are often described as oppressors and conductors of assimilation (the Russian-language printing press seldom presents Estonians as belonging to other social groups). Those non-Estonians who are willing to collaborate with Estonians are sometimes called 'traitors to the Russian people', 'so-called Russian-speaking actors', etc. When Russian-language journalism tries to depict non-Estonians and Estonians as opponents (both on the community and the individual level), Russian-language television often aims to depict them as partners (Iljina and Jakobson 2000: 108).

According to the media monitoring surveys conducted at the turn of the present century, Russian-language television journalism experienced a different type of development. The primary conclusion drawn by the media monitoring survey of 1999 was that Russian-language television in Estonia has (unlike the printed press) a clearly positive view on integration and has formed specific practices for constructing integration. Authors of programmes are more often than not integrated non-Estonians, who are trying to include their viewers in the integration process. However, based on the discourse analysis of Russian-language television journalism, Kõuts noted that

The relationships between local communities are presented as conflict free, and the focus is on a single good and fair individual. [...] In its concept of its viewer, the latter is an *object* of integration and other social processes. This likely expresses the peculiarity of the entire integration discourse present in Estonia. We cannot discuss the noteworthy success of integration until the concept has been altered to acknowledge the active social role of the non-Estonians as fellow citizens; both in the media and in a broader social context.

(Kõuts 2001: 40–46)

When reflecting on the situation in the second half of the 1990s, which preceded the preparation of the first integration programme (2000–07), the authors of the newest Estonian integration monitoring survey (Lauristin et al. 2011) admit that the first integration programme was based on defining the minorities' own position in the integration policy as passive objects. The subject of the policy was the state and the 'Non-Estonian Integration Foundation', established and managed with the state's partnership, which became the initiator, assessor and inspector of the projects, focusing on the naturalization of non-citizens and, in that context, on the promotion of language skill as the precondition to naturalization. The accession to the European Union even deepened the project-like nature of the integration, aiming to meet some EU standards concerning citizenship and language skill requirements, and simultaneously leaving problems of social cohesion and intercultural dialogue in the background. The research has shown that these policy choices led to the implementation of 'conquering' and 'formalism' scenarios in the integration activities.

Discussion

The European Commission treats the public service media in the same way as all other businesses in the market economy; the European Commission is also willing to put PSB under market rules (European Commission 2009).

The situation can best be described as follows: the political-administrative system primarily views the economy (including the media economy) as liberal and as needing as little regulation as possible; however, regulation is also necessary to guarantee the public sector media (broadcast) activities. The basis of this conflict is the scarce legitimacy of PSB in the political-administrative system. The general EU (economic) policy is oriented towards the enlargement of general liberalization. The European Commission's main policy is to support the common market and secure free competition. Compared to other EU institutions, the European Commission has a stronger influence on the member states with regard to shaping their internal media policies. EU media politics is subordinate to economic politics. In this context, the public service media is treated in a similar manner to any other industry. The task to define PSB's purposes and goals has been given to the sole competency of nation-states, meaning that the European Union will not create any guidelines that would specify the (financial) support contributed to PSB (services) or that would be compulsory for the nation-state's legislation. At the same time, EU media policy does not consider the different historical, political, cultural and economic backgrounds in eastern and central European countries when comparing them to western Europe. Furthermore, EU media policy also does not account for the specific needs of culturally more fragile and vulnerable smaller countries, which possess fewer resources, and is not discussing the need to support the interests of the minorities. Debates over PSB funding, the pressure of cost saving and the need for efficiency are apparent in all European countries (Jõesaar 2011; Lowe and Nissen 2011).

At the same time, the integration of the Russian-speaking community into the Estonian information field requires extra effort (including increased funding). As long as the Estonian government continues to execute liberal economic policy and relies on market forces, major changes in the existing media policy are unlikely. In Estonia, PSB is not considered as highly legitimate among the politicians, and, therefore, it does not have the political support that is required to secure sufficient funding, which is needed for the complete fulfilment of the PSB remit, especially in the area of serving the interest of minorities and enhancing the integration of Estonian-speaking and Russian-speaking communities. This has resulted in a situation where two communities are influenced by different independent information fields; Estonian-speakers (mainly) receive daily information from national broadcasting channels, while Russian-speakers receive such information from Russian Federation TV stations and global TV channels.

This could be acknowledged, if the Russian population's strong beliefs towards foreign television channels did not constantly raise problems with regard to their participation in Estonia's everyday life and the degree to which they are informed about this. It has been hoped that one solution could be the target ordering of specific Russian television series on themes of integration, but their audience is more Estonian- than Russian-speaking. The reasons for this lie in the contents of the broadcasts, as well as in the environment. Media research has claimed that the Russian-speaking audience views itself more like integration objects than subjects in these shows. This is not useful, as it decreases the attractiveness of the programmes. As a rule, these programmes are aired on Estonian-language ETV channels in flexible volumes and slots. Therefore, the Russian-speaking audience has not developed a viewing habit. No agreement has been reached on the strategies or funding of the development of Russian-language television programming. Therefore, there is no reason to believe that anything will change in the (near) future, unless there is a substantial increase in the Russian programme funding that is required for the production of high-quality programming in a considerably large scale.

Conclusion

The development of the tradition of Russian-language television journalism was fairly insignificant in Soviet Estonia. This was partly due to the extensive programme offering from the Central Television, and partly due to the lack of policies concerning the national minorities in the USSR. While Estonian-language analytical-political television journalism underwent rapid development in the 1990s, the Russian-language equivalent languished. Furthermore, the political leadership of the newly restored Republic of Estonia was somewhat distrusting of the domestic Russian-language media at that time. The journalists sensed that they were suspected of disloyalty towards Estonia, which in turn lead to the frequent avoidance of complex political and social topics, particularly those concerning the relationships between the nations. Due to these taboos, Russian-speaking television journalism attempted to follow the official integration discourse, meaning that the choice of topics and their treatment was approved by Estonians, but was not supported by the non-Estonian audiences.

Due to the market size, broadcasters have no commercial interest in increasing programming in Russian. The insufficient funding of the public service and ETV's dismissal of the importance of programme production in Russian has led to a situation where the majority of these programmes, aired on ETV and on other domestic TV channels, are funded from external sources, for example, from public funds, budgets of ministries and the financial resources of Tallinn's local administration. Programmes are produced by independent producers under project contracts; there is no centre of competence that would develop a strategy for Russian-language television programming from the viewpoint of the non-Estonian audience.

The merging of Estonian- and Russian-speaking information fields is currently in progress, but it has been slower than expected. In addition, no political will has been expressed to provide extra funding for original Russian-language programmes. Rather, some voices still claim that spending money on Russian-language television will not yield viewers because of high competition and entrenched media-consuming habits. As long as no expectations for minority broadcasting are expressed, and/or the European Commission, the most influential authority for member states, does not provide any support guidelines or initiatives, there is little hope that media policy will ever break the never-ending circle.

References

Ajutrust Konsultatsioonid (2007), *Teostatavusuuring Venekeelse elektroonilise meedia tarbijate infovajaduse rahuldamise võimalustest: Aruanne Rahvastikuministri büroole/ Electronic information needs of Russian speaking audience: Feasibility study*, Tallinn: Ajutrust Konsultatsioonid.

ERR (Eesti Rahvusringhääling/Estonian Public Broadcasting) (2002), *Eesti Raadio ja Eesti Televisiooni Arengukava Aastateks 2003–2005/Development Plan for Estonian Radio and Estonian Television 2003–2005*, Tallinn: Riigikantselei, https://www. riigiteataja.ee/akt/174019. Accessed 15 October 2012.

ERR (Eesti Rahvusringhääling/Estonian Public Broadcasting) (2005), *Eesti Televisiooni ja Eesti Raadio ühine arengukava aastateks 2006–2008/Common development plan for Estonian Radio and Estonian Television for 2006–2008*, http://www.etv.ee/aruanded/ ETV_ja_ER_yhine_arengukava_2.pdf. Accessed 15 October 2012.

ERR (Eesti Rahvusringhääling/Estonian Public Broadcasting) (2009), *Eesti Rahvusringhäälingu arengukava 2010–2013/Estonian National Public Broadcasting's development plan for years 2010–2013*, http://www.err.ee/files/ERR_ arengukava_2010-2013.pdf. Accessed 15 October 2012.

ERR (Eesti Rahvusringhääling/Estonian Public Broadcasting) (2010), *Eesti Rahvusringhäälingu arengukava 2011–2014/Estonian National Public Broadcasting's development plan for years 2011–2014*, http://www.err.ee/files/ERR_arengukava_2011-2014.pdf. Accessed 15 October 2012.

ERR (Eesti Rahvusringhääling/Estonian Public Broadcasting) (2011), *Eesti Rahvusringhäälingu arengukava 2012–2015/Estonian National Public Broadcasting's development plan for years 2012–2015*, http://www.err.ee/files/ERR_arengukava_2012-2015.pdf. Accessed 15 October 2012.

ERR (Eesti Rahvusringhääling/Estonian Public Broadcasting) (2012), *Eesti Rahvusringhäälingu arengukava 2013–2016/Estonian National Public Broadcasting's development plan for years 2013–2016*, http://www.err.ee/files/ERR_arengukava_2013-2016.pdf. Accessed 15 October 2012.

Estonian Ministry of Foreign Affairs (2007), 'Nädal välismeedias 2.-15. Aprill 2007'/'Week in Foreign Press 2-15 April 2007', http://www.vm.ee/?q=node/7224#pronks. Accessed 4 October 2013.

Estonian Statistics (2012), 'Estonian population', Tallinn: Estonian Statistics. http://pub.stat.ee/px-web.2001/Dialog/varval.asp?ma=RV0222&ti=RAHVASTIK+SO Oper cent2C+RAHVUSE+JA+MAAKONNA+Jper centC4RGIper cent2C+1per cent2E+JAANUAR&path=../Database/Rahvastik/01Rahvastikunaitajad_ja_koosseis/04Rahvaarv_ja_rahvastiku_koosseis/&lang=2. Accessed 4 October 2013.

European Commission (2009), 'Communication from the Commission on the application of State aid rules to public service broadcasting text with EEA relevance', *Official Journal*, C 257, 27 October, pp. 1–14.

Iljina, Jelena and Jakobson, Valeria (2000), 'The reflection of the process of integration in the Russian-language press and using the press as an instrument of integration', in M. Lauristin and R. Vetik (eds), *Integration of Estonian Society: Monitoring 2000*, Tallinn: MEIS, http://old.meis.ee/book.php?ID=100. Accessed 15 October 2012.

Jakobson, Valeria (2004), 'Venekeelse meedia areng Eestis 1987–2004'/'Development on Russian media in Estonia 1987–2004', in P. Vihalemm (ed.), *Meediasüsteem ja Meediakasutus Eestis 1965–2004/Media Systems and Media Usage in Estonia 1965–2004*, Tartu: Tartu Ülikooli Kirjastus, pp. 209–33.

Jõesaar, Andres (2011), 'Different ways, same outcome? Liberal communication policy and development of public broadcasting', *Trames*, 15: 1, pp. 74–101.

Jõesaar, Andres (2009), 'Formation of Estonian broadcasting landscape 1994–2007: Experience of the transition state', *Central European Journal of Communication*, 2: 1(2), pp. 43–62.

Kõuts, Ragne (2001), *Integratsiooniprotsesside Kajastumine Eesti Ajakirjanduses Aastal 2000: Projekti 'Integratsiooni Meediamonitooring' Aruanne/Coverage of Integration Processes in Estonian Press in 2000: Integration Mediamonitoring Report*, Tartu: BAMR, pp. 40–46.

Kõuts, Ragne (2004), *Integratsioonikäsitluse Muutumine Meediapildis: Integratsiooni Meediamonitooring 1999–2003/Change of the Integration Discussions in the Media: Integration's Media Monitoring 1999–2003*, Tartu: Balti Ajakirjandusuurijate Assotsiatsioon Integratsiooni Sihtasutus.

Lauristin, Marju (ed.) (2009), *Eesti Inimarengu Aruanne 2008/Human Development Report 2008*, Tallinn: Eesti Koostöö Kogu.

Lauristin, Marju (2004), 'Hinnangud Eesti ühiskonnas toimunud muutustele'/'Valuation of changes in the Estonian Society', in Veronika Kalmus, Marju Lauristin and Pille Pruulmann-Vengerfeldt (eds), *Eesti Elavik 21. Sajandi Algul: Ülevaade Uurimuse Mina. Maailm. Meedia Tulemustest/Estonian in the Beginning of 21st Century: Overview of Research Results*, Tartu: Tartu Ülikooli Kirjastus, pp. 231–49.

Lauristin, Marju, Kaal, Esta, Kirss, Laura, Kriger, Tanja, Masso, Anu, Kirsti Nurmela, Seppel, Külliki, Tammaru, Tiit, Uus, Maiu, Vihalemm, Peeter and Vihalemm, Triin (2011), *Estonian Integration Monitoring 2011*, Tallinn: Ministry of Culture http://www.kul.ee/webeditor/files/integratsioon/Integratsiooni_monitooring_2011_ENG_lyhiversioon.pdf. Accessed 15 October 2012.

Lowe, Gregory Ferrel and Nissen, Christian S. (eds), *Small Among Giants: Television Broadcasting in Smaller Countries*, Göteborg: Nordicom, University of Gothenburg.

President's Round Table of Minorities (PRTM) (2000), 'Presidendi Ümarlaua Istungi Protokoll 2/2000'/'Protocol of President's Round Table 2/2000', Tallinn: Office of The President, http://vp2001-2006.president.ee/et/institutsioonid/ymarlaud.php?gid=11411. Accessed 4 October 2013.

Raag, Ilmar (2004), 'Potjomkinluse lõpp'/'End of fake show', *Eesti Päevaleht*, 7 April, http://www.epl.ee/artikkel/262057. Accessed 15 October 2012.

Riigikogu (1994), *Ringhäälinguseadus/Broadcasting Act*, Tallinn: Riigikantselei. https://www.riigiteataja.ee/akt/22285. Accessed 15 October 2012.

Riigikogu (2007), *Eesti Rahvusringhäälingu Seadus/Estonian National Public Broadcasting Act*, Tallinn: Riigikantselei, https://www.riigiteataja.ee/akt/106012011027. Accessed 15 October 2012.

Riigikogu (2010), *Meediateenuste Seadus/Mediaservices Act*, Tallinn: Riigikantselei. https://www.riigiteataja.ee/akt/106012011001. Accessed 15 October 2012.

Shein, Hagi (2005), *Suur Teleraamat: 50 Aastat Televisiooni Eestis 1955–2005/Great TV-Book: 50 Years of Television in Estonia*, Tallinn: TEA.

Supreme Council (1989), 'Eesti Nõukogude Sotsialistliku Vabariigi keeleseadus'/'Language Law of Estonian SSR', Tallinn: ENSV ÜN ja Valitsuse Teataja, 4, pp. 81-86, http://homepage2.nifty.com/kmatsum/seadus/keel1989.html.

Tiit, Ene-Margit (2011), *Eesti Rahvastik: Viis Põlvkonda ja Kümme Loendust/Estonian Population: Five Generations, Ten Censuses*, Tallinn: Eesti Statistikaamet.

TNS EMOR (2008), *Teleauditooriumi Mõõdikuuring/TV Audience Survey*, Tallinn: TNS Emor, http://www.emor.ee/teleauditooriumi-moodikuuring-2/. Accessed 15 October 2012.

Tomusk, Ilmar (2009), 'Uus keeleseadus tegemisel'/'Preparation of new language law', *Sirp*, 24 April, http://www.sirp.ee/index.php?option=com_content&view=article&id=8665:uus-keeleseadus-tegemisel&catid=18:varamu&Itemid=15&issue=3249. Accessed 15 October 2012.

Trapido, Denis and Peresild, Olga (2000), 'Eesti televisioonikanalite venekeelsete saadete roll integratsiooniprotsessi kajastamisel võrreldes Eesti trükimeediaga'/'Comparative study of Russian TV-programmes and Estonian print media', in M. Lauristin and R. Vetik (eds), *Integratsioon Eesti Ühiskonnas: Monitooring 2000/Integration in Estonian Society*, Tallinn: TPÜ Rahvusvaheliste ja Sotsiaaluuringute Instituut.

Trapido, Denis (2000), 'The role of Russian-language programs of Estonian television channels in reflecting and shaping the integration process compared to printed media', in M. Lauristin and R. Vetik (eds), *Integration of Estonian Society: Monitoring 2000*, Tallinn: MEIS, http://old.meis.ee/book.php?ID=100. Accessed 15 October 2012.

Vihalemm, Peeter (2008), 'Current trends of media use in Estonia', *Informacijos Mokslai/Information Science*, 47, pp. 112–20.

Vihalemm, Peeter (2008), 'The infosphere and media use of Estonian Russians', in M. Heidmets (ed.), *Estonian Human Development Report 2007*, Tallinn: Eesti Koostöö Kogu, pp. 77–81, http://www.kogu.ee/public/trykised/EIA07_eng.pdf. Accessed 15 October 2012.

Vihalemm, Peeter (2009), 'Evaluation of social changes among Estonian, Latvian and Lithuanian ethnic majorities and Russion-speaking minorities', in M. Lauristin (ed.), *Estonian Human Development Report 2008*, Tallinn: Eesti Koostöö Kogu, pp. 87–90.

Vihalemm, Triin (2012), *Eesti Ühiskonna Integratsiooni Monitooring 2011/Estonian Society Integration Monitoring 2011*, Tallinn: Poliitikauuringute keskus Praxis, TNS Emor, Kultuuriministeerium.

Notes

1. Census 1934: Estonians 88.1 per cent, Russians 8.2 per cent, Germans 1.5 per cent. Census 1959: Russians 20 per cent, Ukrainians 1.3 per cent, Byelorussians 1 per cent. In 1970, the ratio of Russian-speaking non-Estonians was 30.2 per cent; in 1979, 32 per cent; in 1989, 35.2 per cent (Tiit 2011).
2. The Singing Revolution is a commonly used name for events in 1987–91 that led to the restoration of the independence of Estonia.
3. *Estonia.eu*: http://estonia.eu/about-estonia/society/citizenship.html. Accessed 4 October 2013.
4. Until 2005, only PBK and RTR Planeta were reported separately in TNS EMOR's 'people meter surveys', other channels were summarized.

5. On 27 April 2007, the government decided to move a World War II monument, colloquially named 'The Bronze Soldier', from the city centre to the Army Cemetery. This event caused a very strong reaction among the Russian-speaking people. For two nights, thousands protested against the sitting government. Such a strong and violent reaction shocked the whole society.

6. Broadcasting media is regulated by the Media Services Act (Riigikogu 2010) and there is a separate law on Estonian public service broadcasting (Riigikogu 2007).

Afterword

'And That's Goodnight From Us': Cultural Diversity and its Challenge for Public Service Media

Andrew Jakubowicz (University of Technology, Sydney)

Europe's four challenges to public service media

Four major challenges confront 'public service media in a culturally diverse Europe'; they go to the heart of the very possibility of the survival of the relationships that have underpinned public broadcasting in the post-war period. While public sector broadcasting remains a resilient and important part of the typical media and government framework throughout Europe, its public service dimension may well be facing its most threatening set of problems since inception. Put simply, each component has become problematized, as the post-war view of the public realm has been transformed by the end of the Soviet bloc; the reconstitution of Europe's populations through emigration and immigration; and global economic repositioning. The public sphere and the public 'project' have both been challenged by neo-liberal political agendas and public sector financial crises. Technological change has transformed the meaning of 'media', destroying the verities of highly differentiated twentieth-century concepts (broadcasting, the press) and facilitating a convergence of delivery systems and a diversification of content, sources and media consumption opportunities. As Born noted in her discussion of the British Broadcasting Corporation (BBC) a decade ago, 'each term of the phrase – "public", "service" and "broadcasting" has been cast in doubt, undermined by social and technological changes' (Born 2004: 7).

Meanwhile the European commitment to 'multiculturalism' as a policy perspective has become fragmented, not only through the formal rejection of the terminology by many governments (the United Kingdom, Germany, France and the Netherlands) but also from internal conflicts over the management of diversity, especially that produced by immigration of Muslim populations and others from former European colonies. Increasingly Europe appears to be suffering from an attack of 'too much diversity'; in many ways key population groups are gravitating to political movements that detest diversity, and reject any mode of governmentality that provides it with support. Apart from these issues internal to societies but generated by global population movements and diasporic settlement, Europe itself is shaking at the seams, the global financial crisis revealing that the European model of social democracy and welfare capitalism cannot easily survive as a continental norm, while earlier cultural conceptions of Europe (of west, north and south) fit uneasily with the expanded community of the east and south-east.

'Public' is used here in two distinct but clearly related ways. Public refers in some sense to the mass of citizenry as reflected in their access to and engagement with the public sphere. As Habermas (Calhoun 1992: *passim*) has described it, this is a space of potentially undistorted communication among the citizenry and other authorized participants – public here means something like 'civil society'. But public can also mean that aspect of a society that is owned in some way by government. That is public can also mean 'the state'. Indeed some would argue that the public interest (in the first sense) is best protected by the application of public authority (in the second). But then others would argue exactly the opposite, and there is the nub of the public sector media debate.

This book has laid out the broad picture of northern European broadcasting, essentially framing the debate within the cultural mores of the European North. Such a distinction is important, because the forms of government, the modes of democratic governance, and the conception of the public sphere change quite substantially as the focus moves towards societies which have evinced the greatest economic difficulties: it is the 'southern' European countries that are most markedly demonstrating crises in the public sphere – ranging from the decline in the economic market and employment, through crises in public finance, to major crises of state legitimacy. The role of government, its relation to democracy, the patterns of social group representation, all play a role in helping us understand the ways in which culture is reproduced, contested and transformed. For European societies, there are three (sometimes four) major trajectories of social transformation under way, often pulling against each other.

The press for a European consciousness, a pan-national orientation aimed to overcome past historical inter-country tensions, presents a 'universal European' model of human rights and social well-being. However as economic crises deepen, antipathy to historically hostile nations returns, often through the guise of a local hyper-nationalism. Meanwhile the impact of immigration fragments what had once been imagined as culturally-uniform societies (though often not now for some generations), demanding a governmental response that is both inclusive and respectful of difference, yet confronted by an increasing transnational network of diasporic communities. In some countries the role of the media in sustaining the distinctiveness of some national minorities through language maintenance and documentation and support for cultural heritage practices (e.g. regional and traditional ethno-cultural) confronts the media role in building national trans-ethnic identities, which marginalize or contain threatening minority cultures (the Romany being the most dramatic example). Together these currents produce whirlpools of tension within societies, and more broadly across the European project.

Country insights

Such tensions are evident in the chapters contributed for this book. Sarita Malik rightly points to the three complementary meanings of 'representation', to argue for greater focus on these issues in public service media in the United Kingdom. She firstly identifies the representation of the existence of diverse audiences in the strategic orientation of media planners and programmers. Put simply, how do the people who make the media imagine the society that is consuming it? What roles do they expect, assume or desire media products will play in ameliorating (or intensifying) the wider social tensions implicit in the complex diversity of contemporary Britain?

The media offer but do not necessarily deliver the opportunities for relationships that might produce a more integrated and inclusive society (if indeed that is the goal of the public sector) – but how should this best be done? Here representation in texts becomes crucial: who are the key characters in the social narratives, from whence comes the authoritative voice? Are the stories targeted to audiences within their own ethno-cultural cocoon, essentially geared to sustaining separate communities? Or are they more explorative of the synergies of modern society, where cultures interact to produce innovation and insight into difference and its feasible accommodations? Are minorities, as has long been recognized, most notable by their presence as threat or as sportspeople, or as marginal characters?

How are the diverse communities represented among the creators of media content in the public sector? Have they been so excluded and their narratives so marginalized, that they along with the mass of diasporic communities are seeking out and finding opportunities to tell their stories to each other on their own terms? Have the public sector media been so beholden to the states that support them, that they have lost contact with the new populations of the nations they are expected to service? Karina Horsti acknowledges the difficulty of this nexus of issues in her discussion of the wider European context. She charts the ways in which various trans-European and national public broadcasting bodies have sought to articulate the diversity question, including the implicit limits they set to where the discourse might lead. As multiculturalism (associated wrongly I would suggest with claims that it seeks to facilitate separation of and antagonisms between ethno-cultural groups) has been overwhelmed by increasing concerns for social cohesion and the threats of home-grown terrorism, so more emphasis has been placed on the control element in media practice. The media increasingly provide the 'field' for the ongoing battle over meaning and identity in Europe, with many parties involved, from the most extreme anti-immigrant (captured graphically on Norwegian TV via the murders of Anders Breivik in 2011) to those who support the diverse presence; to the minorities themselves in all their varieties and internal inconsistencies.

Horsti focuses on the tension between anti-racist strategies in media development, and those seeking to enhance the acceptance and viability of cultural diversity approaches and rhetorics. She suggests that this transformation has been accompanied by and provided support to a number of features of wider European social conflict. The down-playing of racism as a societal problem was achieved through a focus on it as a characteristic of neo-Nazis and extremists, who could be corralled through effective legislative tactics, rather than a quality of postcolonial metropolitan societies, which in fact defined much of the European environment.

Cultural diversity talk re-directs attention to the distinctiveness and qualities of groups, rather than the power relations that constrain and often discriminate against them. The onus thereby shifts to their failings and difficulties in assimilating, rather than to the structures of power and the limits on opportunities available to them. Rather than the race question calling up an examination of the wider society and its inequalities, it reduces the focus of attention to the apparent inadequacies of the minorities. Furthermore the development of more race-aware discourses in management has not delivered very much more in terms of career opportunities in the media for minorities. Indeed the state media are ever more embedded as part of the defence of privilege by long-established ruling elites, who today confront new challengers who seek to share their privileges, in this case the freedom to communicate and disseminate values and ideas, as widely as possible.

We are led then to consider how public service media both might fit the ideals of democratic-egalitarian inclusive and responsive theory, and be understood as a strategic space for maintaining dominant discourses and their associated material interests. Tarlach McGonagle posits as the underlying dilemma of the relationship between media and democracy that of access to wider public debates through media, and the much deeper challenge of citizen (and non-citizen) involvement in creating media. In Europe the Commission and the Council have significant roles to play in framing the goals and governance processes of public sector media, viewing the media as tools through which wider social goals can be pursued. Yet clarifying, guiding and successfully implementing rules for such a range of countries and traditions (and societal idiosyncratic prejudices) has as yet escaped the bureaucratic forms – which are the most troubled now by the advent of citizen media and the dissolution of the dominant limited broadcast model.

Bi-cultural nations have additional issues when they try to address incoming minorities or Indigenous communities. Belgium with its French–Flemish hallmark dichotomy and a big multi-generational immigrant-descended population provides a valuable case study in how these tensions are exposed, explained and resolved (or not). For the Flemish national group, state broadcasting has historically been a key defender of its cultural space against feared French attempts at hegemonic expansion. Alexander Dhoest points to the self/other dichotomy that also exists, between 'us' (auto) and 'other' (allo) populations. Given the struggle by Flemish people for their own identity, they are not well armed to recognize other identities within their space as legitimate. Moreover once driven towards multiculturalism as a philosophy by political pressures, they now find a changing European discourse that seeks to abandon both the term and its implications. As the public broadcaster was driven towards a more corporate identity, it was also asked by government to both support Flemish identity, and service all communities. However despite the rhetoric it appears that most diversity comes from outside Flanders, in imported programming. The need to defend Flemish identity appears to trump the effective integration of cultural diversity.

One of the consequences of the shift to the right in some European nations (documented so clearly in the Dutch context by Isabel Awad and Jiska Engelbert) has been a focus on the public broadcaster as the heartland of political correctness, and in particular, support for multiculturalism. Hard-line rightist parties talk of multiculturalism as a catastrophe, focusing on the transfer effects of 'native born' taxpayers supporting immigrant and alien (usually Muslim) welfare dependants. However while the public sector organizations may give space to those who support multiculturalism, as is evident elsewhere in Europe, the practice is marginal. That is, the look and feel of the media organizations' public output does not reflect the application in toto of the multicultural agendas they are accused of promoting.

Nevertheless, they are being subjected to significant funding reductions, often in the name of testing their alleged preferences in the marketplace of audience choice. Given the Reithian tradition of claiming to give the people what they need rather than what they want, the Dutch scenario is probably the most dramatic case of attempts by political groups to fracture the whole public service edifice through the application of public prejudice about diversity. Thus those who would defend diversity within the public sector are forced to make a business case – that is, that diversity issues, perspectives and participation increase audiences and generate revenues. The Dutch example has some other peculiarities – it is 'pluriform', in order to reflect the historic compromise between the pre-immigration forces in Dutch society. Thus the religious/political silos are protected from having to address cultural diversity, while the cultural diversity issues essentially are bundled within one silo, which has become more integrationist as it has repositioned itself in seeking working-class right-wing viewers.

Ireland's rise and fall as the economic tiger of Europe brought with it significant immigration, and inevitably the potential for fractious intercultural relations as the economy soured. Gavan Titley argues that Irish national broadcasting was caught up in the middle of these complex social movements, and like many parts of Europe was confronted with challenges it could not easily resolve. With a legacy of bilingual broadcasting, and broadcasting in a politically divided society, the national broadcaster was admonished not to discriminate against any part of the society. Faced with significant sociocultural diversity, this was clearly an impossible task, an impossibility compounded by confusion over whether diversity programming was for the minorities, or for everyone to understand every minority. Ultimately many of the initiatives that flowered through the Tiger period came to an abrupt halt as the economy crashed, and the enduring diversity in the population was played down. In common with many other European responses to the crisis of multiculturalism, Irish national broadcasting switched to a 'mainstreaming' rationale.

Sweden has been affected by similar pressures to those elsewhere in Europe – economic in relation to finding and building audiences, and sociopolitical in terms of advancing a more integrationist national agenda. Gunilla Hultén shows that while initially Sweden was seen as a landmark in the building of a multicultural polity in Europe, recent anti-immigrant movements and economic problems have re-shaped the national broadcaster as a much more low-key advocate. Indeed multiculturalism has dissolved to be replaced by a broader diversity rubric. While there has been a small attempt to recruit minority-background journalists and broadcasters, the results have been limited. One of the issues, remarked on elsewhere, remains the reluctance of many ethnic communities to send their children into media, especially if they have achieved tertiary level education that would see them move into high paying and powerful professions. The reluctance of course is intensified by the lack of role models, and the systematic racism that minorities believe is spread through the media.

Where European countries are at least bi-cultural (Belgium and Finland) many of the media institutions have had to deal with a structural reality of ethno-cultural difference for generations. In Finland where Swedish has its own broadcast network, and the Sami have Indigenous rights, such accommodations have been well-tested and are constantly negotiated. Even though there is only a fairly small proportion of foreign-born residents, the nationalist tendencies evident elsewhere in Europe have also been allied with anti-immigrant and especially anti-Muslim sentiment. Whereas traditionally the public sector has presented anti-immigrant attitudes as racist, damaging and deplorable, more recently a 'rational' discourse based on environmental and social cohesion arguments has garnered widespread support.

In Finland as elsewhere in Europe a combination of economic, technical and political factors drive this opening up to populist hostilities as a supposedly legitimate expression of public concern as documented by Karina Horsti. Media convergence and the eruption of Internet alternatives to the national broadcaster; economic cut-backs in funding to the public sector; and economic competition from immigrants for scarcer jobs (often combined with prejudice against them for being welfare dependants) erodes the standing of public media; reduces its resource-base; and further marginalizes diversity as a mainstream pre-occupation.

Norway has become the location of the case par excellence of European racism. The murderous attacks in Oslo by Andreas Breivik in 2011 in support of a notion of white European culture horrified the world. They were rationalized by the perpetrator as a response to the pervasiveness of multicultural values in contemporary Norway, for which in part he held the media to be responsible. Gunn Bjørnsen suggests that something rather different was happening – that cultural diversity was not a feature of prime-time mainstream broadcasting. As is evident elsewhere in Europe (and indeed in Australia), the national broadcaster's obligation to support Norwegian identity and culture confronts it with choices about what such a task means when the society is poly-ethnic and increasingly tense around cultural boundaries.

While the state recognizes diversity, racial discrimination is reinforced by media stereotyping, and it has not yet produced effective strategies to fully incorporate cultural diversity into its programming and employment practices. While Indigenous broadcasting is corralled in Sami Radio, legislative requirements direct the broadcaster to take account of and employ linguistic and national minorities – who had in the past been mainly from long established 'foreign' groups. Over the decade from 2001, the broadcaster was changed in two important ways – first, it paid increasing attention to the communication needs of newer minorities especially from Pakistan, while also adopting affirmative action in recruitment. Second, it moved away from programmes for minorities to a far greater focus on 'integrationist' priorities, communicating about diversity to all Norwegians. This emphasis on 'multiculturalism for all Norwegians' may well have fuelled the sentiment for Breivik's dramatic confrontation with the realities of the diverse society.

While the well-established democratic countries of western Europe have had to struggle with variations on the common theme of sustainable poly-ethnicity within a constitutional and human rights framework, the Estonian case demonstrates the issues that arise when a former empire (Russia) withdraws from a colonized state. Apparently having abandoned the colonial state to its own devices, the enduring presence of Russian-speaking citizens will raise challenges for the national broadcaster of the emerging nation and its significant Russian minority. The new Estonian state thus confronts three inter-related challenges to its authority and legitimacy: Russian as the prior official language, the language of the large quasi-imperial neighbour, and the widespread lingua franca of the Russian diaspora; a government goal for Estonian culture, language and national world-view to be inculcated among all Estonians; and the economic rationalism imposed by the European Commission as well as local political decisions.

Europe's public service and sector media reflect a somewhat common history of an unresolved set of tensions between expressed policies that foreground human rights and the recognition of minorities within a framework of social inclusion, which is nevertheless constantly tested against increasing hostility to immigrants, opposition to multiculturalism, ethno-nationalist reassertion and a critique of cosmopolitan perspectives on social issues. These sociocultural conflicts are framed by political and economic concerns with crisis and free markets, and the reduction in state expenditures.

An Australian reflection

Australia shares many of these challenges, though without the continental imperatives of the greater Europe project; it has responded to them in its own historically-determined ways (Jakubowicz 2006). In particular, the movement of economic power from North America and Europe towards the east and south – China and India, and South America, has been to Australia's shorter-term overall economic benefit. These changes have been accompanied by major changes in the make-up of the immigrant intake, with increasing numbers of new residents coming from Asia to a country that two generations ago prided itself on its 'whiteness'. Even so fiscal crises affecting government are also apparent, especially as scarce public resources are reallocated towards 'pump priming' mass employment options, and away from infrastructure and services. All of these factors have been occurring as media forms converge and questions of media freedom and responsibility press into greater public view.

The public service media (broadcast – there is no print, though with convergence this distinction is dissolving) tradition in Australia is based on the Reithian priorities of the BBC yet has operated since its inception, originally as the Australian Broadcasting

Company in 1929 then as the wholly-Commonwealth-owned Australian Broadcasting Commission (in 1932), as a minority broadcaster in a competitive commercial environment. The commercial framework was recognized by the reconstitution of the Commission as a corporation (ABC) in 1983, even though it still does not carry paid advertising. The system bifurcated in 1980, when a specific multicultural broadcaster was established (the Special Broadcasting Service – SBS), carrying paid advertising since about 1989. The two agencies report to the same minister but have their own boards. The ABC Board does not usually contain people of non-European or Indigenous background, whose segregated participation by regular government practice but never pronouncement is confined to the Board of SBS.

Australia's reassertion in 2011 of multiculturalism as a central organizing principle for government came at the European nadir of formal support for the term and its associated policies. Whereas Europe's announcement of multiculturalism's failure was accepted by Australian commentators as an accurate reflection of the outcome of three decades there of highly criticized immigrant settlement management practices, the Australian experience was deemed to be exceptional and fundamentally different to the European models that were held in such disdain (Jakubowicz 2013). Australia, it was argued, had managed to avoid many of the problems of Europe, in part through luck, and partly through planning. Yet while Australian governments were celebrating the success of the Australian model, the realities were, not unexpectedly, more complicated, less successful and more fraught with tensions. Indeed the public service media provided an apt demonstration of exactly how these contradictions were being played out.

The first major wave that established multiculturalism in Australian political life crested quite early, in the late 1970s. In a very short period Australia abandoned its racially-based immigration policy, White Australia, that had been its standard for three generations, then moved on to establish a series of multicultural institutions. One of the most significant of these was the SBS, a multilingual and multicultural broadcaster created when the national broadcaster, the ABC, proved reluctant to take on the demands of government for it to become a more pluralist and representative venue for Australian diversity (McClean 2013). The separation of the multicultural from the national initiated a rather curious framework for diversity in public sector media. On the one hand the ABC charter (Australian Broadcasting Corporation: 1983/2013) 1(a) i requires that the ABC 'contribute to a sense of national identity [...] [and] reflect the cultural diversity of the Australian community'. Whatever else it does, the ABC is also instructed by the parliament 'to take account of the multicultural character of the Australian community' (2[a] iv).

These charter obligations were introduced after the creation of SBS, and after the adoption of multiculturalism by the conservative coalition government under Malcolm Fraser as prime minister. So the relation between SBS and the ABC was in a sense designed to be fraught, though the expectation might have been that the ABC, once its charter obligated it to accept multiculturalism, would become more amenable to and more capable of responding to these priorities. However this was not to be, and despite numerous inquiries in the 1980s and attempts to amalgamate the organizations by political fiat, the bodies remain separate, with SBS resolutely defending its independence and the ABC somewhat reluctantly responding to what it sees as 'mainstream' elements of multiculturalism (for instance, the modern Australian TV drama series *The Slap*,[2011] which involves a multicultural cast in a typical suburban and primarily English-speaking setting).

In effect the division between the ABC and SBS, while never mandated, has become in practice the representation of two Australias. The ABC's Australia, through its radio and TV arms, and to a degree in its online text services (e.g. *The Drum*) (http://abc.net.au/news/thedrum), channels the values, attitudes and debates of English-speaking middle-class Australians, who may be of non-Anglo background (though not in the proportion of longer-established groups). With the advent of digital cable TV, the ABC has created additional channels for more esoteric (usually BBC and archival content) and children and youth programming in English. Only in 'ABC OPEN', a digital sound and image project that supports citizen production, does one witness some of the cultural diversity of Australia; paradoxically, even though OPEN seeks out minorities, its brief is restricted to non-capital cities, so the places where most newer immigrants live have no access.

SBS on the other hand, shaped in part by how the organization perceived the role of the UK Channel 4, and forced in part by its complementary audience requirements (multilingual radio and multicultural television), has developed a different perspective. SBS has created three additional outlets, one that is free to air and provides access to less popular materials (e.g. much of the daily newscasting from across the world in original languages, more minority interest cinema), and two special-interest pay channels, Studio (music and the arts), and World Movies (including the only regular R-rated programming on Australian cable).

Taking its multicultural brief seriously, SBS has focused on forum, reality TV and documentary productions that involve people from minority communities in 'mainstream' issue debates (McClean 2013). It has been particularly successful in its *Go Back to Where You Came From* (2011, 2012), where English-speaking Australians (some of immigrant origin) are sent to places from where Australia's refugees originate. The participants include some who are opposed to accepting refugees, and others who are in favour. The on-air, social media and newspaper discussions of the attitudes and the experiences have been profoundly important in influencing wider public opinion, even though the broad debate on these issues has become increasingly heated and public attitudes quite divided.

One example of how SBS has addressed the diversity issue can be found in its four-season documentary series, *Once Upon a Time in...* (2012-2016). Seeking to solve the audience issue of limited interest in multicultural topics, the channel decided to merge two genres: crime and social documentary. Aware that public interest in on-screen crime stories leads the programming of most broadcasters, SBS shaped a brief that used crime and populism as a tool to bring audiences to engage with more serious questions. The first series, *Once Upon a Time in Cabramatta*, was broadcast in early 2012 to both critical and audience acclaim. It drew on the arrival in Australia of Vietnamese refugees in the immediate wake of the end of White Australia, and in parallel to the development of multiculturalism. While the first refugees arrived in 1975/76, by 1990 there were tens of thousands (arriving through orderly departure and family reunion) in suburbs like Sydney's Cabramatta ('Vietnamatta') that previously had only known European immigrants. Cabramatta had however become known as a drug haven and site of murder, assault, extortion and heroin overdoses.

The three-part series asked, 'how did this place turn into the drug capital of Sydney, and how come today it is renowned as a generally peaceful tourist destination full of restaurants, shopping and cultural events?' Working from an original paper by this author (Jakubowicz 2004), the production team worked up a theme: 'when immigrants first arrive, all is chaos, and in chaos the first thing to get organized is crime.' Recognizing that crime and criminality exist and gain rapid public notoriety, recognizing that the majority of victims are within communities, the producers sought out families where drugs and crime had come close to the heart. Interviewing, in Vietnamese and in English, ex-criminals, druggies and their parents, local police, politicians and academics, the documentary rooted the wider social reality through the pain and tensions within families. It also looked to the Vietnamese to tell their own stories and provide their own interpretations. Allied to the TV broadcast, the programme had its own website, blog and community storytelling project.

How to explain the turnaround? The focus was put on a Vietnamese Australian local politician, who pressed for inquiries into the quality of policing in Cabramatta. How could an Australian community, and the Vietnamese asserted this is what they were – citizens and participants – be thus abandoned by its police? Three versions of the TV documentary were shown: in English with English subtitles for Vietnamese-speaking participants; in Vietnamese; and subtitled in Arabic (online). A wider community project was initiated in which local people offered their own narratives of life and how things had changed. The programmes were available online for replay, and out-takes of interviews were available online. The programme averaged over 600,000 through a summer period, with over 800,000 watching the opening night; on average 50,000 people watched the Vietnamese version (about one-quarter of about 220,000 Vietnamese speakers nationally). The online site drew 30,000 unique visitors in the first week, while there were over 100,000 online views of the streaming video. While SBS remains a minority-audience broadcaster, normally drawing about 5 per cent of total audience (the ABC gets 12–20 per cent), for this series and those from the same 'multicultural documentaries' stable, the register stood above 10 per cent.

While the Vietnamese story was challenging enough, including as it did the assassination of a local politician and serious corruption, its successor tackled an even more difficult issue: the conflicts associated with Sydney's Lebanese community. While the Lebanese are both Muslim and Christian, both groups have been touched by public images of criminality, violence and extremism. Lebanese immigration dates back to the 'Syrians' of the nineteenth century, though Muslim arrivals were primarily generated by the chaos of the 1976 Civil War period. Since that time Lebanese Muslims and Christians have become increasingly important political players in Sydney's changing environment, providing both a focus for anti-multicultural sentiments, and a driver for an increasing response by the political system to ethno-cultural diversity. A series of rapes and murders associated with crime and drug figures in the community have exacerbated public hostility. However unlike the action by reformist Vietnamese to clear out the criminal gangs, the Lebanese communities have become their targets, trapped between mainstream racism on the one hand, and stand-over tactics, drug trafficking and extortion from 'Leb' gangs on the other.

The popular media in Australia have traditionally addressed these issues in a very sensational manner, playing up the perceived threats to and fears among the wider population. While public-sector media have undertaken some investigations into organized crime and corruption, they have not really sought to understand the social dynamics that lie behind the tabloid headlines. Thus documentaries that tell the story from within the Lebanese communities, leavened with insights from police, politicians and the odd academic (including the present author) have been rare. Even so comic representations of ethnic groups do appear in more socially edgy melodramas such as 'Housies' (about a multi-ethnic public housing estate and its denizens) and the comedy programme 'Legally Brown'.

A rather different 'break-out' at SBS has been the major success of the very low-budget Sunday TV morning music programme, *SBSPopAsia* [2011-]. Sourced from music channels in South Korea, Japan, Hong Kong, Thailand and elsewhere in Asia, it features endless boy and girl bands singing romantic ditties to very boppy music. SBS has tied this compilation programming to a Twitter and Facebook feed, and garnered over 60,000 'likes' by October 2013. The programme runs on SBS TV free-to-air, on YouTube and online, and on digital radio. The Facebook page takes song titles in Chinese script and the programmers have access to the multi-lingual translators' pool operated by SBS. SBS has also trialled a specific Mandarin broadcast news service of its own, which generated Australian material to contest the ceaseless pressures from Chinese-generated media and news that flood through satellite and online feeds. The broadcast version was not successful, but an online version persists.

Australia and Europe in dialogue on diversity

The Australian example (and the focus on SBS might well distort the failings of the other national broadcaster, and the very poor response to cultural diversity that operates on the commercial free-to-air and most of the cable channels) does serve to highlight the transformations that are occurring in most advanced western capitalist societies. Most of such societies are now fully embedded in globalization, with its accelerated flow of culture, capital and people across borders that are becoming less and less of a barrier. Mobile populations are increasingly diasporic, dragging with them their cultural artefacts and forms of belief and daily life. Their partly assimilated children adopt syncretic forms of traditional and contemporary cultures, producing manifestations of belief and creativity that bypass the old modes of governance and control.

Where the media are charged with recognizing and engaging creatively with these changes as part of the contemporary modernity of these complex societies, what had been bizarre or deviant instead becomes reprocessed and integrated into current narratives. Interestingly in the Australian media the programmes that are most likely to promote cultural diversity as a societal good can be found in reality TV, where people of colour, of odd shapes and sizes, and of new eclectic creativities, can emerge as cultural heroes. While such appearances have so long been part of the US imaginative domain as today to be almost unremarkable, in Europe and Australia people who are evidently not of the heritage cultural group are unlikely to emerge as key public figures from whom the population seek security and certainty.

Increasingly too, as the SBS and ABC cases demonstrate, the media convergence process has shaken the very bases of public service media. 'The Australian' newspaper, flagship of the Murdoch News Ltd corporation in Australia, carries video on its website sourced from other media companies in the News Ltd. stable; its columnists blog and its material ends up in radio. Specialist journalists are bought in, and it soon becomes impossible to distinguish what is 'print' and what is 'video' or 'online'. Similarly the ABC now delivers online text that appears on smartphones, tablets and computers, with its radio national talk programmes embedded inside Facebook and Twitter. Whereas SBS has both public funding and advertising-generated income, the ABC depends on government funding and programme sales. As more conservative political groups take aim at the public spending on public service media, the pressure also increases to justify investment, demonstrate diversity and deliver audiences.

Australia's political landscape is changing rapidly as new generations of voters reflect the cultural diversity of recent decades of Asian, Middle Eastern and African immigration. Their integration into Australian mores depends in part on how they use the media, and how therefore the media sees and reflects them. As the tensions in European public media demonstrate, the transformations in global populations, the huge displacement of refugees and economic immigrants, and the pending pressures from environmental, political, economic and social crises, suggest that the public media have an increasingly important part to play. They will need to explain, interpret, engage with and inform many different people, and do so in ways that remain respectful, authoritative and effective. The evidence suggests that, unless they seriously rethink their roles in maintaining social cohesion and ensuring communication rights, they will have their work cut out for them. Given current regimes and modes of dealing with diversity across Europe, the apparently failing faith in public service media from some of their erstwhile supporters and the many enemies hoping to bring them down, the public service media will need to reframe both the meanings of 'public' on which they depend.

References

Australian Broadcasting Corporation (1983/2013) 'Charter of the Corporation', Section 6, *Australian Broadcasting Corporation Act 1983*, http://www.comlaw.gov.au/Details/C2013C00136/Html/Text#_Toc353360751. Accessed 15 July 2013.

Born, G. (2004), *Uncertain Vision: Birt, Dyke and the Reinvention of the BBC*, London: Secker & Warburg.

Calhoun, C. (ed.) (1992), *Habermas and the Public Sphere*, Cambridge, MA: MIT Press.

Jakubowicz, A. (2004), 'Vietnamese in Australia: A quintessential collision', http://andrewjakubowicz.com/publications/vietnamese-in-australia-a-quintessential-collision/. Accessed 15 July 2013.

Jakubowicz, A. (2006), 'Anglo-multiculturalism: Contradictions in the politics of cultural diversity as risk', *International Journal of Media and Cultural Politics*, 2 (3), 249-266.

Jakubowicz, A. (2008), 'Australia', in R. Schaefer (ed.), *Encyclopedia of Race, Ethnicity and Society*, London: Sage.

Jakubowicz, A. (2013), 'Comparing Australian multiculturalism: The international dimension', in A. Jakubowicz and C. Ho (eds), *'For Those Who've Come Across the Seas': Australian Multicultural Policy and Practice*, Melbourne: Australian Scholarly Press, pp.15–30.

McClean, G. (2013), 'National Communication and Diversity: The Story of SBS', in A. Jakubowicz and C. Ho (eds), *'For Those Who've Come Across the Seas': Australian Multicultural Policy and Practice*, Melbourne: Australian Scholarly Press, pp. 45–56.

Index